*Everyman, I will go with thee,
and be thy guide*

THE EVERYMAN
LIBRARY

*The Everyman Library was founded by J. M. Dent
in 1906. He chose the name Everyman because he wanted
to make available the best books ever written in every
field to the greatest number of people at the cheapest possible
price. He began with Boswell's 'Life of Johnson';
his one-thousandth title was Aristotle's 'Metaphysics',
by which time sales exceeded forty million.*

*Today Everyman paperbacks remain true to
J. M. Dent's aims and high standards, with a wide range
of titles at affordable prices in editions which address
the needs of today's readers. Each new text is reset to give
a clear, elegant page and to incorporate the latest thinking
and scholarship. Each book carries the pilgrim logo,
the character in 'Everyman', a medieval morality play,
a proud link between Everyman
past and present.*

HENRY WADSWORTH LONGFELLOW

SELECTED POEMS

Selected and introduced by
ANTHONY THWAITE

Consultant Editor for this Volume
CHRISTOPHER BIGSBY
University of East Anglia

EVERYMAN
J. M. DENT · LONDON
CHARLES E. TUTTLE
VERMONT

First published in Everyman in 1993

Selection and introduction © J. M. Dent 1993
Reissued 1996

Printed in Great Britain by
The Guernsey Press Co. Ltd, Guernsey, C.I.

J. M. Dent Ltd
Orion Publishing Group, Orion House
5 Upper St Martin's Lane, London WC2H 9EA
and Charles E. Tuttle Co. Inc.
28 South Main Street, Rutland,
Vermont 05701, USA

All rights reserved. No part of this publication
may be reproduced, stored in a retrieval system,
or transmitted, in any form or by any means,
electronic, mechanical, photocopying, recording
or otherwise, without the prior permission of
J. M. Dent Ltd.

This book if bound as a paperback is subject to
the condition that it may not be issued on loan
or otherwise except in its original binding.

British Library Cataloguing-in-Publication Data
is available upon request.

ISBN 0 460 87229 X

CONTENTS

Contents

NOTE ON THE EDITOR

ANTHONY THWAITE was born in 1930 in England. He spent the years 1940-44 as a wartime evacuee in the USA. He graduated from Christ Church, Oxford, in 1955, and was then in turn a lecturer in English literature at Tokyo University, a BBC radio producer, literary editor of the *Listener*, assistant professor of English at the University of Libya, literary editor of the *New Statesman*, and from 1973-85 co-editor of *Encounter*. He has published many books of poetry, most recently *Poems 1953-1988* (1989), and several books of criticism and anthologies. As one of Philip Larkin's literary executors, he edited the *Collected Poems* (1988) and the *Selected Letters* (1992). He spent the spring semester 1992 as Poet in Residence, Vanderbilt University, Tennessee. He is a Fellow of the Royal Society of Literature.

INTRODUCTION

One of the few close friends who came to Longfellow's funeral in 1882 was Emerson, himself to die within a few weeks, and with his mind failing. It is reported that Emerson turned to his daughter Ellen, and said, 'The gentleman we have just been burying was a sweet and beautiful soul; but I forget his name'.

The story is a sad one. So is the fact that Longfellow's name has indeed been – not exactly forgotten, but lost in a serious sense. Everyone knows his name; most have heard of 'The Village Blacksmith', *The Song of Hiawatha*, perhaps *Evangeline* and *The Courtship of Miles Standish*; a few people, mostly now getting old, have read a few of the shorter poems, and probably remember a handful of lines. But the poet who, at his death, was widely regarded as not only the glory of American letters but was also loved as one of the greatest poets of the English language itself, within the next thirty or forty years sank first into contempt, and then into neglect.

Perhaps it was not utter neglect. As a boy of eleven in 1941, a wartime evacuee from Britain, I sat in stupefied boredom in John Marshall Grade School, Virginia, when our unimpressive teacher mechanically thrust in front of us, in turn, *Hiawatha*, *The Courtship of Miles Standish*, *Evangeline*. Teaching at the school was, shall we say, conservative, old-fashioned, perhaps just plain bad. We were supposed to learn passages from these poems. I found them even more insufferable than Walter de la Mare's:

> Slowly, silently, now the moon
> Walks the night in her silver shoon

with which our teacher in England had confronted us, when I was nine – the first time, I think, I had ever been faced with something called 'poetry'. These poems (like all poems, I thought then) were boring, artificial, remote from any glimmer of interest or pleasure.

This personal anecdotal childhood stuff about the condition of poetry-teaching in parts of Britain and America in the late Thirties and early Forties, and my response to it, perhaps doesn't tell one much – except that Longfellow was still evidently current within pedagogy at the time, at least in old-fashioned southern state schools. He had been actually dead for almost sixty years: his poetic reputation among most literary critics, and indeed among most literary readers, had been dead for perhaps half that period. Not only were his name and reputation dead: the poems themselves, as artefacts, seemed beyond redemption. When I. A. Richards in 1929 produced his famous report (*Practical Criticism*) on what guinea-pig readers did with the 'anonymous' poems he put in front of them, it was a Longfellow poem ('In the Churchyard at Cambridge') that provoked some of his guinea-pigs' ripest scorn.

It is only much more recently, and sporadically, that the balance has begun to be adjusted. Even so, the balance is still a bit odd. If one consults recent issues of the annual American MLA International Bibliography, which shows who has published what on whom in learned periodicals during the year, one finds among the few entries on Longfellow a preponderance of work by Germans, Dutch, even Chinese, but only very occasional work by American critics, almost none by British ones. If one takes the MLA publication as a significant register, and looks there at Longfellow's American contemporaries, it is clear that Emerson, for example, is still 'respectable'. But Emily Dickinson is much more than that: a poet whose poems were almost totally unknown in her lifetime is a massive presence in articles, theses, books. Poe and Whitman are copiously pondered over and academically processed.

There have been some exceptions with Longfellow. In his *The Flowering of New England: 1815–1865* (1936), Van Wyck Brooks was a pioneer in magisterially setting him in his historical, cultural and topographical context. Norman Holmes Pearson's 1950 essay, 'Both Longfellows', was and is scrupulously intelligent and just. Introductions by poets to a few selected editions of Longfellow, most brilliantly Howard Nemerov's in 1965, have presented the contemporary reader with admirable, if often tempered, enthusiasm: they have not patronised Longfellow but have pointed out his strengths and deplored his neglect. There must be *some* audience for Longfellow somewhere, otherwise editions such as these – and this present one – would not be called for. Over the years since 1941, my own view of Longfellow has changed. The reassessment, the dusting-off, the refurbishing, continue.

Henry Wadsworth Longfellow was born in 1807 in Portland, Maine (then part of the Commonwealth of Massachusetts). His father was a prosperous lawyer. His mother's father had been a general. The family was cultivated, high-minded but not repressively Puritan, and, by present-day standards, large: there were four boys and four girls, and Henry was the second boy. After dame school and the local Portland Academy, he was sent by his father to Bowdoin College, Brunswick, Maine, in 1822. He graduated in 1825, and was in the same class as Nathaniel Hawthorne, a lifelong friend.

Already he had not only written prose and verse but had published some of it. His literary ambitions began early but, though his father was sympathetic, there was little actual encouragement: literature was a precarious profession, if it could at that time in America be considered a profession at all. Instead, it was decided for him that he would teach – and, amazingly, he was offered a newly established professorship of modern languages at Bowdoin College, the post to be taken up after a period of study in Europe, at his family's expense. He sailed for France in May 1826. He was only nineteen.

The years that followed (1826–9) were important for two reasons, the first of them negative. He could happily postpone the matter of committing himself to the life of a university teacher. More importantly, he acquired a command of languages – in France, Spain and Germany – which was the basis both of his later polyglot skills and of his wide and industrious work as a translator of poetry. His earlier schooling had given him fluency in reading, and writing, Latin and Greek; and now he strengthened and perfected his already precocious knowledge of three modern languages.

On taking up his appointment at Bowdoin when he returned from Europe in 1829, Longfellow found a marked lack of textbooks available to his students, so he conscientiously set to work to write several: grammars, exercises and primers on (and in) French, Spanish and Italian. It was not at all what he had expected, and he became restless. But he was calmed and steadied by his marriage in 1831 to Mary Potter, the daughter of another Portland lawyer.

Soon, in 1834, there came an offer from Harvard to take up the Smith Professorship, nominally of French and Spanish, though the college made a condition that Longfellow should again go to Europe for 'a more perfect attainment of the German'. Early in 1835 he set sail for Europe with his wife and two of her friends. They journeyed through Germany, Denmark, Sweden and Holland. It was in Amsterdam, in October 1835, that Mary had a miscarriage; at the end of November she died in Rotterdam.

It was the first great blow in Longfellow's life, and he took a long time to recover from it. He spent the winter trying to concentrate on his studies in Heidelberg. In the spring of 1836 he went to Switzerland, and it was at Thun that he first met Frances (Fanny) Appleton and her family, Bostonians. Seven years later Fanny was to become his second wife. But first he had to return to Harvard, renting and later buying Craigie House in Cambridge, his home for the rest of his life.

He was apparently a good teacher, determined to interest and enlighten his students rather than impress and intimidate them. But he was also often bored and frustrated, finding his literary ambitions choked by the elementary nature of much of the teaching he had to do, by administration, and by conservatives in the college who disapproved of this new discipline of 'modern languages'. At the same time, Longfellow was frustrated in his wooing of Fanny Appleton, who was almost eleven years younger than he: she seems to have been disinclined to accept his ardent pursuit, and it was not until 1843 that she relented and married him. She in fact became the strongest influence on Longfellow's life, a presence as steady and sustaining in his career as Emily Tennyson's in Alfred's.

It was before this, in 1839, that Longfellow published his first collection of original poems, *Voices of the Night*. Six years earlier he had brought out a collection of prose sketches and stories based on his first European tour, *Outre-Mer*, and earlier in 1839 a short novel, *Hyperion*, neither of which deserves much attention. But *Voices of the Night* included a set of quatrains which became one of his best-known and, later, one of his most notorious poems. 'A Psalm of Life' ('What the Heart of the Young Man Said to the Psalmist') has, if nothing else, embedded much of itself in the memories of many people. As someone reputedly remarked of *Hamlet*, it is full of quotations :

> Tell me not, in mournful numbers,
>   'Life is but an empty dream !'
> For the soul is dead that slumbers,
>   And things are not what they seem.
>
> Life is real ! Life is earnest !
>   And the grave is not its goal ;
> 'Dust thou art, to dust returnest',
>   Was not spoken of the soul . . .
>
> Art is long, and Time is fleeting,
>   And our hearts, though stout and brave,
> Still, like muffled drums, are beating
>   Funeral marches to the grave . . .
>
> Let the dead Past bury its dead !
>
> Lives of great men all remind us
>   We can make our lives sublime,
> And, departing, leave behind us
>   Footprints on the sands of time . . .
>
> Let us, then, be up and doing,
>   With a heart for any fate ;
> Still achieving, still pursuing,
>   Learn to labour and to wait.

These (twenty-one of the poem's thirty-six lines) are memorable, unignorable sentiments – as insidiously so, if you like, as Fitzgerald's *Rubaiyat*. In its clear moral exhortation, it stands alongside not only several other familiar Longfellow pieces which similarly later became by-words for doctrinal awfulness, such as 'Excelsior', but also with certain poems by Browning, Tennyson, even Arnold and Clough. 'A Psalm of Life' anticipates them all. Longfellow was not a plagiarist, whatever Poe snarlingly had to say on the matter. He has to be seen as a pioneer, whether you 'like' the poem or not.

When he published *Voices of the Night* in 1839, Longfellow was not yet a professional poet : he was still chiefly an academic and, though the following years saw the publication of such books as *Ballads and Other Poems* (1841), his first attempt at verse drama (*The Spanish Student*, 1843) and *The Belfry at Bruges and Other Poems* (1845), it was not until 1854, when he was forty-seven, that he felt confident enough to retire from his professorship at Harvard. He edited several anthologies in the 1840s, including the immense *The Poets and Poetry of Europe*, full of his own verse translations from the French, German, Italian, Spanish and Danish.

His enormous popular success began with the publication of *Evangeline* in 1847. I have already mentioned my childhood disgust with the poem, and it is indeed unpromising stuff for a twentieth-century eleven-year-old. But reading and re-reading it fifty years later, I find it altogether more impressive and original. In its use of the English hexameter, it anticipates (and may have influenced) the slightly later narratives by Clough, *The Bothie of Tober-na-Vuolich* (1848) and *Amours de Voyages* (1849). Though it is presented by Longfellow as a story for those who 'believe in the beauty and strength of woman's devotion', it is also a story set in Eden, a vast primal garden which is both wilderness and new-found-land – the America of Longfellow's yesterday. There is 'the forest primeval', but there are also rivers and the sea ; and some of Longfellow's best writing, here and in other poems, draws on the sea, beside which he grew up and from which came many images and cadences.

In the same year that he published *Evangeline*, Longfellow also completed a short novel, *Kavanagh*. Though I want to make no great claims for the book (nothing much happens, characters come and go without much compulsion), it is a charming, shrewd and sometimes sly portrait of a New England village, comparable with Mrs Gaskell's *Cranford*, obviously written with pleasure and good humour. Most interestingly, there is the exchange between Mr Churchill, the amiable village schoolmaster, always about to write 'the great Romance' but never actually getting down to it, and Mr Hathaway, a florid and bombastic would-be man of letters :

'I think, Mr Churchill', said he, 'that we want a national literature commensurate with our mountains and rivers – commensurate with Niagara, and the Alleghenies, and the Great Lakes ! 'Oh !' 'We want a national epic that shall correspond to the size of the country ; that shall be to all other epics what Banvard's Panorama of the Mississippi is to all other paintings – the largest in the world !' 'Ah !' 'We want a national drama in which scope enough shall be given to our gigantic ideas, and to the unparalleled activity and progress of our people !' 'Of course.' 'In a word, we want a national literature altogether shaggy and unshorn, that shall shake the earth, like a herd of buffaloes thundering over the prairies !' 'Precisely,' interrupted Mr Churchill; 'but excuse me ! – are you not confounding things that have no analogy ? Great has a very different meaning when applied to a river, and when applied to a literature. Large and shallow may perhaps be applied to both. Literature is rather an image of the spiritual world, than of the physical, is it not ? – of the internal, rather than the external. Mountains, lakes, and rivers are, after all, only its scenery and decorations, not its substance and essence. A man will not necessarily be a great poet because he lives near a great mountain. Nor, being a poet, will he necessarily write better poems than another, because he lives nearer Niagara.' 'But, Mr Churchill, you do not certainly mean to deny the influence of scenery on the mind ?' 'No, only to deny that it can create genius. At best, it can only develop it. Switzerland has produced no extraordinary poet; nor, as far as I know, have the Andes, or the Himalaya mountains, or the Mountains of the Moon in Africa.' 'But, at all events', urged Mr Hathaway, 'let us have our literature national. If it is not national, it is nothing.'

There is something of Longfellow himself in Mr Churchill, in his dreamy aspirations, his fear of indolence ('up and doing'), and also his common sense in the face of Mr Hathaway's grandiose notions. Longfellow wrote *Kavanagh* six years before Whitman produced *Leaves of Grass*, and almost certainly at that time he was totally unaware of Whitman : it is said that the original he had in mind when he invented Mr Hathaway was Cornelius Mathews, the editor of a magazine called *Yankee Doodle* (Mr Hathaway's projected magazine, which comes to nothing, is to be called 'The Niagara'). But the exchange between Hathaway and Churchill is a gently comical prefiguring, in broad terms, of the universalist Longfellow and the nationalist Whitman.

Longfellow, widely read in many literatures, sought – and for a time won – an international reputation. He drew on many sources, and many of these sources lay far beyond New England in particular and America in general. But at the same time he found ways of consciously using American material and of universalising it. In the year he retired from Harvard, 1854, he read a German translation of the Finnish folk-epic *Kalevala*. Inspired by it, he soon began work on a poem which at first he called 'Manabozho'. This became *The Song of Hiawatha*, published in the autumn of 1855. Longfellow had written in his journal: 'I have at length hit upon a plan for a poem on the American Indians, which seemed to me the right one, and the only. It is to weave together their beautiful traditions into a whole.'

Evangeline used the new-found-land for pastoral, gently dramatic purposes: Acadie is a kind of Arcady. *Hiawatha* plunged more deeply into more indigenous lore. The initial scene-setting in both poems is comparable – 'the forest primeval' in *Evangeline* is part of the panorama of *Hiawatha*'s Introduction; but it *is* only part. The scope is vast, a continent wide.

It is of course difficult, perhaps impossible, to read *Hiawatha* with fresh eyes, or with ears that have not been blunted by the relentless noise of parodies, most famously Lewis Carroll's 'Hiawatha's Photographing', written just two years after the poem it parodied. The trochaic tetrameter was experimental, just as *Evangeline*'s hexameters were experimental. Longfellow seems to have aimed for a measure that was primitive yet noble, supple enough to take in quick narrative, reflection, description, grimness, lyricism, and all of it capable of being convincingly heard as *oral* composition – an 'Indian Edda', as he called it. If it is read monotonously (as I remember it was read in Virginia fifty years ago), it will sound monotonous. But it need not be so. Certainly the measure itself is not irretrievable, and for serious purposes: a century and a quarter later, Philip Larkin somehow found himself using it, very effectively, in his haunting poem 'The Explosion'.

Longfellow's other long narratives, such as *The Courtship of Miles Standish* (another American theme), and his attempts at verse plays, are works I have less confidence in trying to resurrect. Like other poets, more highly regarded now, who became copious, fluent and famous (Wordsworth, Tennyson, Browning), he could certainly be a bore. But many of his shorter poems need rediscovering. Several of the best of them date from his last twenty years, at a time when his reputation seemed assured but when he was often deeply depressed. In 1861, in a domestic accident, his wife Fanny died: she had dropped something burning – wax, or a match – on to her thin summer dress as she sat by an open window in Craigie House, and instantly was consumed in flame. Longfellow rushed in and tried to save her, but it was too late, and he was badly burned on his hands and face. She died the next day. Longfellow's own injuries were painful, and in some ways permanent: it was impossible for him to shave, and he grew the long white beard by which he is remembered in so many portraits and photographs. The burden of Fanny's death never left him.

Out of his grief came such poems as 'Palingenesis', 'The Bridge of Cloud', much later 'The Cross of Snow':

> Such is the cross I wear upon my breast
> These eighteen years, through all the changing scenes
> And seasons, changeless since the day she died.

These are fine poems, as moving as all but the best by Tennyson and Hardy, with some of whose work they can sensibly be compared. Just as fine are a number of poems which, in his old age, drew on memories of his childhood on the coast: 'Four by the Clock', 'Chimes', 'Becalmed', the Dedication of his book of poems *Ultima Thule*, and best of all, 'My Lost Youth' (from which Robert Frost took his title *A Boy's Will*) and the magnificent 'The Tide Rises, the Tide Falls', one of the finest lyrics in English. I would add to these one or two of the sonnets 'On Translating the Divina Commedia', particularly the first; 'The Fire of Drift-Wood'; 'Haunted Houses'; the despised 'In the Churchyard at Cambridge' (and, to be fair, I. A. Richards defended it against the insults of his student guinea-pigs); 'The Two Angels'; 'The Jewish Cemetery at Newport'; 'Aftermath'; and, perhaps the most neglected of all these, the sonnet 'Nature'. I find it surprising that one of Longfellow's most appreciative and acute critics in recent times, Newton Arvin, in his *Longfellow: His Life and Work* (1963), in commenting on the sonnets, includes 'Nature' among 'distinctly inferior poems'. On the contrary, I find the control of the long simile throughout both the octave and the sestet a marvellous technical achievement, and the phrasing and cadences deeply moving. The poem's quiet confidence achieves an adagio-like effect which reverberates and haunts me whenever I read it or remember it.

Longfellow, at the very least, was an adept technician, an alert craftsman who tried many forms as well as many subjects. Some of what he wrote has not survived, and probably cannot be resurrected. But enough remains which is lively, stirring and true for anyone who has not become blind to the well-made poem to find pleasure in reading him. For all the fame and honours that came to him in his lifetime, he was never sure of his own merit: worse poets have felt more confident of themselves than Longfellow. He was never smug, he was never dishonest, in his work or, as far as one can see, in his life. He deserves much better than his present dubious position in the shadows of literary history.

Anthony Thwaite

BRIEF COMPARATIVE CHRONOLOGY

1807   Longfellow born.
US Congress passes the Embargo Act, stopping all foreign trade. President Jefferson takes initiative in banning importation of any more slaves from Africa.
Byron's *Hours of Idleness* published

1825   Longfellow graduates from Bowdoin College.
John Quincey Adams elected President of US.
Peru and Bolivia declare independence from Spain.

1826–9   Longfellow in France, Spain and Germany.
French capture Algiers.
Beethoven dies.
Tennyson's first book published.

1831   Longfellow marries Mary Potter.
Nat Turner, rebel slave, hanged.

1834   Longfellow offered Smith Professorship at Harvard.
Slavery abolished in British colonies.
Death of Coleridge.

1835–6   Longfellow's second journey to Europe: Mary dies in Rotterdam, November 1835.
Mexican troops storm Alamo in Texas.
Browning's *Paracelsus* published.

1839   Longfellow's first collection of poems (*Voices of the Night*) published, a few months after his novel *Hyperion*.

1843   Marries Fanny Appleton.

1847   *Evangeline* and *Kavanagh* published.
US Army storms Mexico City.
Tennyson's *The Princess* published; also Charlotte Bronte's *Jane Eyre* and Emily Bronte's *Wuthering Heights*.

1848   Rebellions and risings in France, Italy, Austria, Hungary, etc.
        Mexico cedes Texas and California to US.
1854   Longfellow resigns from Harvard.
        Light Brigade wiped out at Balaclava.
1855   *The Song of Hiawatha* published.
        French and British capture Sebastopol.
        Whitman publishes *Leaves of Grass*, and Tennyson *Maud and other poems*.
1861   Death of Fanny Longfellow in fire.
        Outbreak of American Civil War.
        Deaths of Elizabeth Barrett Browning and of Clough.
        Palgrave's *Golden Treasury* published.
1868   Longfellow's *Poetical Works* published.
        The Emperor Meiji restored to power in Japan, after over two centuries of rule by the Tokugawa Shogunate.
        Browning publishes *The Ring and the Book*.
1872   Longfellow's second volume of *Poetical Works* published.
        Drought and Stock Exchange panic in the US.
        Samuel Butler publishes *Erewhon*, and Thomas Hardy *Under the Greenwood Tree*.
1880   Longfellow publishes *Ultima Thule*.
        British troops lift siege of Kandahar in Afghanistan.
        Ned Kelly executed in Australia.
        George Eliot dies.
1882   Death of Longfellow.

SELECT BIBLIOGRAPHY

POETRY.
Voices of the Night, 1839; *Ballads and Other Poems*, 1842; *Poems on Slavery*, 1842; *Poems*, 1845; *The Belfry of Bruges and Other Poems*, 1845; *Evangeline: A Tale of Acadie*, 1847; *Poems, Lyrical and Dramatic*, 1848; *The Seaside and the Fireside*, 1849; *The Golden Legend*, 1851; *The Song of Hiawatha*, 1855; *Poetical Works*, 1858; *The Courtship of Miles Standish*, 1858; *Tales of a Wayside Inn*, 1863; *Household Poems*, 1865; *Flower-de-Luce*, 1867; *The New England Tragedies*, 1868; *Poetical Works*, 1868; *The Divine Tragedy*, 1871; *Three Books of Song*, 1872; *Christus: A Mystery*, 1872; *Poetical Works*, 1872; *Aftermath*, 1873; *The Hanging of the Crane*, 1874; *The Masque of Pandora and Other Poems*, 1875; *Keramos and Other Poems*, 1878; *Ultima Thule*, 1880; *In the Harbor: Ultima Thule — Part II*, 1882; *Michael Angelo*, 1882–3.

PLAY.
The Spanish Student, 1843.

MISCELLANEOUS PROSE.
Outre-Mer: A Pilgrimage Beyond the Sea, 1833–4; *Hyperion: A Romance*, 1839; *Kavanagh: A Tale*, 1849.

TRANSLATIONS.
The Poets and Poetry of Europe, 1845; Dante's *Divine Comedy*, 1867.

COLLECTIONS.
The Works and *Final Memorials* (ed. Samuel Longfellow), 14 vols, 1886–7; *Works*, 10 vols, 1909; *The Letters* (ed. Andrew Hilen), 4 vols, 1966–72.

BIOGRAPHY AND CRITICISM.
Samuel Longfellow, *Life of Henry Wadsworth Longfellow*, 2 vols, 1886; Lawrance Thompson, *Young Longfellow, 1807–1843*, 1938; Edward Wagenknecht, *Longfellow: A Full-Length Portrait*, 1955, and *Longfellow: Portrait of an American Humanist*, 1966; Newton Arvin,

Longfellow: His Life and Work, 1963 ; Cecil B. Williams, *Longfellow*, 1964 ; E. L. Hirsch, *Longfellow*, 1964 ; Eric S. Robertson, *Life of Longfellow*, 1972 ; Lawrence Buell, *Henry Wadsworth Longfellow: Selected Poems*, 1988.

SELECTED POEMS

Prelude

Pleasant it was, when woods were green
   And winds were soft and low,
To lie amid some sylvan scene,
Where, the long drooping boughs between,
Shadows dark and sunlight sheen
   Alternate come and go;

Or where the denser grove receives
   No sunlight from above,
But the dark foliage interweaves
In one unbroken roof of leaves,
Underneath whose sloping eaves
   The shadows hardly move.

Beneath some patriarchal tree
   I lay upon the ground;
His hoary arms uplifted he,
And all the broad leaves over me
Clapped their little hands in glee,
   With one continuous sound; –

A slumberous sound, a sound that brings
   The feelings of a dream,
As of innumerable wings,
As, when a bell no longer swings,
Faint the hollow murmur rings
   O'er meadow, lake, and stream.

And dreams of that which cannot die,
   Bright visions, came to me,
As lapped in thought I used to lie,
And gaze into the summer sky,
Where the sailing clouds went by,
   Like ships upon the sea;

Dreams that the soul of youth engage
   Ere Fancy has been quelled;
Old legends of the monkish page,

Traditions of the saint and sage,
Tales that have the rime of age,
    And chronicles of eld.

And, loving still these quaint old themes,
    Even in the city's throng
I feel the freshness of the streams,
That, crossed by shades and sunny gleams,
Water the green land of dreams,
    The holy land of song.

Therefore, at Pentecost, which brings
    The Spring, clothed like a bride,
When nestling buds unfold their wings,
And bishop's-caps have golden rings,
Musing upon many things,
    I sought the woodlands wide.

The green trees whispered low and mild;
    It was a sound of joy!
They were my playmates when a child,
And rocked me in their arms so wild!
Still they looked at me and smiled,
    As if I were a boy;

And even whispered, mild and low,
    'Come, be a child once more!'
And waved their long arms to and fro,
And beckoned solemnly and slow;
Oh, I could not choose but go
    Into the woodlands hoar, –

Into the blithe and breathing air,
    Into the solemn wood,
Solemn and silent everywhere!
Nature with folded hands seemed there,
Kneeling at her evening prayer!
    Like one in prayer I stood.

Before me rose an avenue
    Of tall and sombrous pines;

Abroad their fan-like branches grew,
And, where the sunshine darted through,
Spread a vapour soft and blue,
  In long and sloping lines.

And, falling on my weary brain,
  Like a fast-falling shower,
The dreams of youth came back again, –
Low lispings of the summer rain,
Dropping on the ripened grain,
  As once upon the flower.

Visions of childhood ! Stay, oh, stay !
  Ye were so sweet and wild !
And distant voices seemed to say,
'It cannot be ! They pass away !
Other themes demand thy lay ;
  Thou art no more a child !

'The land of Song within thee lies,
  Watered by living springs ;
The lids of Fancy's sleepless eyes
Are gates unto that Paradise ;
Holy thoughts, like stars, arise ;
  Its clouds are angels' wings.

'Learn, that henceforth thy song shall be,
  Not mountains capped with snow,
Nor forests sounding like the sea,
Nor rivers flowing ceaselessly,
Where the woodlands bend to see
  The bending heavens below.

'There is a forest where the din
  Of iron branches sounds !
A mighty river roars between,
And whosoever looks therein
Sees the heavens all black with sin,
  Sees not its depths, nor bounds.

'Athwart the swinging branches cast,
   Soft rays of sunshine pour;
Then comes the fearful wintry blast;
Our hopes, like withered leaves, fall fast;
Pallid lips say, "It is past!
   We can return no more!"

'Look, then, into thine heart, and write!
   Yes, into Life's deep stream!
All forms of sorrow and delight,
All solemn Voices of the Night,
That can soothe thee, or affright, —
   Be these henceforth thy theme.'

Hymn to the Night

I heard the trailing garments of the Night
   Sweep through her marble halls!
I saw her sable skirts all fringed with light
   From the celestial walls!

I felt her presence, by its spell of might,
   Stoop o'er me from above;
The calm, majestic presence of the Night,
   As of the one I love.

I heard the sounds of sorrow and delight,
   The manifold, soft chimes,
That fill the haunted chambers of the Night,
   Like some old poet's rhymes.

From the cool cisterns of the midnight air
   My spirit drank repose;
The fountain of perpetual peace flows there, —
   From those deep cisterns flows.

O holy Night! from thee I learn to bear
   What man has borne before!
Thou layest thy finger on the lips of Care,
   And they complain no more.

Peace! Peace! Orestes-like I breathe this prayer!
   Descend with broad-winged flight,
The welcome, the thrice-prayed for, the most fair,
   The best-beloved Night!

A Psalm of Life

WHAT THE HEART OF THE YOUNG MAN
SAID TO THE PSALMIST

Tell me not, in mournful numbers,
   'Life is but an empty dream!'
For the soul is dead that slumbers,
   And things are not what they seem.

Life is real! Life is earnest!
   And the grave is not its goal;
'Dust thou art, to dust returnest,'
   Was not spoken of the soul.

Not enjoyment, and not sorrow,
   Is our destined end or way;
But to act, that each to-morrow
   Finds us farther than to-day.

Art is long, and Time is fleeting,
   And our hearts, though stout and brave,
Still, like muffled drums, are beating
   Funeral marches to the grave.

In the world's broad field of battle,
   In the bivouac of Life,
Be not like dumb, driven cattle!
   Be a hero in the strife!

Trust no Future, howe'er pleasant!
   Let the dead Past bury its dead!
Act, – act in the living Present!
   Heart within, and God o'erhead!

Lives of great men all remind us
   We can make our lives sublime,
And, departing, leave behind us
   Footprints on the sands of time;

Footprints, that perhaps another,
   Sailing o'er life's solemn main,
A forlorn and shipwrecked brother,
   Seeing, shall take heart again.

Let us, then, be up and doing,
   With a heart for any fate;
Still achieving, still pursuing,
   Learn to labour and to wait.

The Reaper and the Flowers

There is a Reaper, whose name is Death,
    And, with his sickle keen,
He reaps the bearded grain at a breath,
    And the flowers that grow between.

'Shall I have nought that is fair?' saith he,
    'Have nought but the bearded grain?
Though the breath of these flowers is sweet to me,
    I will give them all back again.'

He gazed at the flowers with tearful eyes,
    He kissed their drooping leaves;
It was for the Lord of Paradise
    He bound them in his sheaves.

'My Lord has need of these flowerets gay,'
    The Reaper said, and smiled;
'Dear tokens of the earth are they,
    Where he was once a child.

'They shall all bloom in fields of light,
    Transplanted by my care,
And saints, upon their garments white,
    These sacred blossoms wear.'

And the mother gave, in tears and pain,
    The flowers she most did love;
She knew she should find them all again,
    In the fields of light above.

O, not in cruelty, not in wrath,
    The Reaper came that day;
'Twas an angel visited the green earth,
    And took the flowers away.

The Light of Stars

The night is come, but not too soon;
  And sinking silently,
All silently, the little moon
  Drops down behind the sky.

There is no light in earth or heaven,
  But the cold light of stars;
And the first watch of night is given
  To the red planet Mars.

Is it the tender star of love?
  The star of love and dreams?
O no! from that blue tent above,
  A hero's armour gleams.

And earnest thoughts within me rise,
  When I behold afar,
Suspended in the evening skies,
  The shield of that red star.

O star of strength! I see thee stand
  And smile upon my pain;
Thou beckonest with thy mailed hand,
  And I am strong again.

Within my breast there is no light,
  But the cold light of stars;
I give the first watch of the night
  To the red planet Mars.

The star of the unconquered will,
  He rises in my breast,
Serene, and resolute, and still,
  And calm, and self-possessed.

And thou, too, whosoe'er thou art,
That readest this brief psalm,

As one by one thy hopes depart,
   Be resolute and calm.

O fear not in a world like this,
   And thou shalt know ere long,
Know how sublime a thing it is
   To suffer and be strong.

Footsteps of Angels

When the hours of Day are numbered,
   And the voices of the Night
Wake the better soul, that slumbered,
   To a holy, calm delight;

Ere the evening lamps are lighted,
   And, like phantoms grim and tall,
Shadows from the fitful firelight
   Dance upon the parlour wall;

Then the forms of the departed
   Enter at the open door;
The beloved, the true-hearted,
   Come to visit me once more;

He, the young and strong, who cherished
   Noble longings for the strife,
By the roadside fell and perished,
   Weary with the march of life!

They, the holy ones and weakly,
   Who the cross of suffering bore,
Folded their pale hands so meekly,
   Spake with us on earth no more!

And with them the Being Beauteous,
   Who unto my youth was given,
More than all things else to love me,
   And is now a saint in heaven.

With a slow and noiseless footstep
   Comes that messenger divine,
Takes the vacant chair beside me,
   Lays her gentle hand in mine.

And she sits and gazes at me
   With those deep and tender eyes,

Like the stars, so still and saint-like,
   Looking downward from the skies.

Uttered not, yet comprehended,
   Is the spirit's voiceless prayer,
Soft rebukes, in blessings ended,
   Breathing from her lips of air.

O, though oft depressed and lonely,
   All my fears are laid aside,
If I but remember only
   Such as these have lived and died!

Burial of the Minnisink

On sunny slope and beechen swell,
The shadowed light of evening fell ;
And, where the maple's leaf was brown,
With soft and silent lapse came down
The glory, that the wood receives,
At sunset, in its brazen leaves.

Far upward in the mellow light
Rose the blue hills. One cloud of white,
Around a far uplifted cone,
In the warm blush of evening shone ;
An image of the silver lakes,
By which the Indian's soul awakes.

But soon a funeral hymn was heard
Where the soft breath of evening stirred
The tall, gray forest ; and a band
Of stern in heart, and strong in hand,
Came winding down beside the wave,
To lay the red chief in his grave.

They sang, that by his native bowers
He stood, in the last moon of flowers,
And thirty snows had not yet shed
Their glory on the warrior's head ;
But, as the summer fruit decays,
So died he in those naked days.

A dark cloak of the roebuck's skin
Covered the warrior, and within
Its heavy folds the weapons, made
For the hard toils of war, were laid ;
The cuirass, woven of plaited reeds,
And the broad belt of shells and beads.

Before, a dark-haired virgin train
Chanted the death dirge of the slain ;
Behind, the long procession came

Of hoary men and chiefs of fame,
With heavy hearts, and eyes of grief,
Leading the war-horse of their chief.

Stripped of his proud and martial dress,
Uncurbed, unreined, and riderless,
With darting eye, and nostril spread,
And heavy and impatient tread,
He came ; and oft that eye so proud
Asked for his rider in the crowd.

They buried the dark chief, they freed
Beside the grave his battle steed ;
And swift an arrow cleaved its way
To his stern heart ! One piercing neigh
Arose, – and, on the dead man's plain,
The rider grasps his steed again.

The Indian Hunter

When the summer harvest was gather'd in,
And the sheaf of the gleaner grew white and thin,
And the ploughshare was in its furrow left,
Where the stubble land had been lately cleft,
An Indian hunter, with unstrung bow,
Look'd down where the valley lay stretch'd below.

He was a stranger there, and all that day,
Had been out on the hills, a perilous way,
But the foot of the deer was far and fleet,
And the wolf kept aloof from the hunter's feet,
And bitter feelings pass'd o'er him then,
As he stood by the populous haunts of men.

The winds of autumn came over the woods
As the sun stole out from their solitudes,
The moss was white on the maple's trunk,
And dead from its arms the pale vine shrunk,
And ripen'd the mellow fruit hung, and red
Were the tree's wither'd leaves round it shed.

The foot of the reaper moved slow on the lawn,
And the sickle cut down the yellow corn, –
The mower sung loud by the meadow-side,
Where the mists of evening were spreading wide,
And the voice of the herdsman came up the lea,
And the dance went round by the greenwood tree.

Then the hunter turn'd away from that scene,
Where the home of his fathers once had been,
And heard by the distant and measured stroke,
That the woodman hew'd down the giant oak,
And burning thoughts flash'd over his mind,
Of the white man's faith, and love unkind.

The moon of the harvest grew high and bright,
As her golden horn pierced the cloud of white, –
A footstep was heard in the rustling brake,

Where the beech overshadow'd the misty lake,
And a mourning voice, and a plunge from the shore; –
And the hunter was seen on the hills no more.

When years had pass'd on, by that still lake-side
The fisher look'd down through the silver tide,
And there on the smooth yellow sand display'd,
A skeleton wasted and white was laid,
And 'twas seen, as the waters moved deep and slow,
That the hand was still grasping a hunter's bow.

The Skeleton in Armour

[The following Ballad was suggested to me
while riding on the seashore at Newport. A
year or two previous a skeleton had been
dug up at Fall River, clad in broken and
corroded armour ; and the idea occurred to
me of connecting it with the Round Tower
at Newport, generally known hitherto as the
Old Wind-Mill, though now claimed by the
Danes as a work of their early ancestors.]

'Speak ! speak ! thou fearful guest !
Who, with thy hollow breast
Still in rude armour drest,
   Comest to daunt me !
Wrapt not in Eastern balms,
But with thy fleshless palms
Stretched, as if asking alms,
   Why dost thou haunt me ?'

Then, from those cavernous eyes
Pale flashes seemed to rise,
As when the Northern skies
   Gleam in December ;
And, like the water's flow
Under December's snow,
Came a dull voice of woe
   From the heart's chamber.

'I was a Viking old !
My deeds, though manifold,
No Skald in song has told,
   No Saga taught thee !
Take heed, that in thy verse
Thou dost the tale rehearse,
Else dread a dead man's curse ;
   For this I sought thee.

'Far in the Northern Land,
By the wild Baltic's strand,

I, with my childish hand,
   Tamed the gerfalcon;
And, with my skates fast-bound,
Skimmed the half-frozen Sound,
That the poor whimpering hound
   Trembled to walk on.

'Oft to his frozen lair
Tracked I the grisly bear,
While from my path the hare
   Fled like a shadow;
Oft through the forest dark
Followed the were-wolf's bark,
Until the soaring lark
   Sang from the meadow.

'But when I older grew,
Joining a corsair's crew,
O'er the dark sea I flew
   With the marauders.
Wild was the life we led;
Many the souls that sped,
Many the hearts that bled,
   By our stern orders.

'Many a wassail-bout
Wore the long Winter out;
Often our midnight shout
   Set the cocks crowing,
As we the Berserk's tale
Measured in cups of ale,
Draining the oaken pail,
   Filled to o'erflowing.

'Once as I told in glee
Tales of the stormy sea,
Soft eyes did gaze on me,
   Burning yet tender;
And as the white stars shine
On the dark Norway pine,

On that dark heart of mine
  Fell their soft splendour.

'I wooed the blue-eyed maid,
Yielding, yet half afraid,
And in the forest's shade
  Our vows were plighted.
Under its loosened vest
Fluttered her little breast,
Like birds within their nest
  By the hawk frighted.

'Bright in her father's hall
Shields gleamed upon the wall,
Loud sang the minstrels all,
  Chaunting his glory;
When of old Hildebrand
I asked his daughter's hand,
Mute did the minstrels stand
  To hear my story.

'While the brown ale he quaffed,
Loud then the champion laughed.
And as the wind gusts waft
  The sea-foam brightly,
So the loud laugh of scorn,
Out of those lips unshorn,
From the deep drinking-horn,
  Blew the foam lightly.

'She was a Prince's child,
I but a Viking wild,
And though she blushed and smiled,
  I was discarded!
Should not the dove so white
Follow the sea-mew's flight,
Why did they leave that night
  Her nest unguarded?

'Scarce had I put to sea,
Bearing the maid with me, —

Fairest of all was she
   Among the Norsemen ! –
When on the white sea-strand,
Waving his armèd hand,
Saw we old Hildebrand,
   With twenty horsemen.

'Then launched they to the blast,
Bent like a reed each mast,
Yet we were gaining fast,
   When the wind failed us ;
And with a sudden flaw
Came round the gusty Skaw,
So that our foe we saw
   Laugh as he hailed us.

'And as to catch the gale
Round veered the flapping sail,
Death ! was the helmsman's hail,
   Death without quarter !
Mid-ships with iron keel
Struck we her ribs of steel ;
Down her black hulk did reel
   Through the black water !

'As with his wings aslant,
Sails the fierce cormorant,
Seeking some rocky haunt,
   With his prey laden,
So toward the open main,
Beating to sea again,
Through the wild hurricane
   Bore I the maiden.

'Three weeks we westward bore,
And when the storm was o'er,
Cloud-like we saw the shore
   Stretching to lee-ward ;
There for my lady's bower
Built I the lofty tower,

Which, to this very hour,
  Stands looking seaward.

'There lived we many years;
Time dried the maiden's tears;
She had forgot her fears
  She was a mother;
Death closed her mild blue eyes,
Under that tower she lies;
Ne'er shall the sun arise
  On such another!

'Still grew my bosom then,
Still as a stagnant fen!
Hateful to me were men,
  The sunlight hateful!
In the vast forest here,
Clad in my warlike gear,
Fell I upon my spear,
  O, death was grateful!

'Thus, seamed with many scars
Bursting these prison bars,
Up to its native stars
  My soul ascended!
There from the flowing bowl
Deep drinks the warrior's soul,
Skoal! to the Northland! *skoal!*'
  — Thus the tale ended.

The Wreck of the Hesperus

It was the schooner Hesperus,
    That sailed the wintry sea ;
And the skipper had taken his little daughtèr,
    To bear him company.

Blue were her eyes as the fairy-flax,
    Her cheeks like the dawn of day,
And her bosom white as the hawthorn buds
    That ope in the month of May.

The skipper he stood beside the helm,
    His pipe was in his mouth,
And he watched how the veering flaw did blow
    The smoke now West, now South.

Then up and spake an old Sailòr,
    Had sailed the Spanish Main,
'I pray thee, put into yonder port,
    For I fear a hurricane.

'Last night the moon had a golden ring,
    And to-night no moon we see !'
The skipper he blew a whiff from his pipe,
    And a scornful laugh laughed he.

Colder and colder blew the wind,
    A gale from the North-east ;
The snow fell hissing in the brine,
    And the billows frothed like yeast.

Down came the storm, and smote amain,
    The vessel in its strength ;
She shuddered and paused, like a frightened steed,
    Then leaped her cable's length.

'Come hither ! come hither ! my little daughtèr,
    And do not tremble so ;

For I can weather the roughest gale,
  That ever wind did blow.'

He wrapped her warm in his seaman's coat
  Against the stinging blast;
He cut a rope from a broken spar,
  And bound her to the mast.

'O father! I hear the church-bells ring,
  O say, what may it be?'
''Tis a fog-bell on a rock-bound coast!' –
  And he steered for the open sea.

'O father! I hear the sound of guns,
  O say, what may it be?'
'Some ship in distress, that cannot live
  In such an angry sea!'

'O father! I see a gleaming light,
  O say, what may it be?'
But the father answered never a word,
  A frozen corpse was he.

Lashed to the helm, all stiff and stark,
  With his face turned to the skies,
The lantern gleamed through the gleaming snow
  On his fixed and glassy eyes.

Then the maiden clasped her hands and prayed
  That savèd she might be;
And she thought of Christ, who stilled the wave,
  On the Lake of Galilee.

And fast through the midnight dark and drear,
  Through the whistling sleet and snow,
Like a sheeted ghost, the vessel swept
  Towards the reef of Norman's Woe.

And ever the fitful gusts between
  A sound came from the land;

It was the sound of the trampling surf,
　　On the rocks and the hard sea-sand.

The breakers were right beneath her bows,
　　She drifted a dreary wreck,
And a whooping billow swept the crew
　　Like icicles from her deck.

She struck where the white and fleecy waves
　　Looked soft as carded wool,
But the cruel rocks, they gored her side
　　Like the horns of an angry bull.

Her rattling shrouds, all sheathed in ice,
　　With the masts went by the board;
Like a vessel of glass, she stove and sank,
　　Ho! ho! the breakers roared!

At daybreak, on the bleak sea-beach,
　　A fisherman stood aghast,
　　To see the form of a maiden fair,
　　Lashed close to a drifting mast.

The salt sea was frozen on her breast,
　　The salt tears in her eyes;
And he saw her hair, like the brown sea-weed,
　　On the billows fall and rise.

Such was the wreck of the Hesperus,
　　In the midnight and the snow!
Christ save us all from a death like this
　　On the reef of Norman's Woe!

Evangeline

A TALE OF ACADIE

1847

This is the forest primeval. The murmuring pines and the
    hemlocks,
Bearded with moss, and in garments green, indistinct in the
    twilight,
Stand like Druids of old, with voices sad and prophetic,
Stand like harpers hoar, with beards that rest on their bosoms.
Loud from its rocky caverns, the deep-voiced neighbouring
    ocean
Speaks, and in accents disconsolate answers the wail of the
    forest.

  This is the forest primeval; but where are the hearts that
    beneath it
Leaped like the roe, when he hears in the woodland the voice of
    the huntsman?
Where is the thatch-roofed village, the home of Acadian
    farmers, –
Men whose lives glided on like rivers that water the woodlands,

Darkened by shadows of earth, but reflecting an image of
    heaven?
Waste are those pleasant farms, and the farmers forever
    departed!
Scattered like dust and leaves, when the mighty blasts of October
Seize them, and whirl them aloft, and sprinkle them far o'er the
    ocean.
Naught but tradition remains of the beautiful village of Grand-
    Pré.

  Ye who believe in affection that hopes, and endures, and is
    patient,
Ye who believe in the beauty and strength of woman's devotion,
List to the mournful tradition still sung by the pines of the
    forest;
List to a Tale of Love in Acadie, home of the happy.

PART THE FIRST

I

In the Acadian land, on the shores of the Basin of Minas
Distant, secluded, still, the little village of Grand-Pré
Lay in the fruitful valley. Vast meadows stretched to the
    eastward,
Giving the village its name, and pasture to flocks without
    number.
Dikes, that the hands of the farmers had raised with labour
    incessant,
Shut out the turbulent tides; but at stated seasons the flood-
    gates
Opened, and welcomed the sea to wander at will o'er the
    meadows.
West and south there were fields of flax, and orchards and corn-
    fields
Spreading afar and unfenced o'er the plain; and away to the
    northward
Blomidon rose, and the forests old, and aloft on the mountains
Sea-fogs pitched their tents, and mists from the mighty Atlantic
Looked on the happy valley, but ne'er from their station
    descended.
There, in the midst of its farms, reposed the Acadian village.
Strongly built were the houses, with frames of oak and of
    chestnut,
Such as the peasants of Normandy built in the reign of the
    Henries.
Thatched were the roofs, with dormer-windows; and gables
    projecting
Over the basement below protected and shaded the door-way.
There in the tranquil evenings of summer, when brightly the
    sunset
Lighted the village street, and gilded the vanes on the chimneys,
Matrons and maidens sat in snow-white caps and in kirtles
Scarlet and blue and green, with distaffs spinning the golden
Flax for the gossiping looms, whose noisy shuttles within doors
Mingled their sound with the whir of the wheels and the songs
    of the maidens.
Solemnly down the street came the parish priest, and the
    children

Paused in their play to kiss the hand he extended to bless them.
Reverend walked he among them; and up rose matrons and
    maidens,
Hailing his slow approach with words of affectionate welcome.
Then came the labourers home from the field, and serenely the
    sun sank
Down to his rest, and twilight prevailed. Anon from the belfry
Softly the Angelus sounded, and over the roofs of the village
Columns of pale blue smoke, like clouds of incense ascending,
Rose from a hundred hearths, the homes of peace and
    contentment.
Thus dwelt together in love these simple Acadian farmers, –
Dwelt in the love of God and of man. Alike were they free from
Fear, that reigns with the tyrant, and envy, the vice of republics.
Neither locks had they to their doors, nor bars to their
    windows;
But their dwellings were open as day and the hearts of the
    owners;
There the richest was poor, and the poorest lived in abundance.

  Somewhat apart from the village, and nearer the Basin of
    Minas,
Benedict Bellefontaine, the wealthiest farmer of Grand-Pré,
Dwelt on his goodly acres; and with him, directing his
    household,
Gentle Evangeline lived, his child, and the pride of the village.
Stalworth and stately in form was the man of seventy winters;
Hearty and hale was he, an oak that is covered with snowflakes;
White as the snow were his locks, and his cheeks as brown as
    the oak-leaves.
Fair was she to behold, that maiden of seventeen summers.
Black were her eyes as the berry that grows on the thorn by the
    wayside,
Black, yet how softly they gleamed beneath the brown shade of
    her tresses!
Sweet was her breath as the breath of kine that feed in the
    meadows.
When in the harvest heat she bore to the reapers at noontide
Flagons of home-brewed ale, ah! fair in sooth was the maiden!
Fairer was she when, on Sunday morn, while the bell from its
    turret

Sprinkled with holy sounds the air, as the priest with his hyssop
Sprinkles the congregation, and scatters blessings upon them.
Down the long street she passed, with her chaplet of beads and
　　her missal,
Wearing her Norman cap, and her kirtle of blue, and the ear-
　　rings,
Brought in the olden time from France, and since, as an
　　heirloom,
Handed down from mother to child, through long generations.
But a celestial brightness — a more ethereal beauty —
Shone on her face and encircled her form, when, after
　　confession,
Homeward serenely she walked with God's benediction upon
　　her.
When she had passed, it seemed like the ceasing of exquisite
　　music.

　Firmly builded with rafters of oak, the house of the farmer
Stood on the side of a hill commanding the sea; and a shady
Sycamore grew by the door, with a woodbine wreathing around
　　it.
Rudely carved was the porch, with seats beneath; and a
　　footpath
Led through an orchard wide, and disappeared in the meadow.
Under the Sycamore-tree were hives overhung by a penthouse,
Such as the traveller sees in regions remote by the roadside,
Built o'er a box for the poor, or the blessed image of Mary.
Farther down, on the slope of the hill, was the well with its
　　moss-grown
Bucket, fastened with iron, and near it a trough for the horses.
Shielding the house from storms, on the north, were the barns
　　and the farmyard.
There stood the broad-wheeled wains and the antique ploughs
　　and the harrows;
There were the folds for the sheep; and there, in his feathered
　　seraglio,
Strutted the lordly turkey, and crowed the cock, with the
　　selfsame
Voice that in ages of old had startled the penitent Peter.
Bursting with hay were the barns, themselves a village. In each
　　one

Far o'er the gable projected a roof of thatch; and a staircase,
Under the sheltering eaves, led up to the odorous corn-loft.
There too the dove-cot stood, with its meek and innocent inmates
Murmuring ever of love; while above in the variant breezes
Numberless noisy weathercocks rattled and sang of mutation.

Thus, at peace with God and the world, the farmer of Grand-Pré
Lived on his sunny farm, and Evangeline governed his household.
Many a youth, as he knelt in the church and opened his missal,
Fixed his eyes upon her, as the saint of his deepest devotion;
Happy was he who might touch her hand or the hem of her garment!
Many a suitor came to her door, by the darkness befriended,
And as he knocked and waited to hear the sound of her footsteps,
Knew not which beat the louder, his heart or the knocker of iron;
Or at the joyous feast of the Patron Saint of the village,
Bolder grew, and pressed her hand in the dance as he whispered
Hurried words of love, that seemed a part of the music.
But, among all who came, young Gabriel only was welcome;
Gabriel Lajeunesse, the son of Basil the blacksmith,
Who was a mighty man in the village, and honoured of all men;
For since the birth of time, throughout all ages and nations,
Has the craft of the smith been held in repute by the people.
Basil was Benedict's friend. Their children from earliest childhood
Grew up together as brother and sister; and Father Felician,
Priest and pedagogue both in the village, had taught them their letters
Out of the selfsame book, with the hymns of the church and the plain-song.
But when the hymn was sung, and the daily lesson completed,
Swiftly they hurried away to the forge of Basil the blacksmith.
There at the door they stood, with wondering eyes to behold him
Take in his leathern lap the hoof of the horse as a plaything,

Nailing the shoe in its place; while near him the tire of the cart-
    wheel
Lay like a fiery snake, coiled round in a circle of cinders.
Oft on autumnal eves, when without in the gathering darkness
Bursting with light seemed the smithy, through every cranny
    and crevice,
Warm by the forge within they watched the labouring bellows,
And as its panting ceased, and the sparks expired in the ashes,
Merrily laughed, and said they were nuns going into the chapel.
Oft on sledges in winter, as swift as the swoop of the eagle,
Down the hillside bounding, they glided away o'er the meadow.
Oft in the barns they climbed to the populous nests on the
    rafters,
Seeking with eager eyes that wondrous stone, which the swallow
Brings from the shore of the sea to restore the sight of its
    fledglings;
Lucky was he who found that stone in the nest of the swallow!
Thus passed a few swift years, and they no longer were children.
He was a valiant youth, and his face, like the face of the
    morning,
Gladdened the earth with its light, and ripened thought into
    action.
She was a woman now, with the heart and hopes of a woman.
'Sunshine of Saint Eulalie' was she called; for that was the
    sunshine
Which, as the farmers believed, would load their orchards with
    apples;
She, too, would bring to her husband's house delight and
    abundance,
Filling it full of love and the ruddy faces of children.

II

  Now had the season returned, when the nights grow colder
    and longer,
And the retreating sun the sign of the Scorpion enters.
Birds of passage sailed through the leaden air from the ice-
    bound,
Desolate northern bays to the shores of tropical islands.
Harvests were gathered in; and wild with the winds of
    September

Wrestled the trees of the forest, as Jacob of old with the angel.
All the signs foretold a winter long and inclement.
Bees, with prophetic instinct of want, had hoarded their honey
Till the hives overflowed; and the Indian hunters asserted
Cold would the winter be, for thick was the fur of the foxes.
Such was the advent of autumn. Then followed that beautiful
    season,
Called by the pious Acadian peasants the Summer of All-Saints!
Filled was the air with a dreamy and magical light; and the
    landscape
Lay as if new-created in all the freshness of childhood.
Peace seemed to reign upon earth, and the restless heart of the
    ocean
Was for a moment consoled. All sounds were in harmony
    blended.
Voices of children at play, the crowing of cocks in the farm-
    yards,
Whir of wings in the drowsy air, and the cooing of pigeons,
All were subdued and low as the murmurs of love, and the great
    sun
Looked with the eye of love through the golden vapours around
    him;
While arrayed in its robes of russet and scarlet and yellow,
Bright with the sheen of the dew, each glittering tree of the
    forest
Flashed like the plane-tree the Persian adorned with mantles and
    jewels.

  Now recommenced the reign of rest and affection and
    stillness.
Day with its burden and heat had departed, and twilight
    descending
Brought back the evening star to the sky, and the herds to the
    homestead.
Pawing the ground they came, and resting their necks on each
    other,
And with their nostrils distended inhaling the freshness of
    evening.
Foremost, bearing the bell, Evangeline's beautiful heifer,
Proud of her snow-white hide, and the ribbon that waved from
    her collar,

Quietly paced and slow, as if conscious of human affection.
Then came the shepherd back with his bleating flock from the
 seaside,
Where was their favourite pasture. Behind them followed the
 watch-dog,
Patient, full of importance, and grand in the pride of his instinct,
Walking from side to side with a lordly air, and superbly
Waving his bushy tail, and urging forward the stragglers;
Regent of flocks was he when the shepherd slept; their
 protector,
When from the forest at night, through the starry silence the
 wolves howled.
Late, with the rising moon, returned the wains from the marshes,
Laden with briny hay, that filled the air with its odour.
Cheerily neighed the steeds, with dew on their manes and their
 fetlocks,
While aloft on their shoulders the wooden and ponderous
 saddles,
Painted with brilliant dyes, and adorned with tassels of crimson,
Nodded in bright array, like hollyhocks heavy with blossoms.
Patiently stood the cows meanwhile, and yielded their udders
Unto the milkmaid's hand; whilst loud and in regular cadence
Into the sounding pails the foaming streamlets descended.
Lowing of cattle and peals of laughter were heard in the
 farmyard,
Echoed back by the barns. Anon they sank into stillness;
Heavily closed, with a jarring sound, the valves of the barn-
 doors,
Rattled the wooden bars, and all for a season was silent.

 Indoors, warm by the wide-mouthed fireplace, idly the farmer
Sat in his elbow-chair, and watched how the flames and the
 smoke wreaths
Struggled together like foes in a burning city. Behind him,
Nodding and mocking along the wall, with gestures fantastic,
Darted his own huge shadow, and vanished away into darkness.
Faces, clumsily carved in oak, on the back of his arm-chair
Laughed in the flickering light, and the pewter plates on the
 dresser
Caught and reflected the flame, as shields of armies the sunshine.
Fragments of song the old man sang, and carols of Christmas,

Such as at home, in the olden time, his fathers before him
Sang in their Norman orchards and bright Burgundian
  vineyards.
Close at her father's side was the gentle Evangeline seated,
Spinning flax for the loom, that stood in the corner behind her.
Silent awhile were its treadles, at rest was its diligent shuttle,
While the monotonous drone of the wheel, like the drone of a
  bagpipe,
Followed the old man's song, and united the fragments together.
As in a church, when the chant of the choir at intervals ceases,
Footfalls are heard in the aisles, or words of the priest at the
  altar,
So, in each pause of the song, with measured motion the clock
  clicked.

Thus as they sat, there were footsteps heard, and, suddenly
  lifted,
Sounded the wooden latch, and the door swung back on its
  hinges.
Benedict knew by the hob-nailed shoes it was Basil the
  blacksmith,
And by her beating heart Evangeline knew who was with him.
'Welcome!' the farmer exclaimed, as their footsteps paused on
  the threshold,
'Welcome, Basil, my friend! Come, take thy place on the settle
Close by the chimney-side, which is always empty without thee;
Take from the shelf overhead thy pipe and the box of tobacco;
Never so much thyself art thou as when through the curling
Smoke of the pipe or the forge thy friendly and jovial face
  gleams
Round and red as the harvest moon through the mist of the
  marshes.'
Then, with a smile of content, thus answered Basil the
  blacksmith,
Taking with easy air the accustomed seat by the fireside: —
'Benedict Bellefontaine, thou hast ever thy jest and thy ballad!
Ever in cheerfullest mood art thou, when others are filled with
Gloomy forebodings of ill, and see only ruin before them.
Happy art thou, as if every day thou hadst picked up a horse-
  shoe.'

Pausing a moment, to take the pipe that Evangeline brought
    him,
And with a coal from the embers had lighted, he slowly
    continued : —
'Four days now are passed since the English ships at their
    anchors
Ride in the Gaspereau's mouth, with their cannon pointed
    against us.
What their design may be is unknown ; but all are commanded
On the morrow to meet in the church, where his Majesty's
    mandate
Will be proclaimed as law in the land. Alas ! in the mean time
Many surmises of evil alarm the hearts of the people.'
Then made answer the farmer : — 'Perhaps some friendlier
    purpose
Brings these ships to our shores. Perhaps the harvests in England
By the untimely rains or untimelier heat have been blighted,
And from our bursting barns they would feed their cattle and
    children.'
'Not so thinketh the folk in the village,' said, warmly, the
    blacksmith.
Shaking his head, as in doubt ; then, heaving a sigh, he con-
    tinued : —
'Louisburg is not forgotten, nor Beau Séjour, nor Port Royal.
Many already have fled to the forest, and lurk on its outskirts,
Waiting with anxious hearts the dubious fate of to-morrow.
Arms have been taken from us, and warlike weapons of all
    kinds ;
Nothing is left but the blacksmith's sledge and the scythe of the
    mower.'
Then with a pleasant smile made answer the jovial farmer : —
'Safer are we unarmed, in the midst of our flocks and our corn-
    fields,
Safer within these peaceful dikes, besieged by the ocean,
Than were our fathers in forts, besieged by the enemy's cannon.
Fear no evil, my friend, and to-night may no shadow of sorrow
Fall on this house and hearth ; for this is the night of the
    contract.
Built are the house and the barn. The merry lads of the village
Strongly have built them and well ; and, breaking the glebe
    round about them,

Filled the barn with hay, and the house with food for a
    twelvemonth.
René Leblanc will be here anon, with his papers and inkhorn.
Shall we not then be glad, and rejoice in the joy of our children ?'
As apart by the window she stood, with her hand in her lover's,
Blushing Evangeline heard the words that her father had spoken,
And as they died on his lips the worthy notary entered.

III

Bent like a labouring oar, that toils in the surf of the ocean,
Bent, but not broken, by age was the form of the notary public ;
Shocks of yellow hair, like the silken floss of the maize, hung
Over his shoulders ; his forehead was high ; and glasses with
    horn bows
Sat astride on his nose, with a look of wisdom supernal.
Father of twenty children was he, and more than a hundred
Children's children rode on his knee, and heard his great watch
    tick.
Four long years in the times of the war had he languished a
    captive,
Suffering much in an old French fort as the friend of the English.
Now, though warier grown, without all guile or suspicion,
Ripe in wisdom was he, but patient, and simple, and childlike.
He was beloved by all, and most of all by the children ;
For he told them tales of the Loup-garou in the forest,
And of the goblin that came in the night to water the horses,
And of the white Létiche, the ghost of a child who unchristened
Died, and was doomed to haunt unseen the chambers of
    children ;
And how on Christmas eve the oxen talked in the stable,
And how the fever was cured by a spider shut up in a nutshell
And of the marvellous powers of four-leaved clover and horse-
    shoes,
With whatsoever else was writ in the lore of the village.
Then up rose from his seat by the fireside Basil the blacksmith,
Knocked from his pipe the ashes, and slowly extending his right
    hand,
'Father Leblanc,' he exclaimed, 'thou hast heard the talk in the
    village,

And, perchance, canst tell us some news of these ships and their
    errand.'
  Then with modest demeanour made answer the notary
    public, –
'Gossip enough have I heard, in sooth, yet am never the wiser;
And what their errand may be I know not better than others.
Yet am I not of those who imagine some evil intention
Brings them here, for we are at peace; and why then molest us?'
'God's name!' shouted the hasty and somewhat irascible
    blacksmith;
'Must we in all things look for the how, and the why, and the
    wherefore?
Daily injustice is done, and might is the right of the strongest!'
But, without heeding his warmth, continued the notary
    public, –
'Man is unjust, but God is just; and finally justice
Triumphs; and well I remember a story, that often consoled me,
When as a captive I lay in the old French fort at Port Royal.'
This was the old man's favourite tale, and he loved to repeat it
When his neighbours complained that any injustice was done
    them.
'Once in an ancient city, whose name I no longer remember,
Raised aloft on a column, a brazen statue of Justice
Stood in the public square, upholding the scales in its left hand,
And in its right a sword, as an emblem that justice presided
Over the laws of the land, and the hearts and homes of the
    people.
Even the birds had built their nests in the scales of the balance,
Having no fear of the sword that flashed in the sunshine above
    them.
But in the course of time the laws of the land were corrupted;
Might took the place of right, and the weak were oppressed,
    and the mighty
Ruled with an iron rod. Then it chanced in a nobleman's palace
That a necklace of pearls was lost, and ere long a suspicion
Fell on an orphan girl who lived as maid in the household.
She, after form of trial condemned to die on the scaffold,
Patiently met her doom at the foot of the statue of Justice.
As to her Father in heaven her innocent spirit ascended,
Lo! o'er the city a tempest rose; and the bolts of the thunder

Smote the statue of bronze, and hurled in wrath from its left
    hand
Down on the pavement below the clattering scales of the
    balance,
And in the hollow thereof was found the nest of a magpie,
Into whose clay-built walls the necklace of pearls was inwoven.'
Silenced, but not convinced, when the story was ended, the
    blacksmith
Stood like a man who fain would speak, but findeth no
    language;
All his thoughts were congealed into lines on his face, as the
    vapours
Freeze in fantastic shapes on the window-panes in the winter.

   Then Evangeline lighted the brazen lamp on the table,
Filled, till it overflowed, the pewter tankard with home-brewed
Nut-brown ale, that was famed for its strength in the village of
    Grand-Pré;
While from his pocket the notary drew his papers and inkhorn,
Wrote with a steady hand the date and the age of the parties,
Naming the dower of the bride in flocks of sheep and in cattle.
Orderly all things proceeded, and duly and well were completed,
And the great seal of the law was set like a sun on the margin.
Then from his leathern pouch the farmer threw on the table
Three times the old man's fee in solid pieces of silver;
And the notary rising, and blessing the bride and the
    bridegroom,
Lifted aloft the tankard of ale and drank to their welfare.
Wiping the foam from his lip, he solemnly bowed and departed,
While in silence the others sat and mused by the fireside,
Till Evangeline brought the draught-board out of its corner.
Soon was the game begun. In friendly contention the old men
Laughed at each lucky hit, or unsuccessful manœuvre,
Laughed when a man was crowned, or a breach was made in
    the king-row.
Meanwhile apart, in the twilight gloom of a window's
    embrasure,
Sat the lovers, and whispered together, beholding the moon rise
Over the pallid sea and the silvery mist of the meadows.
Silently, one by one, in the infinite meadows of heaven,
Blossomed the lovely stars, the forget-me-nots of the angels.

Thus passed the evening away. Anon the bell from the belfry
Rang out the hour of nine, the village curfew, and straightway
Rose the guests and departed; and silence reigned in the
     household.
Many a farewell word and sweet good-night on the door-step
Lingered long in Evangeline's heart, and filled it with gladness.
Carefully then were covered the embers that glowed on the
     hearth-stone,
And on the oaken stairs resounded the tread of the farmer.
Soon with a soundless step the foot of Evangeline followed.
Up the staircase moved a luminous space in the darkness,
Lighted less by the lamp than the shining face of the maiden.
Silent she passed through the hall, and entered the door of her
     chamber.
Simple that chamber was, with its curtains of white, and its
     clothes-press
Ample and high, on whose spacious shelves were carefully
     folded
Linen and woollen stuffs, by the hand of Evangeline woven.
This was the precious dower she would bring to her husband in
     marriage,
Better than flocks and herds, being proofs of her skill as a
     housewife.
Soon she extinguished her lamp, for the mellow and radiant
     moonlight
Streamed through the windows, and lighted the room, till the
     heart of the maiden
Swelled and obeyed its power, like the tremulous tides of the
     ocean.
Ah! she was fair, exceeding fair to behold, as she stood with
Naked snow-white feet on the gleaming floor of her chamber!
Little she dreamed that below, among the trees of the orchard,
Waited her lover and watched for the gleam of her lamp and her
     shadow.
Yet were her thoughts of him, and at times a feeling of sadness
Passed o'er her soul, as the sailing shade of clouds in the
     moonlight
Flitted across the floor and darkened the room for a moment.
And as she gazed from the window she saw serenely the moon
     pass

Forth from the folds of a cloud, and one star follow her
    footsteps,
As out of Abraham's tent young Ishmael wandered with Hagar!

IV

  Pleasantly rose next morn the sun on the village of Grand-Pré.
Pleasantly gleamed in the soft, sweet air the Basin of Minas,
Where the ships, with their wavering shadows, were riding at
    anchor.
Life had long been astir in the village, and clamorous labour
Knocked with its hundred hands at the golden gates of the
    morning.
Now from the country around, from the farms and the neigh-
    bouring hamlets,
Came in their holiday dresses the blithe Acadian peasants.
Many a glad good-morrow and jocund laugh from the young
    folk
Made the bright air brighter, as up from the numerous
    meadows,
Where no path could be seen but the track of wheels in the
    greensward,
Group after group appeared, and joined, or passed on the
    highway.
Long ere noon, in the village all sounds of labour were silenced.
Thronged were the streets with people; and noisy groups at the
    house-doors
Sat in the cheerful sun, and rejoiced and gossiped together.
Every house was an inn, where all were welcomed and feasted;
For with this simple people, who lived like brothers together,
All things were held in common, and what one had was
    another's.
Yet under Benedict's roof hospitality seemed more abundant:
For Evangeline stood among the guests of her father;
Bright was her face with smiles, and words of welcome and
    gladness
Fell from her beautiful lips, and blessed the cup as she gave it.

  Under the open sky, in the odorous air of the orchard,
Bending with golden fruit, was spread the feast of betrothal.

There in the shade of the porch were the priest and the notary
    seated;
There good Benedict sat, and sturdy Basil the blacksmith.
Not far withdrawn from these, by the cider-press and the bee-
    hives,
Michael the fiddler was placed, with the gayest of hearts and of
    waistcoats.
Shadow and light from the leaves alternately played on his
    snow-white
Hair, as it waved in the wind, and the jolly face of the fiddler
Glowed like a living coal when the ashes are blown from the
    embers
Gayly the old man sang to the vibrant sound of his fiddle,
Tous les Bourgeois de Chartres, and *Le Carillon de Dunkerque*,
And anon with his wooden shoes beat time to the music.
Merrily, merrily whirled the wheels of the dizzying dances
Under the orchard-trees and down the path to the meadows;
Old folk and young together, and children mingled among them.
Fairest of all the maids was Evangeline, Benedict's daughter!
Noblest of all the youths was Gabriel, son of the blacksmith!

So passed the morning away. And lo! with a summons
    sonorous
Sounded the bell from its tower, and over the meadows a drum
    beat,
Thronged ere long was the church with men. Without, in the
    churchyard,
Waited the women. They stood by the graves, and hung on the
    headstones
Garlands of autumn leaves and evergreens fresh from the forest.
Then came the guard from the ships, and marching proudly
    among them
Entered the sacred portal. With loud and dissonant clangour
Echoed the sound of their brazen drums from ceiling and
    casement, –
Echoed a moment only, and slowly the ponderous portal
Closed, and in silence the crowd awaited the will of the soldiers.
Then up rose their commander, and spake from the steps of the
    altar,
Holding aloft in his hands, with its seals, the royal commission,
'You are convened this day,' he said, 'by his Majesty's orders.

Clement and kind has he been; but how you have answered his
    kindness,
Let your own hearts reply! To my natural make and my temper
Painful the task is I do, which to you I know must be grievous.
Yet must I bow and obey, and deliver the will of our monarch;
Namely, that all your lands, and dwellings, and cattle of all kinds
Forfeited be to the crown; and that you yourselves from this
    province
Be transported to other lands. God grant you may dwell there
Ever as faithful subjects, a happy and peaceable people!
Prisoners now I declare you; for such is his Majesty's pleasure!'
As, when the air is serene in the sultry solstice of summer,
Suddenly gathers a storm, and the deadly sling of the hailstones
Beats down the farmer's corn in the field and shatters his
    windows,
Hiding the sun, and strewing the ground with thatch from the
    house-roofs,
Bellowing fly the herds, and seek to break their inclosures;
So on the hearts of the people descended the words of the
    speaker.
Silent a moment they stood in speechless wonder, and then rose
Louder and ever louder a wail of sorrow and anger,
And, by one impulse moved, they madly rushed to the doorway.
Vain was the hope of escape; and cries and fierce imprecations
Rang through the house of prayer; and high o'er the heads of
    the others
Rose, with his arms uplifted, the figure of Basil the blacksmith,
As, on a stormy sea, a spar is tossed by the billows.
Flushed was his face and distorted with passion; and wildly he
    shouted, —
'Down with the tyrants of England! we never have sworn them
    allegiance!
Death to these foreign soldiers, who seize on our homes and our
    harvests!'
More he fain would have said, but the merciless hand of a
    soldier
Smote him upon the mouth, and dragged him down to the
    pavement.

    In the midst of the strife and tumult of angry contention,
Lo! the door of the chancel opened, and Father Felician

Entered, with serious mien, and ascended the steps of the altar.
Raising his reverend hand, with a gesture he awed into silence
All that clamorous throng; and thus he spake to his people;
Deep were his tones and solemn; in accents measured and mournful
Spake he, as, after the tocsin's alarum, distinctly the clock strikes.
'What is this that ye do, my children? what madness has seized you?
Forty years of my life have I laboured among you, and taught you,
Not in word alone, but in deed, to love one another!
Is this the fruits of my toils, of my vigils and prayers and privations?
Have you so soon forgotten all lessons of love and forgiveness?
This is the house of the Prince of Peace, and would you profane it
Thus with violent deeds and hearts overflowing with hatred?
Lo! where the crucified Christ from his cross is gazing upon you!
See! in those sorrowful eyes what meekness and holy compassion!
Hark! how those lips still repeat the prayer, "O Father, forgive them!"
Let us repeat that prayer in the hour when the wicked assail us,
Let us repeat it now, and say, "O Father, forgive them!"'
Few were his words of rebuke, but deep in the hearts of his people
Sank they, and sobs of contrition succeeded that passionate outbreak;
And they repeated his prayer, and said 'O Father, forgive them!'

Then came the evening service. The tapers gleamed from the altar.
Fervent and deep was the voice of the priest, and the people responded,
Not with their lips alone, but their hearts; and the Ave Maria
Sang they, and fell on their knees, and their souls, with devotion translated,
Rose on the ardour of prayer, like Elijah ascending to heaven.

Meanwhile had spread in the village the tidings of ill, and on all sides
Wandered, wailing, from house to house the women and children.
Long at her father's door Evangeline stood, with her right hand
Shielding her eyes from the level rays of the sun, that, descending,
Lighted the village street with mysterious splendour, and roofed each
Peasant's cottage with golden thatch, and emblazoned its windows.
Long within had been spread the snow-white cloth on the table;
There stood the wheaten loaf, and the honey fragrant with wild flowers;
There stood the tankard of ale, and the cheese fresh brought from the dairy,
And at the head of the board the great armchair of the farmer.
Thus did Evangeline wait at her father's door, as the sunset
Threw the long shadows of trees o'er the broad ambrosial meadows.
Ah! on her spirit within a deeper shadow had fallen,
And from the fields of her soul a fragrance celestial ascended, –
Charity, meekness, love, and hope, and forgiveness, and patience!
Then, all-forgetful of self, she wandered into the village,
Cheering with looks and words the disconsolate hearts of the women
As o'er the darkening fields with lingering steps they departed,
Urged by their household cares, and the weary feet of their children.
Down sank the great red sun, and in golden, glimmering vapours
Veiled the light of his face, like the Prophet descending from Sinai.
Sweetly over the village the bell of the Angelus sounded.

Meanwhile, amid the gloom, by the church Evangeline lingered.
All was silent within; and in vain at the door and the windows
Stood she, and listened and looked, until, overcome by emotion
'Gabriel!' cried she aloud with tremulous voice; but no answer

Came from the graves of the dead, nor the gloomier grave of the
    living.
Slowly at length she returned to the tenantless house of her
    father.
Smouldered the fire on the hearth, on the board stood the supper
    untasted,
Empty and drear was each room, and haunted with phantoms
    of terror.
Sadly echoed her step on the stair and the floor of her chamber.
In the dead of the night she heard the whispering rain fall
Loud on the withered leaves of the Sycamore-tree by the
    window.
Keenly the lightning flashed; and the voice of the echoing
    thunder
Told her that God was in heaven, and governed the world he
    created!
Then she remembered the tale she had heard of the justice of
    heaven;
Soothed was her troubled soul, and she peacefully slumbered till
    morning.

V

  Four times the sun had risen and set; and now on the fifth
    day
Cheerily called the cock to the sleeping maids of the farmhouse.
Soon o'er the yellow fields, in silent and mournful procession,
Came from the neighbouring hamlets and farms the Acadian
    women,
Driving in ponderous wains their household goods to the sea-
    shore,
Pausing and looking back to gaze once more on their dwellings,
Ere they were shut from sight by the winding road and the
    woodland.
Close at their sides their children ran, and urged on the oxen,
While in their little hands they clasped some fragments of
    playthings.

  Thus to the Gaspereau's mouth they hurried; there on the
    sea-beach
Piled in confusion lay the household goods of the peasants.

All day long between the shore and the ships did the boats ply;
All day long the wains came labouring down from the village.
Late in the afternoon, when the sun was near to his setting,
Echoing far o'er the fields came the roll of drums from the
    churchyard.
Thither the women and children thronged. On a sudden the
    church-doors
Opened, and forth came the guard, and marching in gloomy
    procession
Followed the long-prisoned, but patient Acadian farmers.
Even as pilgrims, who journey afar from their homes and their
    country,
Sing as they go, and in singing forget they are weary and
    wayworn,
So with songs on their lips the Acadian peasants descended
Down from the church to the shore, amid their wives and their
    daughters.
Foremost the young men came; and, raising together their
    voices,
Sang they with tremulous lips a chant of the Catholic
    Missions: —
'Sacred heart of the Saviour! O inexhaustible fountain!
Fill our hearts this day with strength and submission and
    patience!'
Then the old men, as they marched, and the women that stood
    by the wayside
Joined in the sacred psalm, and the birds in the sunshine above
    them
Mingled their notes therewith, like voices of spirits departed.

    Half-way down to the shore Evangeline waited in silence,
Not overcome with grief, but strong in the hour of affliction, —
Calmly and sadly waited, until the procession approached her,
And she beheld the face of Gabriel pale with emotion.
Tears then filled her eyes, and eagerly running to meet him,
Clasped she his hands, and laid her head on his shoulder, and
    whispered, —
'Gabriel! be of good cheer! for if we love one another,
Nothing, in truth, can harm us, whatever mischances may
    happen!'

Smiling she spake these words; then suddenly paused, for her
    father
Saw she slowly advancing. Alas! how changed was his aspect!
Gone was the glow from his cheek, and the fire from his eye,
    and his footstep
Heavier seemed with the weight of the weary heart in his bosom.
But with a smile and a sigh, she clasped his neck and embraced
    him,
Speaking words of endearment where words of comfort availed
    not.
Thus to the Gaspereau's mouth moved on that mournful
    procession.

  There disorder prevailed, and the tumult and stir of
    embarking.
Busily plied the freighted boats; and in the confusion
Wives were torn from their husbands, and mothers, too late,
    saw their children
Left on the land, extending their arms, with wildest entreaties.
So unto separate ships were Basil and Gabriel carried,
While in despair on the shore Evangeline stood with her father.
Half the task was not done when the sun went down, and the
    twilight
Deepened and darkened around; and in haste the refluent ocean
Fled away from the shore, and left the line of the sand-beach
Covered with waifs of the tide, with kelp and the slippery
    seaweed.
Farther back in the midst of the household goods and the
    wagons,
Like to a gypsy camp, or a leaguer after a battle,
All escape cut off by the sea, and the sentinels near them,
Lay encamped for the night the houseless Acadian farmers.
Back to its nethermost caves retreated the bellowing ocean,
Dragging adown the beach the rattling pebbles, and leaving
Inland and far up the shore the stranded boats of the sailors.
Then, as the night descended, the herds returned from their
    pastures;
Sweet was the moist still air with the odour of milk from their
    udders;
Lowing they waited, and long, at the well-known bars of the
    farmyard, —

Waited and looked in vain for the voice and the hand of the
    milkmaid.
Silence reigned in the streets; from the church no Angelus
    sounded,
Rose no smoke from the roofs, and gleamed no lights from the
    windows.

  But on the shores meanwhile the evening fires had been
    kindled,
Built of the drift-wood thrown on the sands from wrecks in the
    tempest.
Round them shapes of gloom and sorrowful faces were gathered,
Voices of women were heard, and of men, and the crying of
    children.
Onward from fire to fire, as from hearth to hearth in his parish,
Wandered the faithful priest, consoling and blessing and
    cheering,
Like unto shipwrecked Paul on Melita's desolate seashore.
Thus he approached the place where Evangeline sat with her
    father,
And in the flickering light beheld the face of the old man,
Haggard and hollow and wan, and without either thought or
    emotion,
E'en as the face of a clock from which the hands have been
    taken.
Vainly Evangeline strove with words and caresses to cheer him,
Vainly offered him food; yet he moved not, he looked not, he
    spake not,
But, with a vacant stare, ever gazed at the flickering fire-light.
'*Benedicite!*' murmured the priest, in tones of compassion.
More he fain would have said, but his heart was full, and his
    accents
Faltered and paused on his lips, as the feet of a child on a
    threshold,
Hushed by the scene he beholds, and the awful presence of
    sorrow.
Silently, therefore, he laid his hand on the head of the maiden,
Raising his eyes, full of tears, to the silent stars that above them
Moved on their way, unperturbed by the wrongs and sorrows
    of mortals,
Then sat he down at her side, and they wept together in silence.

Suddenly rose from the south a light, as in autumn the blood-
    red
Moon climbs the crystal walls of heaven, and o'er the horizon
Titan-like stretches its hundred hands upon mountain and
    meadow,
Seizing the rocks and the rivers, and piling huge shadows
    together.
Broader and ever broader it gleamed on the roofs of the village,
Gleamed on the sky and the sea, and the ships that lay in the
    roadstead.
Columns of shining smoke uprose, and flashes of flame were
Thrust through their folds and withdrawn, like the quivering
    hands of a martyr.
Then as the wind seized the gleeds and the burning thatch, and,
    uplifting,
Whirled them aloft through the air, at once from a hundred
    house-tops
Started the sheeted smoke with flashes of flame intermingled.

These things beheld in dismay the crowd on the shore and on
    shipboard.
Speechless at first they stood, then cried aloud in their anguish.
'We shall behold no more our homes in the village of Grand-
    Pré !'
Loud on a sudden the cocks began to crow in the farmyards,
Thinking the day had dawned ; and anon the lowing of cattle
Came on the evening breeze, by the barking of dogs interrupted.
Then rose a sound of dread, such as startles the sleeping
    encampments
Far in the western prairies or forests that skirt the Nebraska,
When the wild horses affrighted sweep by with the speed of the
    whirlwind,
Or the loud bellowing herds of buffaloes rush to the river.
Such was the sound that arose on the night, as the herds and the
    horses
Broke through their folds and fences, and madly rushed o'er the
    meadows.

Overwhelmed with the sight, yet speechless, the priest and the
    maiden

Gazed on the scene of terror that reddened and widened before
   them;
And as they turned at length to speak to their silent companion,
Lo! from his seat he had fallen, and stretched abroad on the
   seashore
Motionless lay his form, from which the soul had departed.
Slowly the priest uplifted the lifeless head, and the maiden
Knelt at her father's side, and wailed aloud in her terror.
Then in a swoon she sank, and lay with her head on his bosom.
Through the long night she lay in deep, oblivious slumber;
And when she woke from the trance, she beheld a multitude
   near her.
Faces of friends she beheld, that were mournfully gazing upon
   her,
Pallid, with tearful eyes, and looks of saddest compassion.
Still the blaze of the burning village illumined the landscape,
Reddened the sky overhead, and gleamed on the faces around
   her,
And like the day of doom it seemed to her wavering senses.
Then a familiar voice she heard, as it said to the people, —
'Let us bury him here by the sea. When a happier season
Brings us again to our homes from the unknown land of our
   exile,
Then shall his sacred dust be piously laid in the churchyard.'
Such were the words of the priest. And there in haste by the
   seaside,
Having the glare of the burning village for funeral torches,
But without bell or book, they buried the farmer of Grand-Pré.
And as the voice of the priest repeated the service of sorrow,
Lo! with a mournful sound, like the voice of a vast
   congregation,
Solemnly answered the sea, and mingled its roar with the dirges.
'Twas the returning tide, that afar from the waste of the ocean,
With the first dawn of the day, came heaving and hurrying
   landward.
Then recommenced once more the stir and noise of embarking;
And with the ebb of that tide the ships sailed out of the harbour,
Leaving behind them the dead on the shore, and the village in
   ruins.

PART THE SECOND

I

Many a weary year had passed since the burning of Grand-Pré,
When on the falling tide the freighted vessels departed,
Bearing a nation, with all its household goods, into exile,
Exile without an end, and without an example in story.
Far asunder, on separate coasts, the Acadians landed;
Scattered were they, like flakes of snow, when the wind from the northeast
Strikes aslant through the fogs that darken the Banks of Newfoundland.
Friendless, homeless, hopeless, they wandered from city to city,
From the cold lakes of the North to sultry Southern savannas, –
From the bleak shores of the sea to the lands where the Father of Waters
Seizes the hills in his hands, and drags them down to the ocean,
Deep in their sands to bury the scattered bones of the mammoth.
Friends they sought and homes; and many, despairing, heartbroken,
Asked of the earth but a grave, and no longer a friend nor a fireside.
Written their history stands on tablets of stone in the churchyards.
Long among them was seen a maiden who waited and wandered,
Lowly and meek in spirit, but patiently suffering all things.
Fair was she and young; but, alas! before her extended,
Dreary and vast and silent, the desert of life, with its pathway
Marked by the graves of those who had sorrowed and suffered before her,
Passions long extinguished, and hopes long dead and abandoned,
As the emigrant's way o'er the Western desert is marked by
Camp-fires long consumed, and bones that bleach in the sunshine.
Something there was in her life incomplete, imperfect, unfinished;
As if a morning of June, with all its music and sunshine,
Suddenly paused in the sky, and, fading, slowly descended
Into the east again, from whence it late had arisen.

Sometimes she lingered in towns, till, urged by the fever within
    her,
Urged by a restless longing, the hunger and thirst of the spirit,
She would commence again her endless search and endeavour;
Sometimes in churchyards strayed, and gazed on the crosses and
    tombstones,
Sat by some nameless grave, and thought that perhaps in its
    bosom
He was already at rest, and she longed to slumber beside him.
Sometimes a rumour, a hearsay, an inarticulate whisper,
Came with its airy hand to point and beckon her forward.
Sometimes she spake with those who had seen her beloved and
    known him,
But it was long ago, in some far-off place or forgotten.
'Gabriel Lajeunesse!' said they; 'O, yes! we have seen him.
He was with Basil the blacksmith, and both have gone to the
    prairies;
Coureurs-des-Bois are they, and famous hunters and trappers.'
'Gabriel Lajeunesse!' said others; 'O, yes! we have seen him.
He is a *Voyageur* in the lowlands of Louisiana.'
Then would they say, – 'Dear child! why dream and wait for
    him longer?
Are there not other youths as fair as Gabriel? others
Who have hearts as tender and true, and spirits as loyal?
Here is Baptiste Leblanc, the notary's son, who has loved thee
Many a tedious year; come, give him thy hand and be happy!
Thou art too fair to be left to braid St Catherine's tresses.'
Then would Evangeline answer, serenely but sadly, – 'I cannot!
Whither my heart has gone, there follows my hand, and not
    elsewhere.
For when the heart goes before, like a lamp, and illumines the
    pathway,
Many things are made clear, that else lie hidden in darkness.'
And thereupon the priest, her friend and father-confessor,
Said, with a smile, – 'O daughter! thy God thus speaketh within
    thee!
Talk not of wasted affection, affection never was wasted;
If it enrich not the heart of another, its waters, returning
Back to their springs, like the rain, shall fill them full of
    refreshment;

That which the fountain sends forth returns again to the
    fountain.
Patience; accomplish thy labour; accomplish thy work of
    affection!
Sorrow and silence are strong, and patient endurance is godlike.
Therefore accomplish thy labour of love, till the heart is made
    godlike,
Purified, strengthened, perfected, and rendered more worthy of
    heaven!'
Cheered by the good man's words, Evangeline laboured and
    waited.
Still in her heart she heard the funeral dirge of the ocean,
But with its sound there was mingled a voice that whispered,
    'Despair not!'
Thus did that poor soul wander in want and cheerless
    discomfort,
Bleeding, barefooted, over the shards and thorns of existence.
Let me essay, O Muse! to follow the wanderer's footsteps; –
Not through each devious path, each changeful year of
    existence;
But as a traveller follows a streamlet's course through the valley:
Far from its margin at times, and seeing the gleam of its water
Here and there, in some open space, and at intervals only;
Then drawing nearer its banks, through sylvan glooms that
    conceal it,
Though he behold it not, he can hear its continuous murmur;
Happy, at length, if we find the spot where it reaches an outlet.

II

    It was the month of May. Far down the Beautiful River,
Past the Ohio shore and past the mouth of the Wabash,
Into the golden stream of the broad and swift Mississippi,
Floated a cumbrous boat, that was rowed by Acadian boatmen.
It was a band of exiles: a raft, as it were, from the shipwrecked
Nation, scattered along the coast, now floating together,
Bound by the bonds of a common belief and a common
    misfortune;
Men and women and children, who, guided by hope or by
    hearsay,
Sought for their kith and their kin among the few-acred farmers

On the Acadian coast, and the prairies of fair Opelousas.

With them Evangeline went, and her guide, the Father Felician.

Onward o'er sunken sands, through a wilderness sombre with forests,

Day after day they glided adown the turbulent river;

Night after night, by their blazing fires, encamped on its borders.

Now through rushing chutes, among green islands, where plume-like

Cotton-trees nodded their shadowy crests, they swept with the current.

Then emerged into broad lagoons, where silvery sand-bars

Lay in the stream, and along the wimpling waves of their margin,

Shining with snow-white plumes, large flocks of pelicans waded.

Level the landscape grew, and along the shores of the river,

Shaded by china-trees, in the midst of luxuriant gardens,

Stood the houses of planters, with negro-cabins and dove-cots.

They were approaching the region where reigns perpetual summer,

Where through the Golden Coast, and groves of orange and citron,

Sweeps with majestic curve the river away to the eastward.

They, too, swerved from their course; and, entering the Bayou of Plaquemine,

Soon were lost in a maze of sluggish and devious waters,

Which, like a network of steel, extended in every direction.

Over their heads the towering and tenebrous boughs of the cypress

Met in a dusky arch, and trailing mosses in mid-air

Waved like banners that hang on the walls of ancient cathedrals.

Deathlike the silence seemed, and unbroken, save by the herons

Home to their roosts in the cedar-trees returning at sunset,

Or by the owl, as he greeted the moon with demoniac laughter.

Lovely the moonlight was as it glanced and gleamed on the water,

Gleamed on the columns of cypress and cedar sustaining the arches,

Down through whose broken vaults it fell as through chinks in a ruin.

Dreamlike, and indistinct, and strange were all things around them;

And o'er their spirits there came a feeling of wonder and
    sadness, --
Strange forebodings of ill, unseen and that cannot be compassed.
As, at the tramp of a horse's hoof on the turf of the prairies,
Far in advance are closed the leaves of the shrinking mimosa,
So, at the hoof-beats of fate, with sad forebodings of evil,
Shrinks and closes the heart, ere the stroke of doom has attained
    it.
But Evangeline's heart was sustained by a vision, that faintly
Floated before her eyes, and beckoned her on through the
    moonlight.
It was the thought of her brain that assumed the shape of a
    phantom.
Through those shadowy aisles had Gabriel wandered before her,
And every stroke of the oar now brought him nearer and nearer.

  Then, in his place, at the prow of the boat, rose one of the
    oarsmen,
And, as a signal sound, if others like them peradventure
Sailed on those gloomy and midnight streams, blew a blast on
    his bugle.
Wild through the dark colonnades and corridors leafy the blast
    rang,
Breaking the seal of silence, and giving tongues to the forest.
Soundless above them the banners of moss just stirred to the
    music.
Multitudinous echoes awoke and died in the distance,
Over the watery floor, and beneath the reverberant branches;
But not a voice replied; no answer came from the darkness;
And when the echoes had ceased, like a sense of pain was the
    silence.
Then Evangeline slept; but the boatmen rowed through the
    midnight,
Silent at times, then singing familiar Canadian boat-songs,
Such as they sang of old on their own Acadian rivers.
And through the night were heard the mysterious sounds of the
    desert,
Far off, indistinct, as of wave or wind in the forest,
Mixed with the whoop of the crane and the roar of the grim
    alligator.

Thus ere another noon they emerged from those shades; and
   before them
Lay, in the golden sun, the lakes of the Atchafalaya.
Water-lilies in myriads rocked on the slight undulations
Made by the passing oars, and, resplendent in beauty, the lotus
Lifted her golden crown above the heads of the boatmen.
Faint was the air with the odorous breath of magnolia blossoms,
And with the heat of noon; and numberless sylvan islands,
Fragrant and thickly embowered with blossoming hedges of
   roses,
Near to whose shores they glided along, invited to slumber.
Soon by the fairest of these their weary oars were suspended.
Under the boughs of Wachita willows, that grew by the margin,
Safely their boat was moored; and scattered about on the
   greensward,
Tired with their midnight toil, the weary travellers slumbered.
Over them vast and high extended the cope of a cedar.
Swinging from its great arms, the trumpet-flower and the grape-
   vine
Hung their ladder of ropes aloft like the ladder of Jacob,
On whose pendulous stairs the angels ascending, descending,
Were the swift humming-birds, that flitted from blossom to
   blossom.
Such was the vision Evangeline saw as she slumbered beneath it.
Filled was her heart with love, and the dawn of an opening
   heaven
Lighted her soul in sleep with the glory of regions celestial.

Nearer and ever nearer, among the numberless islands,
Darted a light, swift boat, that sped away o'er the water,
Urged on its course by the sinewy arms of hunters and trappers.
Northward its prow was turned, to the land of the bison and
   beaver.
At the helm sat a youth, with countenance thoughtful and
   careworn.
Dark and neglected locks overshadowed his brow, and a sadness
Somewhat beyond his years on his face was legibly written.
Gabriel was it, who, weary with waiting, unhappy and restless,
Sought in the Western wilds oblivion of self and of sorrow.
Swiftly they glided along, close under the lee of the island,
But by the opposite bank, and behind a screen of palmettos,

So that they saw not the boat, where it lay concealed in the willows,
And undisturbed by the dash of their oars, and unseen, were the sleepers;
Angel of God was there none to awaken the slumbering maiden.
Swiftly they glided away, like the shade of a cloud on the prairie.
After the sound of their oars on the tholes had died in the distance,
As from a magic trance the sleepers awoke, and the maiden
Said with a sigh to the friendly priest, – 'O Father Felician!
Something says in my heart that near me Gabriel wanders.
Is it a foolish dream, an idle and vague superstition?
Or has an angel passed, and revealed the truth to my spirit?'
Then, with a blush, she added, – 'Alas for my credulous fancy!
Unto ears like thine such words as these have no meaning.'
But made answer the reverend man, and he smiled as he answered, –
'Daughter, thy words are not idle; nor are they to me without meaning.
Feeling is deep and still; and the word that floats on the surface
Is as the tossing buoy, that betrays where the anchor is hidden.
Therefore trust to thy heart, and to what the world calls illusions.
Gabriel truly is near thee; for not far away to the southward,
On the banks of the Têche, are the towns of St Maur and St Martin.
There the long-wandering bride shall be given again to her bridegroom,
There the long-absent pastor regain his flock and his sheepfold.
Beautiful is the land, with its prairies and forests of fruit-trees;
Under the feet a garden of flowers, and the bluest of heavens
Bending above, and resting its dome on the walls of the forest.
They who dwell there have named it the Eden of Louisiana.'

And with these words of cheer they arose and continued their journey.
Softly the evening came. The sun from the western horizon
Like a magician extended his golden wand o'er the landscape;
Twinkling vapours arose; and sky and water and forest
Seemed all on fire at the touch, and melted and mingled together.
Hanging between two skies, a cloud with edges of silver,

Floated the boat, with its dripping oars, on the motionless
    water.
Filled was Evangeline's heart with inexpressible sweetness.
Touched by the magic spell, the sacred fountains of feeling
Glowed with the light of love, as the skies and waters around
    her.
Then from a neighbouring thicket the mocking-bird, wildest of
    singers,
Swinging aloft on a willow spray that hung o'er the water,
Shook from his little throat such floods of delirious music,
That the whole air and the woods and the waves seemed silent
    to listen.
Plaintive at first were the tones and sad ; then soaring to madness
Seemed they to follow or guide the revel of frenzied Bacchantes.
Single notes were then heard, in sorrowful, low lamentation ;
Till, having gathered them all, he flung them abroad in derision,
As when, after a storm, a gust of wind through the tree-tops
Shakes down the rattling rain in a crystal shower on the
    branches.
With such a prelude as this, hearts that throbbed with emotion,
Slowly they entered the Têche, where it flows through the green
    Opelousas,
And through the amber air, above the crest of the woodland,
Saw the column of smoke that arose from a neighbouring
    dwelling; —
Sounds of a horn they heard, and the distant lowing of cattle.

III

  Near to the bank of the river, o'ershadowed by oaks, from
    whose branches
Garlands of Spanish moss and of mystic mistletoe flaunted,
Such as the Druids cut down with golden hatchets at Yule-tide,
Stood secluded and still, the house of the herdsman. A garden
Girded it round about with a belt of luxuriant blossoms,
Filling the air with fragrance. The house itself was of timbers
Hewn from the cypress-tree, and carefully fitted together.
Large and low was the roof ; and on slender columns supported,
Rose-wreathed, vine-encircled, a broad and spacious veranda,
Haunt of the humming-bird and the bee, extended around it.
At each end of the house, amid the flowers of the garden,

Stationed the dove-cots were, as love's perpetual symbol,
Scenes of endless wooing, and endless contentions of rivals.
Silence reigned o'er the place. The line of shadow and sunshine
Ran near the tops of the trees; but the house itself was in
  shadow,
And from its chimney-top, ascending and slowly expanding
Into the evening air, a thin blue column of smoke rose.
In the rear of the house, from the garden gate, ran a pathway
Through the great groves of oak to the skirts of the limitless
  prairie,
Into whose sea of flowers the sun was slowly descending.
Full in his track of light, like ships with shadowy canvas
Hanging loose from their spars in a motionless calm in the
  tropics,
Stood a cluster of trees, with tangled cordage of grape-vines.

  Just where the woodlands met the flowery surf of the prairie,
Mounted upon his horse, with Spanish saddle and stirrups,
Sat a herdsman, arrayed in gaiters and doublet of deerskin.
Broad and brown was the face that from under the Spanish
  sombrero
Gazed on the peaceful scene, with the lordly look of its master.
Round about him were numberless herds of kine, that were
  grazing
Quietly in the meadows, and breathing the vapoury freshness
That uprose from the river, and spread itself over the landscape.
Slowly lifting the horn that hung at his side, and expanding
Fully his broad, deep chest, he blew a blast, that resounded
Wildly and sweet and far, through the still damp air of the
  evening.
Suddenly out of the grass the long white horns of the cattle
Rose like flakes of foam on the adverse currents of ocean.
Silent a moment they gazed, then bellowing rushed o'er the
  prairie,
And the whole mass became a cloud, a shade in the distance.
Then, as the herdsman turned to the house, through the gate of
  the garden
Saw he the forms of the priest and the maiden advancing to
  meet him.
Suddenly down from his horse he sprang in amazement, and
  forward

Rushed with extended arms and exclamations of wonder;
When they beheld his face, they recognised Basil the blacksmith.
Hearty his welcome was, as he led his guests to the garden.
There in an arbour of roses with endless question and answer
Gave they vent to their hearts, and renewed their friendly embraces,
Laughing and weeping by turns, or sitting silent and thoughtful.
Thoughtful, for Gabriel came not; and now dark doubts and misgivings
Stole o'er the maiden's heart; and Basil, somewhat embarrassed,
Broke the silence and said, — 'If you came by the Atchafalaya,
How have you nowhere encountered my Gabriel's boat on the bayous?'
Over Evangeline's face at the words of Basil a shade passed.
Tears came into her eyes, and she said, with a tremulous accent, —
'Gone? is Gabriel gone?' and, concealing her face on his shoulder,
All her o'erburdened heart gave way and she wept and lamented.
Then the good Basil said, — and his voice grew blithe as he said it, —
'Be of good cheer, my child; it is only to-day he departed.
Foolish boy! he has left me alone with my herds and my horses.
Moody and restless grown, and, tried and troubled, his spirit
Could no longer endure the calm of this quiet existence.
Thinking ever of thee, uncertain and sorrowful ever,
Ever silent, or speaking only of thee and his troubles,
He at length had become so tedious to men and to maidens,
Tedious even to me, that at length I bethought me, and sent him
Unto the town of Adayes to trade for mules with the Spaniards.
Thence he will follow the Indian trails to the Ozark Mountains,
Hunting for furs in the forests, on rivers trapping the beaver.
Therefore be of good cheer; we will follow the fugitive lover;
He is not far on his way, and the Fates and the streams are against him.
Up and away to-morrow, and through the red dew of the morning
We will follow him fast, and bring him back to his prison.'

Then glad voices were heard, and up from the banks of the river,

Borne aloft on his comrades' arms, came Michael the fiddler.
Long under Basil's roof had he lived like a god on Olympus,
Having no other care than dispensing music to mortals.
Far renowned was he for his silver locks and his fiddle.
'Long live Michael,' they cried, 'our brave Acadian minstrel!'
As they bore him aloft in triumphal procession; and straightway
Father Felician advanced with Evangeline, greeting the old man
Kindly and oft, and recalling the past, while Basil, enraptured,
Hailed with hilarious joy his old companions and gossips,
Laughing loud and long, and embracing mothers and daughters.
Much they marvelled to see the wealth of the ci-devant
     blacksmith,
All his domains and his herds, and his patriarchal demeanour;
Much they marvelled to hear his tales of the soil and the climate,
And of the prairies, whose numberless herds were his who
     would take them;
Each one thought in his heart, that he, too, would go and do
     likewise.
Thus they ascended the steps, and, crossing the airy veranda,
Entered the hall of the house, where already the supper of Basil
Waited his late return; and they rested and feasted together.

   Over the joyous feast the sudden darkness descended.
All was silent without, and, illuming the landscape with silver,
Fair rose the dewy moon and the myriad stars; but within
     doors,
Brighter than these, shone the faces of friends in the glimmering
     lamplight.
Then from his station aloft, at the head of the table, the
     herdsman
Poured forth his heart and his wine together in endless
     profusion.
Lighting his pipe, that was filled with sweet Natchitoches
     tobacco,
Thus he spake to his guests, who listened, and smiled as they
     listened: —
'Welcome once more, my friends, who so long have been
     friendless and homeless,
Welcome once more to a home, that is better perchance than
     the old one!
Here no hungry winter congeals our blood like the rivers;

Here no stony ground provokes the wrath of the farmer;
Smoothly the ploughshare runs through the soil as a keel
  through the water.
All the year round the orange-groves are in blossom; and grass
  grows
More in a single night than a whole Canadian summer.
Here, too, numberless herds run wild and unclaimed in the
  prairies;
Here, too, lands may be had for the asking, and forests of timber
With a few blows of the axe are hewn and framed into houses.
After your houses are built, and your fields are yellow with
  harvests,
No King George of England shall drive you away from your
  homesteads,
Burning your dwellings and barns, and stealing your farms and
  your cattle.'
Speaking these words, he blew a wrathful cloud from his
  nostrils,
And his huge, brawny hand came thundering down on the table,
So that the guests all started; and Father Felician, astonished,
Suddenly paused, with a pinch of snuff half-way to his nostrils.
But the brave Basil resumed, and his words were milder and
  gayer: —
'Only beware of the fever, my friends, beware of the fever!
For it is not like that of our cold Acadian climate,
Cured by wearing a spider hung round one's neck in a nutshell!'
Then there were voices heard at the door, and footsteps
  approaching
Sounded upon the stairs and floor of the breezy veranda.
It was the neighbouring Creoles and small Acadian planters,
Who had been summoned all to the house of Basil the
  Herdsman.
Merry the meeting was of ancient comrades and neighbours:
Friend clasped friend in his arms; and they who before were as
  strangers,
Meeting in exile, became straightway as friends to each other,
Drawn by the gentle bond of a common country together.
But in the neighbouring hall a strain of music, proceeding
From the accordant strings of Michael's melodious fiddle,
Broke up all further speech. Away, like children delighted,

All things forgotten beside, they gave themselves to the maddening
Whirl of the dizzy dance, as it swept and swayed to the music,
Dreamlike, with beaming eyes and the rush of fluttering garments.

 Meanwhile, apart, at the head of the hall, the priest and the herdsman
Sat, conversing together of past and present and future;
While Evangeline stood like one entranced, for within her
Olden memories rose, and loud in the midst of the music
Heard she the sound of the sea, and an irrepressible sadness
Came o'er her heart, and unseen she stole forth into the garden.
Beautiful was the night. Behind the black wall of the forest,
Tipping its summit with silver, arose the moon. On the river
Fell here and there through the branches a tremulous gleam of the moonlight,
Like the sweet thoughts of love on a darkened and devious spirit,
Nearer and round about her, the manifold flowers of the garden
Poured out their souls in odours, that were their prayers and confessions
Unto the night, as it went its way, like a silent Carthusian.
Fuller of fragrance than they, and as heavy with shadows and night-dews,
Hung the heart of the maiden. The calm and the magical moonlight
Seemed to inundate her soul with indefinable longings,
As, through the garden gate, beneath the brown shade of the oak-trees,
Passed she along the path to the edge of the measureless prairie.
Silent it lay, with a silvery haze upon it, and fire-flies
Gleaming and floating away in mingled and infinite numbers.
Over her head the stars, the thoughts of God in the heavens,
Shone on the eyes of man, who had ceased to marvel and worship,
Save when a blazing comet was seen on the walls of that temple,
As if a hand had appeared and written upon them, 'Upharsin.'
And the soul of the maiden, between the stars and the fire-flies,
Wandered alone, and she cried, – 'O Gabriel! O my beloved!
Art thou so near unto me, and yet I cannot behold thee?

Art thou so near unto me, and yet thy voice does not reach me?
Ah! how often thy feet have trod this path to the prairie!
Ah! often thine eyes have looked on the woodlands around me!
Ah! how often beneath this oak, returning from labour,
Thou hast lain down to rest, and to dream of me in thy slumbers.
When shall these eyes behold, these arms be folded about thee?'
Loud and sudden and near the note of a whippoorwill sounded
Like a flute in the woods; and anon, through the neighbouring thickets,
Farther and farther away it floated and dropped into silence.
'Patience!' whispered the oaks from oracular caverns of darkness;
And, from the moonlit meadow, a sigh responded, 'To-morrow!'

Bright rose the sun next day; and all the flowers of the garden
Bathed his shining feet with their tears, and anointed his tresses
With the delicious balm that they bore in their vases of crystal.
'Farewell!' said the priest, as he stood at the shadowy threshold;
'See that you bring us the Prodigal Son from his fasting and famine,
And, too, the Foolish Virgin, who slept when the bridegroom was coming.'
'Farewell!' answered the maiden, and, smiling, with Basil descended
Down to the river's brink, where the boatmen already were waiting,
Thus beginning their journey with morning, and sunshine, and gladness,
Swiftly they followed the flight of him who was speeding before them,
Blown by the blast of fate like a dead leaf over the desert.
Not that day, nor the next, nor yet the day that succeeded,
Found they trace of his course, in lake or forest or river,
Nor, after many days, had they found him; but vague and uncertain
Rumours alone were their guides through a wild and desolate country;
Till, at the little inn of the Spanish town of Adayes,
Weary and worn, they alighted, and learned from the garrulous landlord

That on the day before, with horses and guides and companions,
Gabriel left the village, and took the road to the prairies.

IV

Far in the West there lies a desert land, where the mountains
Lift, through perpetual snows, their lofty and luminous summits.
Down from their jagged, deep ravines, where the gorge, like a
      gateway,
Opens a passage rude to the wheels of the emigrant's wagon,
Westward the Oregon flows and the Walleway and Owyhee.
Eastward, with devious course, among the Wind-river
      Mountains,
Through the Sweet-water Valley precipitate leaps the Nebraska;
And to the south, from Fontaine-qui-bout and the Spanish
      sierras,
Fretted with sands and rocks, and swept by the wind of the
      desert,
Numberless torrents, with ceaseless sound, descend to the ocean,
Like the great chords of a harp, in loud and solemn vibrations.
Spreading between these streams are the wondrous, beautiful
      prairies,
Billowy bays of grass ever rolling in shadow and sunshine,
Bright with luxuriant clusters of roses and purple amorphas.
Over them wander the buffalo herds, and the elk and the
      roebuck;
Over them wander the wolves, and herds of riderless horses;
Fires that blast and blight, and winds that are weary with travel;
Over them wander the scattered tribes of Ishmael's children,
Staining the desert with blood; and above their terrible war-
      trails
Circles and sails aloft, on pinions majestic, the vulture,
Like the implacable soul of a chieftain slaughtered in battle,
By invisible stairs ascending and scaling the heavens.
Here and there rise smokes from the camps of these savage
      marauders;
Here and there rise groves from the margins of swift-running
      rivers;
And the grim, taciturn bear, the anchorite monk of the desert,
Climbs down their dark ravines to dig for roots by the
      brookside,

And over all is the sky, the clear and crystalline heaven,
Like the protecting hand of God inverted above them.

   Into this wonderful land, at the base of the Ozark Mountains,
Gabriel far had entered, with hunters and trappers behind him.
Day after day, with their Indian guides, the maiden and Basil
Followed his flying steps, and thought each day to o'ertake him.
Sometimes they saw, or thought they saw, the smoke of his
    camp-fire
Rise in the morning air from the distant plain; but at nightfall,
When they had reached the place, they found only embers and
    ashes.
And, though their hearts were sad at times and their bodies were
    weary,
Hope still guided them on, as the magic Fata Morgana
Showed them her lakes of light, that retreated and vanished
    before them.

   Once, as they sat by their evening fire, there silently entered
Into the little camp an Indian woman, whose features
Wore deep traces of sorrow, and patience as great as her sorrow.
She was a Shawnee woman returning home to her people,
From the far-off hunting-grounds of the cruel Camanches,
Where her Canadian husband, a Coureur-des-Bois, had been
    murdered.
Touched were their hearts at her story, and warmest and
    friendliest welcome
Gave they, with words of cheer, and she sat and feasted among
    them
On the buffalo-meat and the venison cooked on the embers,
But when their meal was done, and Basil and all his companions,
Worn with the long day's march and the chase of the deer and
    the bison,
Stretched themselves on the ground, and slept where the quiver-
    ing firelight
Flashed on their swarthy cheeks, and their forms wrapped up in
    their blankets,
Then at the door of Evangeline's tent she sat and repeated
Slowly, with soft, low voice, and the charm of her Indian accent,
All the tale of her love, with its pleasures, and pains, and
    reverses.

Much Evangeline wept at the tale, and to know that another
Hapless heart like her own had loved and had been
    disappointed.
Moved to the depths of her soul by pity and woman's
    compassion,
Yet in her sorrow pleased that one who had suffered was near
    her,
She in turn related her love and all its disasters.
Mute with wonder the Shawnee sat, and when she had ended
Still was mute; but at length, as if a mysterious horror
Passed through her brain, she spake, and repeated the tale of the
    Mowis;
Mowis, the bridegroom of snow, who won and wedded a
    maiden,
But, when the morning came, arose and passed from the
    wigwam,
Fading and melting away and dissolving into the sunshine,
Till she beheld him no more, though she followed far into the
    forest.
Then, in those sweet, low tones, that seemed like a weird
    incantation,
Told she the tale of the fair Lilinau, who was wooed by a
    phantom,
That, through the pines o'er her father's lodge, in the hush of
    the twilight,
Breathed like the evening wind, and whispered love to the
    maiden,
Till she followed his green and waving plume through the forest,
And never more returned, nor was seen again by her people.
Silent with wonder and strange surprise, Evangeline listened
To the soft flow of her magical words, till the region around her
Seemed like enchanted ground, and her swarthy guest the
    enchantress.
Slowly over the tops of the Ozark Mountains the moon rose,
Lighting the little tent, and with a mysterious splendour
Touching the sombre leaves, and embracing and filling the
    woodland.
With a delicious sound the brook rushed by, and the branches
Swayed and sighed overhead in scarcely audible whispers.
Filled with the thoughts of love was Evangeline's heart, but a
    secret,

Subtile sense crept in of pain and indefinite terror,
As the cold, poisonous snake creeps into the nest of the swallow.
It was no earthly fear. A breath from the region of spirits
Seemed to float in the air of night; and she felt for a moment
That, like the Indian maid, she, too, was pursuing a phantom.
And with this thought she slept, and the fear and the phantom
  had vanished.

  Early upon the morrow the march was resumed; and the
    Shawnee
Said, as they journeyed along, – 'On the western slope of these
    mountains
Dwells in his little village the Black Robe chief of the Mission.
Much he teaches the people, and tells them of Mary and Jesus;
Loud laugh their hearts with joy, and weep with pain, as they
    hear him.'
Then, with a sudden and secret emotion, Evangeline answered, –
'Let us go to the Mission, for there good tidings await us!'
Thither they turned their steeds; and behind a spur of the
    mountains,
Just as the sun went down, they heard a murmur of voices,
And in a meadow green and broad, by the bank of a river,
Saw the tents of the Christians, the tents of the Jesuit Mission.
Under a towering oak, that stood in the midst of the village,
Knelt the Black Robe chief with his children. A crucifix fastened
High on the trunk of the tree, and overshadowed by grape-
    vines,
Looked with its agonised face on the multitude kneeling beneath
    it.
This was their rural chapel. Aloft, through the intricate arches
Of its aërial roof, arose the chant of their vespers,
Mingling its notes with the soft susurrus and sighs of the
    branches.
Silent, with heads uncovered, the travellers, nearer approaching,
Knelt on the swarded floor, and joined in the evening devotions.
But when the service was done, and the benediction had fallen
Forth from the hands of the priest, like seed from the hands of
    the sower,
Slowly the reverend man advanced to the strangers, and bade
    them

Welcome; and when they replied, he smiled with benignant
    expression
Hearing the homelike sounds of his mother-tongue in the forest,
And with words of kindness conducted them into his wigwam.
There upon mats and skins they reposed, and on cakes of the
    maize-ear
Feasted, and slaked their thirst from the water-gourd of the
    teacher.
Soon was their story told; and the priest with solemnity
    answered : –
'Not six suns have risen and set since Gabriel, seated
On this mat by my side, where now the maiden reposes,
Told me this same sad tale; then arose and continued his
    journey !'
Soft was the voice of the priest, and he spake with an accent of
    kindness;
But on Evangeline's heart fell his words as in winter the snow-
    flakes
Fall into some lone nest from which the birds have departed.
'Far to the north he has gone,' continued the priest; 'but in
    autumn,
When the chase is done, will return again to the Mission.'
Then Evangeline said, and her voice was meek and
    submissive, –
'Let me remain with thee, for my soul is sad and afflicted.'
So seemed it wise and well unto all; and betimes on the morrow,
Mounting his Mexican steed, with his Indian guides and
    companions,
Homeward Basil returned, and Evangeline stayed at the Mission.

Slowly, slowly, slowly the days succeeded each other, –
Days and weeks and months; and the fields of maize that were
    springing
Green from the ground when a stranger she came, now waving
    above her,
Lifted their slender shafts, with leaves interlacing, and forming
Cloisters for mendicant crows and granaries pillaged by
    squirrels.
Then in the golden weather the maize was husked, and the
    maidens
Blushed at each blood-red ear, for that betokened a lover,

But at the crooked laughed, and called it a thief in the corn-
field.
Even the blood-red ear to Evangeline brought not her lover.
'Patience !' the priest would say ; 'have faith, and thy prayer will
be answered !
Look at this delicate plant that lifts its head from the meadow,
See how its leaves all point to the north, as true as the magnet ;
It is the compass-flower, that the finger of God has suspended
Here on its fragile stalk, to direct the traveller's journey
Over the sea-like, pathless, limitless waste of the desert.
Such in the soul of man is faith. The blossoms of passion,
Gay and luxuriant flowers, are brighter and fuller of fragrance,
But they beguile us, and lead us astray, and their odour is
deadly.
Only this humble plant can guide us here, and hereafter
Crown us with asphodel flowers, that are wet with the dews of
nepenthe.'

So came the autumn, and passed, and the winter, – yet Gabriel
came not ;
Blossomed the opening spring and the notes of the robin and
blue-bird
Sounded sweet upon wold and in wood, yet Gabriel came not.
But on the breath of the summer winds a rumour was wafted
Sweeter than song of bird, or hue or odour of blossom.
Far to the north and east, it said, in the Michigan forests,
Gabriel had his lodge by the banks of the Saginaw river.
And, with returning guides, that sought the lakes of St Lawrence
Saying a sad farewell, Evangeline went from the Mission.
When over weary ways, by long and perilous marches,
She had attained at length the depths of the Michigan forests,
Found she the hunter's lodge deserted and fallen to ruin !

Thus did the long sad years glide on, and in seasons and
places
Divers and distant far was seen the wandering maiden ; –
Now in the tents of grace of the meek Moravian Missions,
Now in the noisy camps and the battle-fields of the army,
Now in secluded hamlets, in towns and populous cities.
Like a phantom she came, and passed away unremembered.
Fair was she and young, when in hope began the long journey ;

Faded was she and old, when in disappointment it ended.
Each succeeding year stole something away from her beauty,
Leaving behind it, broader and deeper, the gloom and the
    shadow.
Then there appeared and spread faint streaks of gray o'er her
    forehead,
Dawn of another life, that broke o'er her earthly horizon,
As in the eastern sky the first faint streaks of the morning.

V

In that delightful land which is washed by the Delaware's
    waters,
Guarding in sylvan shades the name of Penn the apostle,
Stands on the banks of its beautiful stream the city he founded.
There all the air is balm, and the peach is the emblem of beauty,
And the streets still re-echo the names of the trees of the forest,
As if they fain would appease the Dryads whose haunts they
    molested.
There from the troubled sea had Evangeline landed, an exile,
Finding among the children of Penn a home and a country.
There old René Leblanc had died ; and when he departed,
Saw at his side only one of all his hundred descendants.
Something at least there was in the friendly streets of the city,
Something that spake to her heart, and made her no longer a
    stranger ;
And her ear was pleased with the Thee and Thou of the Quakers,
For it recalled the past, the old Acadian country,
Where all men were equal, and all were brothers and sisters.
So, when the fruitless search, the disappointed endeavour,
Ended, to recommence no more upon earth, uncomplaining,
Thither, as leaves to the light, were turned her thoughts and her
    footsteps.
As from a mountain's top the rainy mists of the morning
Roll away, and afar we behold the landscape below us,
Sun-illumined, with shining rivers and cities and hamlets,
So fell the mists from her mind, and she saw the world far below
    her,
Dark no longer, but all illumined with love ; and the pathway
Which she had climbed so far, lying smooth and fair in the
    distance.

Gabriel was not forgotten. Within her heart was his image,
Clothed in the beauty of love and youth, as last she beheld him,
Only more beautiful made by his deathlike silence and absence.
Into her thoughts of him time entered not, for it was not.
Over him years had no power; he was not changed, but
    transfigured;
He had become to her heart as one who is dead, and not absent;
Patience and abnegation of self, and devotion to others,
This was the lesson a life of trial and sorrow had taught her.
So was her love diffused, but, like to some odorous spices,
Suffered no waste nor loss, though filling the air with aroma.
Other hope had she none, nor wish in life, but to follow
Meekly, with reverent steps, the sacred feet of her Saviour.
Thus many years she lived as a Sister of Mercy; frequenting
Lonely and wretched roofs in the crowded lanes of the city,
Where distress and want concealed themselves from the sunlight,
Where disease and sorrow in garrets languished neglected.
Night after night, when the world was asleep, as the watchman
    repeated
Loud, through the gusty streets, that all was well in the city,
High at some lonely window he saw the light of her taper.
Day after day, in the gray of the dawn, as slow through the
    suburbs
Plodded the German farmer, with flowers and fruits for the
    market,
Met he that meek, pale face, returning home from its watchings.

   Then it came to pass that a pestilence fell on the city,
Presaged by wondrous signs, and mostly by flocks of wild
    pigeons,
Darkening the sun in their flight, with naught in their craws but
    an acorn.
And, as the tides of the sea arise in the month of September,
Flooding some silver stream, till it spreads to a lake in the
    meadow,
So death flooded life, and, o'erflowing its natural margin,
Spread to a brackish lake, the silver stream of existence.
Wealth had no power to bribe, nor beauty to charm, the
    oppressor;
But all perished alike beneath the scourge of his anger; —
Only, alas! the poor, who had neither friends nor attendants,

Crept away to die in the almshouse, home of the homeless.
Then in the suburbs it stood, in the midst of meadows and
    woodlands; —
Now the city surrounds it ; but still, with its gateway and wicket
Meek, in the midst of splendour, its humble walls seem to echo
Softly the words of the Lord : — 'The poor ye always have with
    you.'
Thither, by night and by day, came the Sister of Mercy. The
    dying
Looked up into her face, and thought, indeed, to behold there
Gleams of celestial light encircle her forehead with splendour,
Such as the artist paints o'er the brows of saints and apostles,
Or such as hangs by night o'er a city seen at a distance.
Unto their eyes it seemed the lamps of the city celestial,
Into whose shining gates ere long their spirits would enter.

    Thus, on a Sabbath morn, through the streets, deserted and
    silent,
Wending her quiet way, she entered the door of the almshouse.
Sweet on the summer air was the odour of flowers in the garden ;
And she paused on her way to gather the fairest among them,
That the dying once more might rejoice in their fragrance and
    beauty.
Then, as she mounted the stairs to the corridors, cooled by the
    east wind,
Distant and soft on her ear fell the chimes from the belfry of
    Christ Church,
While, intermingled with these, across the meadows were wafted
Sounds of psalms, that were sung by the Swedes in the church
    at Wicaco.
Soft as descending wings fell the calm of the hour on her spirit ;
Something within her said, — 'At length thy trials are ended;'
And, with light in her looks, she entered the chambers of
    sickness.
Noiselessly moved about the assiduous, careful attendants,
Moistening the feverish lip, and the aching brow, and in silence
Closing the sightless eyes of the dead, and concealing their faces,
Where on their pallets they lay, like drifts of snow by the
    roadside.
Many a languid head, upraised as Evangeline entered,

Turned on its pillow of pain to gaze while she passed, for her
    presence
Fell on their hearts like a ray of the sun on the walls of a prison.
And, as she looked around, she saw how Death, the consoler,
Laying his hand upon many a heart, had healed it forever.
Many familiar forms had disappeared in the night-time;
Vacant their places were, or filled already by strangers.

   Suddenly, as if arrested by fear or a feeling of wonder,
Still she stood, with her colourless lips apart, while a shudder
Ran through her frame, and forgotten, the flowerets dropped
    from her fingers,
And from her eyes and cheeks the light and bloom of the
    morning.
Then there escaped from her lips a cry of such terrible anguish,
That the dying heard it, and started up from their pillows.
On the pallet before her was stretched the form of an old man.
Long, and thin, and gray were the locks that shaded his temples;
But, as he lay in the morning light, his face for a moment
Seemed to assume once more the forms of its earlier manhood;
So are wont to be changed the faces of those who are dying.
Hot and red on his lips still burned the flush of the fever,
As if life, like the Hebrew, with blood had besprinkled its
    portals,
That the Angel of Death might see the sign, and pass over.
Motionless, senseless, dying, he lay, and his spirit exhausted
Seemed to be sinking down through infinite depths in the
    darkness,
Darkness of slumber and death, forever sinking and sinking.
Then through those realms of shade, in multiplied
    reverberations,
Heard he that cry of pain, and through the hush that succeeded
Whispered a gentle voice, in accents tender and saint like,
'Gabriel! O my beloved!' and died away into silence.
Then he beheld, in a dream, once more the home of his
    childhood;
Green Acadian meadows, with sylvan rivers among them,
Village, and mountain and woodlands; and, walking under their
    shadow,
As in the days of her youth, Evangeline rose in his vision.
Tears came into his eyes; and as slowly he lifted his eyelids,

Vanished the vision away, but Evangeline knelt by his bedside.
Vainly he strove to whisper her name, for the accents unuttered
Died on his lips, and their motion revealed what his tongue
  would have spoken.
Vainly he strove to rise; and Evangeline, kneeling beside him,
Kissed his dying lips, and laid his head on her bosom.
Sweet was the light of his eyes; but it suddenly sank into
  darkness,
As when a lamp is blown out by a gust of wind at a casement.

All was ended now, the hope, and the fear, and the sorrow,
All the aching of heart, the restless, unsatisfied longing,
All the dull, deep pain, and constant anguish of patience!
And, as she pressed once more the lifeless head to her bosom,
Meekly she bowed her own, and murmured, 'Father, I thank
  thee!'

Still stands the forest primeval; but far away from its shadow,
Side by side, in their nameless graves, the lovers are sleeping.
Under the humble walls of the little Catholic churchyard,
In the heart of the city, they lie, unknown and unnoticed.
Daily the tides of life go ebbing and flowing beside them,
Thousands of throbbing hearts, where theirs are at rest and
  forever,
Thousands of aching brains, where theirs no longer are busy,
Thousands of toiling hands, where theirs have ceased from their
  labours,
Thousands of weary feet, where theirs have completed their
  journey!

Still stands the forest primeval; but under the shade of its
  branches
Dwells another race, with other customs and language.
Only along the shores of the mournful and misty Atlantic
Linger a few Acadian peasants whose fathers from exile
Wandered back to their native land to die in its bosom.
In the fisherman's cot the wheel and the loom are still busy;
Maidens still wear their Norman caps and their kirtles of
  homespun,
And by the evening fire repeat Evangeline's story,

While from its rocky caverns the deep-voiced, neighbouring
    ocean
Speaks, and in accents disconsolate answers the wail of the
    forest.

The Courtship of Miles Standish

I

MILES STANDISH

In the Old Colony days, in Plymouth the land of the Pilgrims,
To and fro in a room of his simple and primitive dwelling,
Clad in doublet and hose, and boots of Cordovan leather,
Strode, with a martial air, Miles Standish the Puritan Captain.
Buried in thought he seemed, with his hands behind him, and
pausing
Ever and anon to behold his glittering weapons of warfare,
Hanging in shining array along the walls of the chamber, –
Cutlass and corselet of steel, and his trusty sword of Damascus,
Curved at the point and inscribed with its mystical Arabic
sentence,
While underneath, in a corner, were fowling-piece, musket, and
matchlock.
Short of stature he was, but strongly built and athletic,
Broad in the shoulders, deep-chested, with muscles and sinews
of iron;
Brown as a nut was his face, but his russet beard was already
Flaked with patches of snow, as hedges sometimes in November.
Near him was seated John Alden, his friend, and household
companion,
Writing with diligent speed at a table of pine by the window;
Fair-haired, azure-eyed, with delicate Saxon complexion,
Having the dew of his youth, and the beauty thereof, as the
captives
Whom Saint Gregory saw, and exclaimed, 'Not Angles but
Angels.'
Youngest of all was he of the men who came in the May Flower.

Suddenly breaking the silence, the diligent scribe interrupting,
Spake, in the pride of his heart, Miles Standish the Captain of
Plymouth.
'Look at these arms,' he said, 'the warlike weapons that hang
here
Burnished and bright and clean, as if for parade or inspection!

This is the sword of Damascus I fought with in Flanders; this
    breastplate,
Well I remember the day! once saved my life in a skirmish;
Here in front you can see the very dint of the bullet
Fired point-blank at my heart by a Spanish arcabucero.
Had it not been of sheer steel, the forgotten bones of Miles
    Standish
Would at this moment be mould, in their grave in the Flemish
    morasses.'
Thereupon answered John Alden, but looked not up from his
    writing:
'Truly the breath of the Lord hath slackened the speed of the
    bullet;
He in his mercy preserved you, to be our shield and our
    weapon!'
Still the Captain continued, unheeding the words of the
    stripling:
'See, how bright they are burnished, as if in an arsenal hanging;
That is because I have done it myself, and not left it to others.
Serve yourself, would you be well served, is an excellent adage;
So I take care of my arms, as you of your pens and your inkhorn.
Then, too, there are my soldiers, my great, invincible army,
Twelve men, all equipped, having each his rest and his
    matchlock,
Eighteen shillings a month, together with diet and pillage,
And, like Cæsar, I know the name of each of my soldiers!'
This he said with a smile, that danced in his eyes, as the
    sunbeams
Dance on the waves of the sea, and vanish again in a moment.
Alden laughed as he wrote, and still the Captain continued:
'Look! you can see from this window my brazen howitzer
    planted
High on the roof of the church, a preacher who speaks to the
    purpose,
Steady, straight-forward, and strong, with irresistible logic,
Orthodox, flashing conviction right into the hearts of the
    heathen.
Now we are ready, I think, for any assault of the Indians;
Let them come, if they like, and the sooner they try it the
    better, —

Let them come if they like, be it sagamore, sachem, or pow-
wow,
Aspinet, Samoset, Corbitant, Squanto, or Tokamahamon !'

  Long at the window he stood, and wistfully gazed on the
landscape,
Washed with a cold gray mist, the vapoury breath of the east
wind,
Forest and meadow and hill, and the steel-blue rim of the
ocean,
Lying silent and sad, in the afternoon shadows and sunshine.
Over his countenance flitted a shadow like those on the
landscape,
Gloom intermingled with light ; and his voice was subdued with
emotion,
Tenderness, pity, regret, as after a pause he proceeded :
'Yonder there, on the hill by the sea, lies buried Rose Standish ;
Beautiful rose of love, that bloomed for me by the wayside !
She was the first to die of all who came in the May Flower !
Green above her is growing the field of wheat we have sown
there,
Better to hide from the Indian scouts the graves of our people,
Lest they should count them and see how many already have
perished !'
Sadly his face he averted, and strode up and down, and was
thoughtful.

  Fixed to the opposite wall was a shelf of books, and among
them
Prominent three, distinguished alike for bulk and for binding ;
Bariffe's Artillery Guide, and the Commentaries of Cæsar,
Out of the Latin translated by Arthur Goldinge of London,
And, as if guarded by these, between them was standing the
Bible.
Musing a moment before them, Miles Standish paused, as if
doubtful
Which of the three he should choose for his consolation and
comfort,
Whether the wars of the Hebrews, the famous campaigns of the
Romans,
Or the Artillery practice, designed for belligerent Christians.

Finally down from its shelf he dragged the ponderous Roman,
Seated himself at the window, and opened the book, and in
    silence
Turned o'er the well-worn leaves, where thumb-marks thick on
    the margin,
Like the trample of feet, proclaimed the battle was hottest.
Nothing was heard in the room but the hurrying pen of the
    stripling,
Busily writing epistles important, to go by the May Flower,
Ready to sail on the morrow, or next day at latest, God will-
    ing !
Homeward bound with the tidings of all that terrible winter,
Letters written by Alden, and full of the name of Priscilla.
Full of the name and the fame of the Puritan maiden Priscilla !

II

LOVE AND FRIENDSHIP

Nothing was heard in the room but the hurrying pen of the
    stripling,
Or an occasional sigh from the labouring heart of the Captain,
Reading the marvellous words and achievements of Julius
    Cæsar.
After a while he exclaimed, as he smote with his hand, palm
    downwards,
Heavily on the page : 'A wonderful man was this Cæsar !
You are a writer, and I am a fighter, but here is a fellow
Who could both write and fight, and in both was equally
    skilful !'
Straightway answered and spake John Alden, the comely, the
    youthful :
'Yes, he was equally skilled, as you say, with his pen and his
    weapons.
Somewhere have I read, but where I forget, he could dictate
Seven letters at once, at the same time writing his memoirs.'
'Truly,' continued the Captain, not heeding or hearing the other,
'Truly a wonderful man was Caius Julius Cæsar !
Better be first, he said, in a little Iberian village,
Than be second in Rome, and I think he was right when he said
    it.

Twice was he married before he was twenty, and many times
    after;
Battles five hundred he fought, and a thousand cities he
    conquered;
He, too, fought in Flanders, as he himself has recorded;
Finally he was stabbed by his friend, the orator Brutus!
Now, do you know what he did on a certain occasion in
    Flanders,
When the rear-guard of his army retreated, the front giving way
    too,
And the immortal Twelfth Legion was crowded so closely
    together
There was no room for their swords? Why, he seized a shield
    from a soldier,
Put himself straight at the head of his troops, and commanded
    the captains,
Calling on each by his name, to order forward the ensigns;
Then to widen the ranks, and give more room for their
    weapons;
So he won the day, the battle of something-or-other.
That's what I always say; if you wish a thing to be well done,
You must do it yourself, you must not leave it to others!'

  All was silent again; the Captain continued his reading.
Nothing was heard in the room but the hurrying pen of the
    stripling
Writing epistles important to go next day by the May Flower,
Filled with the name and the fame of the Puritan maiden
    Priscilla;
Every sentence began or closed with the name of Priscilla,
Till the treacherous pen, to which he confided the secret,
Strove to betray it by singing and shouting the name of Priscilla!
Finally closing his book, with a bang of the ponderous cover,
Sudden and loud as the sound of a soldier grounding his musket.
Thus to the young man spake Miles Standish the Captain of
    Plymouth:
'When you have finished your work, I have something important
    to tell you.
Be not however in haste; I can wait; I shall not be impatient!'
Straightway Alden replied, as he folded the last of his letters,
Pushing his papers aside, and giving respectful attention:

'Speak; for whenever you speak, I am always ready to listen,
Always ready to hear whatever pertains to Miles Standish.'
Thereupon answered the Captain, embarrassed, and culling his
    phrases:
''Tis not good for a man to be alone, say the Scriptures.
This I have said before, and again and again I repeat it;
Every hour in the day, I think it, and feel it, and say it.
Since Rose Standish died, my life has been weary and dreary;
Sick at heart have I been, beyond the healing of friendship.
Oft in my lonely hours have I thought of the maiden Priscilla.
She is alone in the world; her father and mother and brother
Died in the winter together; I saw her going and coming,
Now to the grave of the dead, and now to the bed of the dying,
Patient, courageous, and strong, and said to myself, that if ever
There were angels on earth, as there are angels in heaven,
Two have I seen and known: and the angel whose name is
    Priscilla
Holds in my desolate life the place which the other abandoned.
Long have I cherished the thought, but never have dared to
    reveal it,
Being a coward in this, though valiant enough for the most part.
Go to the damsel Priscilla, the loveliest maiden of Plymouth,
Say that a blunt old Captain, a man not of words but of actions,
Offers his hand and his heart, the hand and heart of a soldier.
Not in these words, you know, but this in short is my meaning;
I am a maker of war, and not a maker of phrases.
You, who are bred as a scholar, can say it in elegant language,
Such as you read in your books of the pleadings and wooings of
    lovers,
Such as you think best adapted to win the heart of a maiden.'

  When he had spoken, John Alden, the fairhaired, taciturn
    stripling,
All aghast at his words, surprised, embarrassed, bewildered,
Trying to mask his dismay by treating the subject with lightness,
Trying to smile, and yet feeling his heart stand still in his bosom,
Just as a timepiece stops in a house that is stricken by lightning,
Thus made answer and spake, or rather stammered than
    answered:
'Such a message as that, I am sure I should mangle and mar it;

If you would have it well done, — I am only repeating your
    maxim, —
You must do it yourself, you must not leave it to others !'
But with the air of a man whom nothing can turn from his
    purpose,
Gravely shaking his head, made answer the Captain of Plymouth
'Truly the maxim is good, and I do not mean to gainsay it ;
But we must use it discreetly, and not waste powder for nothing.
Now, as I said before, I was never a maker of phrases.
I can march up to a fortress and summon the place to surrender,
But march up to a woman with such a proposal, I dare not.
I'm not afraid of bullets, nor shot from the mouth of a cannon,
But of a thundering "No !" point-blank from the mouth of a
    woman,
That I confess I'm afraid of, nor am I ashamed to confess it !
So you must grant my request, for you are an elegant scholar,
Having the graces of speech, and skill in the turning of phrases.'
Taking the hand of his friend, who still was reluctant and
    doubtful,
Holding it long in his own, and pressing it kindly, he added :
'Though I have spoken thus lightly, yet deep is the feeling that
    prompts me ;
Surely you cannot refuse what I ask in the name of our
    friendship !'
Then made answer John Alden : 'The name of friendship is
    sacred ;
What you demand in that name, I have not the power to deny
    you !'
So the strong will prevailed, subduing and moulding the gentler,
Friendship prevailed over love, and Alden went on his errand.

III

THE LOVER'S ERRAND

So the strong will prevailed, and Alden went on his errand,
Out of the street of the village, and into the paths of the forest,
Into the tranquil woods, where blue-birds and robins were
    building
Towns in the populous trees, with hanging gardens of verdure,
Peaceful, aerial cities of joy and affection and freedom.

All around him was calm, but within him commotion and
    conflict,
Love contending with friendship, and self with each generous
    impulse
To and fro in his breast his thoughts were heaving and dashing,
As in a foundering ship, with every roll of the vessel,
Washes the bitter sea, the merciless surge of the ocean !
'Must I relinquish it all,' he cried with a wild lamentation,
'Must I relinquish it all, the joy, the hope, the illusion ?
Was it for this I have loved, and waited, and worshipped in
    silence ?
Was it for this I have followed the flying feet and the shadow
Over the wintry sea, to the desolate shores of New England ?
Truly the heart is deceitful, and out of its depths of corruption
Rise, like an exhalation, the misty phantoms of passion ;
Angels of light they seem, but are only delusions of Satan.
All is clear to me now ; I feel it, I see it distinctly !
This is the hand of the Lord ; it is laid upon me in anger,
For I have followed too much the heart's desires and devices,
Worshipping Astaroth blindly, and impious idols of Baal.
This is the cross I must bear ; the sin and the swift retribution.'

  So through the Plymouth woods John Alden went on his
    errand ;
Crossing the brook at the ford, where it brawled over pebble
    and shallow,
Gathering still, as he went, the May-flowers blooming around
    him,
Fragrant, filling the air with a strange and wonderful sweetness,
Children lost in the woods, and covered with leaves in their
    slumber.
'Puritan flowers,' he said, 'and the type of Puritan maidens,
Modest and simple and sweet, the very type of Priscilla !
So I will take them to her ; to Priscilla the May-flower of
    Plymouth,
Modest and simple and sweet, as a parting gift will I take them ;
Breathing their silent farewells, as they fade and wither and
    perish,
Soon to be thrown away as is the heart of the giver.'
So through the Plymouth woods John Alden went on his errand ;
Came to an open space, and saw the disk of the ocean,

Sailless, sombre and cold with the comfortless breath of the east
    wind;
Saw the new-built house, and people at work in a meadow;
Heard, as he drew near the door, the musical voice of Priscilla
Singing the hundredth Psalm, the grand old Puritan anthem,
Music that Luther sang to the sacred words of the Psalmist,
Full of the breath of the Lord, consoling and comforting many.
Then, as he opened the door, he beheld the form of the maiden
Seated beside her wheel, and the carded wool like a snow-drift
Piled at her knee, her white hands feeding the ravenous spindle,
While with her foot on the treadle she guided the wheel in its
    motion.
Open wide on her lap lay the well-worn psalm-book of
    Ainsworth,
Printed in Amsterdam, the words and the music together,
Rough-hewn, angular notes, like stones in the wall of a
    churchyard,
Darkened and overhung by the running vine of the verses.
Such was the book from whose pages she sang the old Puritan
    anthem,
She, the Puritan girl, in the solitude of the forest,
Making the humble house and the modest apparel of home-spun
Beautiful with her beauty, and rich with the wealth of her being!
Over him rushed, like a wind that is keen and cold and relentless,
Thoughts of what might have been, and the weight and woe of
    his errand;
All the dreams that had faded, and all the hopes that had
    vanished,
All his life henceforth a dreary and tenantless mansion,
Haunted by vain regrets, and pallid, sorrowful faces.
Still he said to himself, and almost fiercely he said it,
'Let not him that putteth his hand to the plough look
    backwards;
Though the ploughshare cut through the flowers of life to its
    fountains,
Though it pass o'er the graves of the dead and the hearths of the
    living,
It is the will of the Lord; and his mercy endureth for ever!'

So he entered the house: and the hum of the wheel and the
    singing

Suddenly ceased; for Priscilla, aroused by his step on the threshold,
Rose as he entered, and gave him her hand, in signal of welcome,
Saying, 'I knew it was you, when I heard your step in the passage;
For I was thinking of you, as I sat there singing and spinning.'
Awkward and dumb with delight, that a thought of him had been mingled
Thus in the sacred psalm, that came from the heart of the maiden,
Silent before her he stood, and gave her the flowers for an answer,
Finding no words for his thought. He remembered that day in the winter,
After the first great snow, when he broke a path from the village,
Reeling and plunging along through the drifts that encumbered the doorway,
Stamping the snow from his feet as he entered the house, and Priscilla
Laughed at his snowy locks, and gave him a seat by the fireside,
Grateful and pleased to know he had thought of her in the snow-storm.
Had he but spoken then! perhaps not in vain had he spoken;
Now it was all too late; the golden moment had vanished!
So he stood there abashed, and gave her the flowers for an answer.

Then they sat down and talked of the birds and the beautiful Spring-time,
Talked of their friends at home, and the May Flower that sailed on the morrow.
'I have been thinking all day,' said gently the Puritan maiden,
'Dreaming all night, and thinking all day, of the hedgerows of England, –
They are in blossom now, and the country is all like a garden;
Thinking of lanes and fields, and the song of the lark and the linnet,
Seeing the village street, and familiar faces of neighbours
Going about as of old, and stopping to gossip together,
And, at the end of the street, the village church, with the ivy

Climbing the old gray tower, and the quiet graves in the
    churchyard.
Kind are the people I live with, and dear to me my religion;
Still my heart is so sad, that I wish myself back in Old England.
You will say it is wrong, but I cannot help it: I almost
Wish myself back in Old England, I feel so lonely and wretched.'

    Thereupon answered the youth: — 'Indeed I do not condemn
        you;
Stouter hearts than a woman's have quailed in this terrible
    winter.
Yours is tender and trusting, and needs a stronger to lean on;
So I have come to you now, with an offer and proffer of
    marriage
Made by a good man and true, Miles Standish the Captain of
    Plymouth!'

    Thus he delivered his message, the dexterous writer of
        letters, —
Did not embellish the theme, nor array it in beautiful phrases,
But came straight to the point, and blurted it out like a
    schoolboy;
Even the Captain himself could hardly have said it more bluntly.
Mute with amazement and sorrow, Priscilla the Puritan maiden
Looked into Alden's face, her eyes dilated with wonder,
Feeling his words like a blow, that stunned her and rendered her
    speechless;
Till at length she exclaimed, interrupting the ominous silence:
'If the great Captain of Plymouth is so very eager to wed me,
Why does he not come himself, and take the trouble to woo
    me?
If I am not worth the wooing, I surely am not worth the
    winning!'
Then John Alden began explaining and smoothing the matter,
Making it worse as he went, by saying the Captain was busy, —
Had no time for such things; — such things! the words grating
    harshly
Fell on the ear of Priscilla; and swift as a flash she made answer:
'Has he no time for such things, as you call it, before he is
    married,
Would he be likely to find it, or make it, after the wedding?

That is the way with you men; you don't understand us, you
    cannot.
When you have made up your minds, after thinking of this one
    and that one,
Choosing, selecting, rejecting, comparing one with another,
Then you make known your desire, with abrupt and sudden
    avowal,
And are offended and hurt, and indignant perhaps, that a
    woman
Does not respond at once to a love that she never suspected,
Does not attain at a bound the height to which you have been
    climbing.
This is not right nor just: for surely a woman's affection
Is not a thing to be asked for, and had for only the asking.
When one is truly in love, one not only says it, but shows it.
Had he but waited awhile, had he only showed that he loved
    me,
Even this Captain of yours – who knows ? – at last might have
    won me,
Old and rough as he is; but now it never can happen.'

   Still John Alden went on, unheeding the words of Priscilla,
Urging the suit of his friend, explaining, persuading, expanding;
Spoke of his courage and skill, and of all his battles in Flanders,
How with the people of God he had chosen to suffer affliction,
How, in return for his zeal, they had made him Captain of
    Plymouth;
He was a gentleman born, could trace his pedigree plainly
Back to Hugh Standish of Duxbury Hall, in Lancashire,
    England,
Who was the son of Ralph, and the grandson of Thurston de
    Standish;
Heir unto vast estates, of which he was basely defrauded.
Still bore the family arms, and had for his crest a cock argent
Combed and wattled gules, and all the rest of the blazon.
He was a man of honour, of noble and generous nature;
Though he was rough, he was kindly; she knew how during the
    winter
He had attended the sick, with a hand as gentle as woman's;
Somewhat hasty and hot, he could not deny it, and headstrong,
Stern as a soldier might be, but hearty, and placable always,

Not to be laughed at and scorned, because he was little of
    stature;
For he was great of heart, magnanimous, courtly, courageous;
Any woman in Plymouth, nay, any woman in England,
Might be happy and proud to be called the wife of Miles
    Standish!

But as he warmed and glowed, in his simple and eloquent
    language,
Quite forgetful of self, and full of the praise of his rival,
Archly the maiden smiled, and, with eyes overrunning with
    laughter,
Said, in a tremulous voice, 'Why don't you speak for yourself,
    John?'

IV

JOHN ALDEN

Into the open air John Alden, perplexed and bewildered,
Rushed like a man insane, and wandered alone by the seaside;
Paced up and down the sands, and bared his head to the east
    wind,
Cooling his heated brow, and the fire and fever within him.
Slowly as out of the heavens, with apocalyptical splendours,
Sank the City of God, in the vision of John the Apostle,
So, with its cloudy walls of chrysolite, jasper, and sapphire,
Sank the broad red sun, and over its turrets uplifted
Glimmered the golden reed of the angel who measured the city.

'Welcome, O wind of the East!' he exclaimed in his wild
    exultation,
'Welcome, O wind of the East, from the caves of the misty
    Atlantic!
Blowing o'er fields of dulse, and measureless meadows of sea-
    grass,
Blowing o'er rocky wastes, and the grottos and gardens of
    ocean!
Lay thy cold, moist hand on my burning forehead, and wrap me
Close in thy garments of mist, to allay the fever within me!'

Like an awakened conscience, the sea was moaning and
    tossing,
Beating remorseful and loud the mutable sands of the sea-shore.
Fierce in his soul was the struggle and tumult of passions
    contending;
Love triumphant and crowned, and friendship wounded and
    bleeding,
Passionate cries of desire, and importunate pleadings of duty!
'Is it my fault,' he said, 'that the maiden has chosen between us?
Is it my fault that he failed, — my fault that I am the victor?'
Then within him there thundered a voice, like the voice of the
    Prophet:
'It hath displeased the Lord!' — and he thought of David's
    transgression,
Bathsheba's beautiful face, and his friend in the front of the
    battle!
Shame and confusion of guilt, and abasement and self-
    condemnation,
Overwhelmed him at once; and he cried in the deepest
    contrition:
'It hath displeased the Lord! It is the temptation of Satan!'

Then, uplifting his head, he looked at the sea, and beheld
    there
Dimly the shadowy form of the May Flower riding at anchor,
Rocked on the rising tide, and ready to sail on the morrow;
Heard the voices of men through the mist, the rattle of cordage
Thrown on the deck, the shouts of the mate, and the sailors'
    'Ay, ay, Sir!'
Clear and distinct, but not loud, in the dripping air of the
    twilight.
Still for a moment he stood, and listened, and stared at the
    vessel,
Then went hurriedly on, as one who, seeing a phantom,
Stops, then quickens his pace, and follows the beckoning
    shadow.
'Yes, it is plain to me now,' he murmured; 'the hand of the
    Lord is
Leading me out of the land of darkness, the bondage of error.
Through the sea, that shall lift the walls of its waters around
    me,

Hiding me, cutting me off, from the cruel thoughts that pursue
    me.
Back will I go o'er the ocean, this dreary land will abandon,
Her whom I may not love, and him whom my heart has
    offended.
Better to be in my grave in the green old churchyard in England,
Close by my mother's side, and among the dust of my kindred;
Better be dead and forgotten, than living in shame and
    dishonour!
Sacred and safe and unseen, in the dark of the narrow chamber
With me my secret shall lie, like a buried jewel that glimmers
Bright on the hand that is dust, in the chambers of silence and
    darkness, –
Yes, as the marriage ring of the great espousal hereafter!'

    Thus as he spake, he turned, in the strength of his strong
        resolution,
Leaving behind him the shore, and hurried along in the twilight,
Through the congenial gloom of the forest silent and sombre,
Till he beheld the lights in the seven houses of Plymouth,
Shining like seven stars in the dusk and mist of the evening.
Soon he entered his door, and found the redoubtable Captain
Sitting alone, and absorbed in the martial pages of Cæsar,
Fighting some great campaign in Hainault or Brabant or
    Flanders.
'Long have you been on your errand,' he said with a cheery
    demeanour,
Even as one who is waiting an answer, and fears not the issue.
'Nor far off is the house, although the woods are between us;
But you have lingered so long, that while you were going and
    coming
I have fought ten battles and sacked and demolished a city.
Come, sit down, and in order relate to me all that has happened.'

    Then John Alden spake, and related the wondrous adventure,
From beginning to end, minutely, just as it happened;
How he had seen Priscilla, and how he had sped in his courtship,
Only smoothing a little, and softening down her refusal.
But when he came at length to the words Priscilla had spoken,
Words so tender and cruel: 'Why don't you speak for yourself,
    John?'

Up leaped the Captain of Plymouth, and stamped on the floor, till his armour
Clanged on the wall, where it hung, with a sound of sinister omen.
All his pent-up wrath burst forth in a sudden explosion,
Even as a hand-grenade, that scatters destruction around it.
Wildly he shouted, and loud: 'John Alden! you have betrayed me!
Me, Miles Standish, your friend! have supplanted, defrauded, betrayed me!
One of my ancestors ran his sword through the heart of Wat Tyler;
Who shall prevent me from running my own through the heart of a traitor?
Yours is the greater treason, for yours is a treason to friendship!
You, who lived under my roof, whom I cherished and loved as a brother;
You, who have fed at my board, and drunk at my cup, to whose keeping
I have intrusted my honour, my thoughts the most sacred and secret, —
You, too, Brutus! ah woe to the name of friendship hereafter!
Brutus was Cæsar's friend, and you were mine, but henceforward
Let there be nothing between us save war, and implacable hatred!'

  So spake the Captain of Plymouth, and strode about in the chamber,
Chafing and choking with rage; like cords were the veins on his temples.
But in the midst of his anger a man appeared at the doorway,
Bringing in uttermost haste a message of urgent importance,
Rumours of danger and war and hostile incursions of Indians!
Straightway the Captain paused, and, without further question or parley,
Took from the nail on the wall his sword with its scabbard of iron,
Buckled the belt round his waist, and, frowning fiercely, departed.
Alden was left alone. He heard the clank of the scabbard

Growing fainter and fainter, and dying away in the distance.
Then he arose from his seat, and looked forth into the darkness,
Felt the cool air blow on his cheek, that was hot with the insult,
Lifted his eyes to the heavens, and, folding his hands as in
    childhood,
Prayed in the silence of night to the Father who seeth in secret.

  Meanwhile the choleric Captain strode wrathful away to the
    council,
Found it already assembled, impatiently waiting his coming;
Men in the middle of life, austere and grave in deportment,
Only one of them old, the hill that was nearest to heaven,
Covered with snow, but erect, the excellent Elder of Plymouth.
God had sifted three kingdoms to find the wheat for this
    planting,
Then had sifted the wheat, as the living seed of a nation;
So say the chronicles old, and such is the faith of the people!
Near them was standing an Indian, in attitude stern and defiant,
Naked down to the waist, and grim and ferocious in aspect;
While on the table before them was lying unopened a Bible,
Ponderous, bound in leather, brass-studded, printed in Holland,
And beside it outstretched the skin of a rattlesnake glittered,
Filled, like a quiver, with arrows; a signal and challenge of
    warfare,
Brought by the Indian, and speaking with arrowy tongues of
    defiance.
This Miles Standish beheld, as he entered, and heard them
    debating
What were an answer befitting the hostile message and menace,
Talking of this and of that, contriving, suggesting, objecting;
One voice only for peace, and that the voice of the Elder,
Judging it wise and well that some at least were converted,
Rather than any were slain, for this was but Christian
    behaviour!
Then outspake Miles Standish, the stalwart Captain of
    Plymouth,
Muttering deep in his throat, for his voice was husky with anger,
'What! do you mean to make war with milk and the water of
    roses?
Is it to shoot red squirrels you have your howitzer planted
There on the roof of the church, or is it to shoot red devils?

Truly the only tongue that is understood by a savage
Must be the tongue of fire that speaks from the mouth of the
    cannon !'
Thereupon answered and said the excellent Elder of Plymouth,
Somewhat amazed and alarmed at this irreverent language :
'Not so thought Saint Paul, nor yet the other Apostles ;
Not from the cannon's mouth were the tongues of fire they
    spake with !'
But unheeded fell this mild rebuke on the Captain,
Who had advanced to the table, and thus continued discoursing :
'Leave this matter to me, for to me by right it pertaineth.
War is a terrible trade ; but in the cause that is righteous,
Sweet is the smell of powder ; and thus I answer the challenge !'

Then from the rattlesnake's skin, with a sudden, contemp-
    tuous gesture,
Jerking the Indian arrows, he filled it with powder and bullets
Full to the very jaws, and handed it back to the savage,
Saying, in thundering tones : 'Here, take it ! this is your answer !'
Silently out of the room then glided the glistening savage,
Bearing the serpent's skin, and seeming himself like a serpent,
Winding his sinuous way in the dark to the depths of the forest.

V

THE SAILING OF THE MAY FLOWER

Just in the gray of the dawn, as the mists up-rose from the
    meadows,
There was a stir and a sound in the slumbering village of
    Plymouth ;
Clanging and clicking of arms, and the order imperative,
    'Forward !'
Given in tone suppressed, a tramp of feet, and then silence.
Figures ten, in the mist, marched slowly out of the village.
Standish the stalwart it was, with eight of his valorous army,
Led by their Indian guide, by Hobomok, friend of the white
    men,
Northward marching to quell the sudden revolt of the savage.
Giants they seemed in the mist, or the mighty men of King
    David ;
Giants in heart they were, who believed in God and the Bible, —

Ay, who believed in the smiting of Midianites and Philistines.
Over them gleamed far off the crimson banners of morning;
Under them loud on the sands, the serried billows, advancing,
Fired along the line, and in regular order retreated.

  Many a mile had they marched, when at length the village of
      Plymouth
Woke from its sleep, and arose, intent on its manifold labours.
Sweet was the air and soft; and slowly the smoke from the
      chimneys
Rose over roofs of thatch, and pointed steadily eastward;
Men came forth from the doors, and paused and talked of the
      weather,
Said that the wind had changed, and was blowing fair for the
      May Flower;
Talked of their Captain's departure, and all the dangers that
      menaced,
He being gone, the town, and what should be done in his
      absence.
Merrily sang the birds, and the tender voices of women
Consecrated with hymns the common cares of the household.
Out of the sea rose the sun, and the billows rejoiced at his
      coming;
Beautiful were his feet on the purple tops of the mountains;
Beautiful on the sails of the May Flower riding at anchor,
Battered and blackened and worn by all the storms of the
      winter.
Loosely against her masts was hanging and flapping her canvas,
Rent by so many gales, and patched by the hands of the sailors.
Suddenly from her side, as the sun rose over the ocean,
Darted a puff of smoke, and floated seaward; anon rang
Loud over field and forest the cannon's roar, and the echoes
Heard and repeated the sound, the signal-gun of departure!
Ah! but with louder echoes replied the hearts of the people!
Meekly, in voices subdued, the chapter was read from the Bible,
Meekly the prayer was begun, but ended in fervent entreaty!
Then from their houses in haste came forth the Pilgrims of
      Plymouth,
Men and women and children, all hurrying down to the sea-
      shore,
Eager, with tearful eyes, to say farewell to the May Flower,

Homeward bound o'er the sea, and leaving them here in the
     desert.

  Foremost among them was Alden. All night he had lain
     without slumber,
Turning and tossing about in the heat and unrest of his fever.
He had beheld Miles Standish, who came back late from the
     council,
Stalking into the room, and heard him mutter and murmur,
Sometimes it seemed a prayer, and sometimes it sounded like
     swearing.
Once he had come to the bed, and stood there a moment in
     silence;
Then he had turned away, and said: 'I will not awake him;
Let him sleep on, it is best; for what is the use of more talking!'
Then he extinguished the light, and threw himself down on his
     pallet,
Dressed as he was, and ready to start at the break of the
     morning, –
Covered himself with the cloak he had worn in his campaigns in
     Flanders, –
Slept as a soldier sleeps in his bivouac, ready for action.
But with the dawn he arose; in the twilight Alden beheld him
Put on his corselet of steel, and all the rest of his armour,
Buckle about his waist his trusty blade of Damascus,
Take from the corner his musket, and so stride out of the
     chamber.
Often the heart of the youth had burned and yearned to embrace
     him,
Often his lips had essayed to speak, imploring for pardon;
All the old friendship came back, with its tender and grateful
     emotions;
But his pride overmastered the nobler nature within him, –
Pride, and the sense of his wrong, and the burning fire of the
     insult.
So he beheld his friend departing in anger, but spake not,
Saw him go forth to danger, perhaps to death, and he spake
     not!
Then he arose from his bed, and heard what the people were
     saying,

Joined in the talk at the door, with Stephen and Richard and
    Gilbert,
Joined in the morning prayer, and in the reading of Scripture,
And, with the others, in haste went hurrying down to the sea-
    shore,
Down to the Plymouth Rock, that had been to their feet as a
    door-step
Into a world unknown, — the corner-stone of a nation!

  There with his boat was the Master, already a little impatient
Lest he should lose the tide, or the wind might shift to the
    eastward,
Square-built, hearty, and strong, with an odour of ocean about
    him,
Speaking with this one and that, and cramming letters and
    parcels
Into his pockets capacious, and messages mingled together
Into his narrow brain, till at last he was wholly bewildered.
Nearer the boat stood Alden, with one foot placed on the
    gunwale,
One still firm on the rock, and talking at times with the sailors,
Seated erect on the thwarts, all ready and eager for starting.
He too was eager to go, and thus put an end to his anguish,
Thinking to fly from despair, that swifter than keel is or canvas,
Thinking to drown in the sea the ghost that would rise and
    pursue him.
But as he gazed on the crowd, he beheld the form of Priscilla
Standing dejected among them, unconscious of all that was
    passing.
Fixed were her eyes upon his, as if she divined his intention,
Fixed with a look so sad, so reproachful, imploring, and patient,
That with a sudden revulsion his heart recoiled from its purpose,
As from the verge of a crag, where one step more is destruction.
Strange is the heart of man, with its quick, mysterious instincts!
Strange is the life of man, and fatal or fated are moments,
Whereupon turn, as on hinges, the gates of the wall adamantine!
'Here I remain!' he exclaimed, as he looked at the heavens
    above him,
Thanking the Lord whose breath had scattered the mist and the
    madness,
Wherein, blind and lost, to death he was staggering headlong.

'Yonder snow-white cloud, that floats in the ether above me,
Seems like a hand that is pointing and beckoning over the ocean.
There is another hand, that is not so spectral and ghost-like,
Holding me, drawing me back, and clasping mine for protection.
Float, O hand of cloud, and vanish away in the ether!
Roll thyself up like a fist, to threaten and daunt me; I heed not
Either your warning or menace, or any omen of evil!
There is no land so sacred, no air so pure and so wholesome,
As is the air she breathes, and the soil that is pressed by her
    footsteps.
Here for her sake will I stay, and like an invisible presence
Hover around her for ever, protecting, supporting her
    weakness;
Yes! as my foot was the first that stepped on this rock at the
    landing,
So, with the blessing of God, shall it be the last at the leaving!'

Meanwhile the Master alert, but with dignified air and
    important,
Scanning with watchful eye the tide and the wind and the
    weather,
Walked about on the sands; and the people crowded around
    him
Saying a few last words, and enforcing his careful remembrance.
Then, taking each by the hand, as if he were grasping a tiller,
Into the boat he sprang, and in haste shoved off to his vessel,
Glad in his heart to get rid of all this worry and flurry,
Glad to be gone from a land of sand and sickness and sorrow,
Short allowance of victual, and plenty of nothing but Gospel!
Lost in the sound of the oars was the last farewell of the
    Pilgrims.
O strong hearts and true! not one went back in the May
    Flower!
No, not one looked back, who had set his hand to this
    ploughing!

Soon were heard on board the shouts and songs of the sailors
Heaving the windlass round, and hoisting the ponderous anchor.
Then the yards were braced, and all sails set to the west-wind,
Blowing steady and strong; and the May Flower sailed from the
    harbour,

Rounded the point of the Gurnet, and leaving far to the southward
Island and cape of sand, and the Field of the First Encounter,
Took the wind on her quarter, and stood for the open Atlantic,
Borne on the send of the sea, and the swelling hearts of the Pilgrims.

Long in silence they watched the receding sail of the vessel,
Much endeared to them all, as something living and human ;
Then, as if filled with the spirit, and wrapt in a vision prophetic,
Baring his hoary head, the excellent Elder of Plymouth,
Said, 'Let us pray !' and they prayed, and thanked the Lord and took courage.
Mournfully sobbed the waves at the base of the rock, and above them
Bowed and whispered the wheat on the hill of death, and their kindred
Seemed to awake in their graves, and to join in the prayer that they uttered.
Sun-illumined and white, on the eastern verge of the ocean
Gleamed the departing sail, like a marble slab in a graveyard ;
Buried beneath it lay for ever all hope of escaping.
Lo ! as they turned to depart, they saw the form of an Indian,
Watching them from the hill ; but while they spake with each other,
Pointing with outstretched hands, and saying, 'Look !' he had vanished.
So they returned to their homes ; but Alden lingered a little,
Musing alone on the shore, and watching the wash of the billows
Round the base of the rock, and the sparkle and flash of the sunshine,
Like the spirit of God, moving visibly over the waters.

VI

PRISCILLA

Thus for a while he stood, and mused by the shore of the ocean
Thinking of many things, and most of all of Priscilla ;
And as if thought had the power to draw to itself, like the loadstone,

Whatsoever it touches, by subtile laws of its nature,
Lo ! as he turned to depart, Priscilla was standing beside him.
'Are you so much offended, you will not speak to me ?' said she.
'Am I so much to blame, that yesterday, when you were pleading
Warmly the cause of another, my heart, impulsive and wayward,
Pleaded your own, and spake out, forgetful perhaps of decorum ?
Certainly you can forgive me for speaking so frankly, for saying
What I ought not to have said, yet now I can never unsay it ;
For there are moments in life, when the heart is so full of emotion,
That if by chance it be shaken, or into its depths like a pebble
Drops some careless word, it overflows, and its secret,
Spilt on the ground like water, can never be gathered together.
Yesterday I was shocked, when I heard you speak of Miles Standish
Praising his virtues, transforming his very defects into virtues,
Praising his courage and strength, and even his fighting in Flanders,
As if by fighting alone you could win the heart of a woman,
Quite overlooking yourself and the rest, in exalting your hero.
Therefore I spake as I did, by an irresistible impulse.
You will forgive me, I hope, for the sake of the friendship between us,
Which is too true and too sacred to be so easily broken !'
Thereupon answered John Alden, the scholar, the friend of Miles Standish :
'I was not angry with you, with myself alone I was angry,
Seeing how badly I managed the matter I had in my keeping.'
'No !' interrupted the maiden, with answer prompt and decisive ;
'No ; you were angry with me, for speaking so frankly and freely.
It was wrong, I acknowledge ; for it is the fate of a woman
Long to be patient and silent, to wait like a ghost that is speechless,
Till some questioning voice dissolves the spell of its silence.
Hence is the inner life of so many suffering women
Sunless and silent and deep, like subterranean rivers
Running through caverns of darkness, unheard, unseen, and unfruitful,

Chafing their channels of stone, with endless and profitless
    murmurs.'
Thereupon answered John Alden, the young man, the lover of
    women :
'Heaven forbid it, Priscilla ; and truly they seem to me always
More like the beautiful rivers that watered the garden of Eden,
More like the river Euphrates, through deserts of Havilah
    flowing,
Filling the land with delight, and memories sweet of the garden !'
'Ah, by these words, I can see,' again interrupted the maiden,
'How very little you prize me, or care for what I am saying.
When from the depths of my heart, in pain and with secret
    misgiving,
Frankly I speak to you, asking for sympathy only and kindness,
Straightway you take up my words, that are plain and direct
    and in earnest,
Turn them away from their meaning, and answer with flattering
    phrases.
This is not right, is not just, is not true to the best that is in you ;
For I know and esteem you, and feel that your nature is noble,
Lifting mine up to a higher, a more ethereal level.
Therefore I value your friendship, and feel it perhaps the more
    keenly
If you say aught that implies I am only as one among many,
If you make use of those common and complimentary phrases
Most men think so fine, in dealing and speaking with women,
But which women reject as insipid, if not as insulting.'

  Mute and amazed was Alden ; and listened and looked at
    Priscilla,
Thinking he never had seen her more fair, more divine in her
    beauty.
He who but yesterday pleaded so glibly the cause of another,
Stood there embarrassed and silent, and seeking in vain for an
    answer.
So the maiden went on, and little divined or imagined
What was at work in his heart, that made him so awkward and
    speechless.
'Let us, then, be what we are, and speak what we think, and in
    all things

Keep ourselves loyal to truth, and the sacred professions of friendship.

It is no secret I tell you, nor am I ashamed to declare :

I have liked to be with you, to see you, to speak with you always.

So I was hurt at your words, and a little affronted to hear you

Urge me to marry your friend, though he were the Captain Miles Standish.

For I must tell you the truth : much more to me is your friendship

Than all the love he could give, were he twice the hero you think him.'

Then she extended her hand, and Alden, who eagerly grasped it,

Felt all the wounds in his heart, that were aching and bleeding so sorely,

Healed by the touch of that hand, and he said, with a voice full of feeling :

'Yes, we must ever be friends, and of all who offer you friendship

Let me be ever the first, the truest, the nearest and dearest !'

Casting a farewell look at the glimmering sail of the May Flower,

Distant, but still in sight, and sinking below the horizon,

Homeward together they walked, with a strange, indefinite feeling,

That all the rest had departed and left them alone in the desert.

But, as they went through the fields in the blessing and smile of the sunshine,

Lighter grew their hearts, and Priscilla said very archly :

'Now that our terrible Captain has gone in pursuit of the Indians,

Where he is happier far than he would be commanding a household,

You may speak boldly, and tell me of all that happened between you,

When you returned last night, and said how ungrateful you found me.'

Thereupon answered John Alden, and told her the whole of the story, —

Told her his own despair, and the direful wrath of Miles Standish.

Whereat the maiden smiled, and said between laughing and
     earnest,
'He is a little chimney, and heated hot in a moment !'
But as he gently rebuked her, and told her how much he had
     suffered, –
How he had even determined to sail that day in the May Flower,
And had remained for her sake, on hearing the dangers that
     threatened, –
All her manner was changed, and she said with a faltering
     accent,
'Truly I thank you for this : how good you have been to me
     always !'

Thus, as a pilgrim devout, who toward Jerusalem journeys,
Taking three steps in advance, and one reluctantly backward,
Urged by importunate zeal, and withheld by pangs of contrition ;
Slowly but steadily onward, receding yet ever advancing,
Journeyed this Puritan youth to the Holy Land of his longings
Urged by the fervour of love, and withheld by remorseful
     misgivings.

VII

THE MARCH OF MILES STANDISH

Meanwhile the stalwart Miles Standish was marching steadily
     northward,
Winding through forest and swamp, and along the trend of the
     seashore,
All day long, with hardly a halt, the fire of his anger
Burning and crackling within, and the sulphurous odour of
     powder
Seeming more sweet to his nostrils than all the scents of the
     forest.
Silent and moody he went, and much he revolved his
     discomfort ;
He who was used to success, and to easy victories always,
Thus to be flouted, rejected, and laughed to scorn by a maiden,
Thus to be mocked and betrayed by the friend whom most he
     had trusted !
Ah ! 'twas too much to be borne, and he fretted and chafed in
     his armour !

'I alone am to blame,' he muttered, 'for mine was the folly.
What has a rough old soldier, grown grim and gray in the harness,
Used to the camp and its ways, to do with the wooing of maidens?
'Twas but a dream, – let it pass, – let it vanish like so many others!
What I thought was a flower, is only a weed, and is worthless;
Out of my heart will I pluck it, and throw it away, and henceforward
Be but a fighter of battles, a lover and wooer of dangers!'
Thus he revolved in his mind his sorry defeat and discomfort,
While he was marching by day or lying at night in the forest,
Looking up at the trees, and the constellations beyond them.

After a three days' march he came to an Indian encampment
Pitched on the edge of a meadow, between the sea and the forest;
Women at work by the tents, and the warriors, horrid with war-paint,
Seated about a fire, and smoking and talking together;
Who, when they saw from afar the sudden approach of the white men,
Saw the flash of the sun on breastplate and sabre and musket,
Straightway leaped to their feet, and two, from among them advancing,
Came to parley with Standish, and offer him furs as a present;
Friendship was in their looks, but in their hearts there was hatred.
Braves of the tribe were these, and brothers gigantic in stature,
Huge as Goliath of Gath, or the terrible Og, king of Bashan;
One was Pecksuot named, and the other was called Wattawamat.
Round their necks were suspended their knives in scabbards of wampum,
Two-edged, trenchant knives, with points as sharp as a needle.
Other arms had they none, for they were cunning and crafty.
'Welcome, English!' they said, – these words they had learned from the traders
Touching at times on the coast, to barter and chaffer for peltries.
Then in their native tongue they began to parley with Standish,

Through his guide and interpreter, Hobomok, friend of the
    white man,
Begging for blankets and knives, but mostly for muskets and
    powder,
Kept by the white man, they said, concealed, with the plague, in
    his cellars,
Ready to be let loose, and destroy his brother the red man!
But when Standish refused, and said he would give them the
    Bible,
Suddenly changing their tone, they began to boast and to bluster.
Then Wattawamat advanced with a stride in front of the other,
And, with a lofty demeanour, thus vauntingly spake to the
    Captain:
'Now Wattawamat can see, by the fiery eyes of the Captain,
Angry is he in his heart; but the heart of the brave Wattawamat
Is not afraid at the sight. He was not born of a woman,
But on a mountain, at night, from an oak-tree riven by lightning,
Forth he sprang at a bound, with all his weapons about him,
Shouting, "Who is there here to fight with the brave
    Wattawamat?"'
Then he unsheathed his knife, and, whetting the blade on his
    left hand,
Held it aloft and displayed a woman's face on the handle,
Saying, with bitter expression and look of sinister meaning:
'I have another at home, with the face of a man on the handle;
By and by they shall marry; and there will be plenty of
    children!'

    Then stood Pecksuot forth, self-vaunting, insulting Miles
    Standish:
While with his fingers he patted the knife that hung at his
    bosom,
Drawing it half from its sheath, and plunging it back, as he
    muttered,
'By and by it shall see; it shall eat; ah, ah! but shall speak not!
This is the mighty Captain the white men have sent to destroy
    us!
He is a little man; let him go and work with the women!'

    Meanwhile Standish had noted the faces and figures of Indians
Peeping and creeping about from bush to tree in the forest,

Feigning to look for game, with arrows set on their bow-strings,
Drawing about him still closer and closer the net of their
    ambush.
But undaunted he stood, and dissembled and treated them
    smoothly;
So the old chronicles say, that were writ in the days of the
    fathers.
But when he heard their defiance, the boast, the taunt, and the
    insult,
All the hot blood of his race, of Sir Hugh and of Thurston de
    Standish,
Boiled and beat in his heart, and swelled in the veins of his
    temples.
Headlong he leaped on the boaster, and, snatching his knife
    from its scabbard,
Plunged it into his heart, and, reeling backward, the savage
Fell with his face to the sky, and a fiendlike fierceness upon it.
Straight there arose from the forest the awful sound of the war-
    whoop,
And, like a flurry of snow on the whistling wind of December,
Swift and sudden and keen came a flight of feathery arrows.
Then came a cloud of smoke, and out of the cloud came the
    lightning,
Out of the lightning thunder; and death unseen ran before it.
Frightened the savages fled for shelter in swamp and in thicket,
Hotly pursued and beset; but their sachem, the brave
    Wattawamat,
Fled not; he was dead. Unswerving and swift had a bullet
Passed through his brain, and he fell with both hands clutching
    the greensward,
Seeming in death to hold back from his foe the land of his
    fathers.

  There on the flowers of the meadow the warriors lay, and
    above them,
Silent, with folded arms, stood Hobomok, friend of the white
    man.
Smiling at length he exclaimed to the stalwart Captain of
    Plymouth:
'Pecksuot bragged very loud, of his courage, his strength, and
    his stature, —

Mocked the great Captain, and called him a little man; but I see now

Big enough have you been to lay him speechless before you!'

   Thus the first battle was fought and won by the stalwart Miles Standish.

When the tidings thereof were brought to the village of Plymouth,

And as a trophy of war the head of the brave Wattawamat

Scowled from the roof of the fort, which at once was a church and a fortress,

All who beheld it rejoiced, and praised the Lord, and took courage.

Only Priscilla averted her face from this spectre of terror,

Thanking God in her heart that she had not married Miles Standish;

Shrinking, fearing almost, lest, coming home from his battles,

He should lay claim to her hand, as the prize and reward of his valour.

VIII

THE SPINNING-WHEEL

   Month after month passed away, and in Autumn the ships of the merchants

Came with kindred and friends, with cattle and corn for the Pilgrims.

All in the village was peace; the men were intent on their labours,

Busy with hewing and building, with garden-plot and with merestead,

Busy with breaking the glebe, and mowing the grass in the meadows,

Searching the sea for its fish, and hunting the deer in the forest.

All in the village was peace; but at times the rumour of warfare

Filled the air with alarm, and the apprehension of danger.

Bravely the stalwart Miles Standish was scouring the land with his forces,

Waxing valiant in fight and defeating the alien armies,

Till his name had become a sound of fear to the nations.

Anger was still in his heart, but at times the remorse and contrition
Which in all noble natures succeed the passionate outbreak,
Came like a rising tide, that encounters the rush of a river,
Staying its current awhile, but making it bitter and brackish.

  Meanwhile Alden at home had built him a new habitation,
Solid, substantial, of timber rough-hewn from the firs of the forest.
Wooden-barred was the door, and the roof was covered with rushes;
Latticed the windows were, and the window-panes were of paper,
Oiled to admit the light, while wind and rain were excluded.
There too he dug a well, and around it planted an orchard:
Still may be seen to this day some trace of the well and the orchard.
Close to the house was the stall, where, safe and secure from annoyance,
Raghorn, the snow-white steer, that had fallen to Alden's allotment
In the division of cattle, might ruminate in the night-time
Over the pastures he cropped, made fragrant by sweet pennyroyal.

  Oft when his labour was finished, with eager feet would the dreamer
Follow the pathway that ran through the woods to the house of Priscilla,
Led by illusions romantic and subtile deceptions of fancy,
Pleasure disguised as duty, and love in the semblance of friendship.
Ever of her he thought, when he fashioned the walls of his dwelling;
Ever of her he thought, when he delved in the soil of his garden;
Ever of her he thought, when he read in his Bible on Sunday
Praise of the virtuous woman, as she is described in the Proverbs, —
How the heart of her husband doth safely trust in her always,
How all the days of her life she will do him good, and not evil,

How she seeketh the wool and the flax and worketh with
    gladness,
How she layeth her hand to the spindle and holdeth the distaff,
How she is not afraid of the snow for herself or her household,
Knowing her household are clothed with the scarlet cloth of her
    weaving!

    So as she sat at her wheel one afternoon in the Autumn,
Alden, who opposite sat, and was watching her dexterous
    fingers,
As if the thread she was spinning were that of his life and his
    fortune,
After a pause in their talk, thus spake to the sound of the
    spindle.
'Truly, Priscilla,' he said, 'when I see you spinning and spinning,
Never idle a moment, but thrifty and thoughtful of others,
Suddenly you are transformed, are visibly changed in a moment;
You are no longer Priscilla, but Bertha the Beautiful Spinner.'
Here the light foot on the treadle grew swifter and swifter; the
    spindle
Uttered an angry snarl, and the thread snapped short in her
    fingers
While the impetuous speaker, not heeding the mischief,
    continued:
'You are the beautiful Bertha, the spinner, the queen of
    Helvetia;
She whose story I read at a stall in the streets of Southampton,
Who, as she rode on her palfrey, o'er valley and meadow and
    mountain
Ever was spinning her thread from a distaff fixed to her saddle.
She was so thrifty and good, that her name passed into a
    proverb.
So shall it be with your own, when the spinning-wheel shall no
    longer
Hum in the house of the farmer, and fill its chambers with
    music.
Then shall the mothers, reproving, relate how it was in their
    childhood,
Praising the good old times, and the days of Priscilla the
    spinner!'
Straight uprose from her wheel the beautiful Puritan maiden,

Pleased with the praise of her thrift from him whose praise was
    the sweetest,
Drew from the reel on the table a snowy skein of her spinning,
Thus making answer, meanwhile, to the flattering phrases of
    Alden:
'Come, you must not be idle; if I am a pattern for housewives,
Show yourself equally worthy of being the model of husbands.
Hold this skein on your hands, while I wind it, ready for
    knitting;
Then who knows but hereafter, when fashions have changed
    and the manners,
Fathers may talk to their sons of the good old times of John
    Alden!'
Thus, with a jest and a laugh, the skein on his hands she
    adjusted,
He sitting awkwardly there, with his arms extended before him,
She standing graceful, erect, and winding the thread from his
    fingers.
Sometimes chiding a little his clumsy manner of holding,
Sometimes touching his hands, as she disentangled expertly
Twist or knot in the yarn, unawares – for how could she help
    it? –
Sending electrical thrills through every nerve in his body.

    Lo! in the midst of this scene, a breathless messenger entered,
Bringing in hurry and heat the terrible news from the village.
Yes; Miles Standish was dead! – an Indian had brought them
    the tidings, –
Slain by a poisoned arrow, shot down in the front of the battle,
Into an ambush beguiled, cut off with the whole of his forces;
All the town would be burned, and all the people be murdered!
Such were the tidings of evil that burst on the hearts of the
    hearers.
Silent and statue-like stood Priscilla, her face looking backward
Still at the face of the speaker, her arms uplifted in horror;
But John Alden, upstarting, as if the barb of the arrow
Piercing the heart of his friend had struck his own, and had
    sundered
Once and for ever the bonds that held him bound as a captive,
Wild with excess of sensation, the awful delight of his freedom,

Mingled with pain and regret, unconscious of what he was
    doing,
Clasped, almost with a groan, the motionless form of Priscilla,
Pressing her close to his heart, as for ever his own, and
    exclaiming:
'Those whom the Lord hath united, let no man put them
    asunder!'

  Even as rivulets twain, from distant and separate sources,
Seeing each other afar, as they leap from the rocks, and pursuing
Each one its devious path, but drawing nearer and nearer,
Rush together at last, at their trysting-place in the forest;
So these lives that had run thus far in separate channels,
Coming in sight of each other, then swerving and flowing
    asunder,
Parted by barriers strong, but drawing nearer and nearer,
Rushed together at last, and one was lost in the other.

IX

THE WEDDING-DAY

  Forth from the curtain of clouds, from the tent of purple and
    scarlet,
Issued the sun, the great High-Priest, in his garments
    resplendent,
Holiness unto the Lord, in letters of light, on his forehead,
Round the hem of his robe the golden bells and pomegranates.
Blessing the world he came, and the bars of vapour beneath him
Gleamed like a grate of brass, and the sea at his feet was a
    laver!

This was the wedding-morn of Priscilla the Puritan maiden.
Friends were assembled together; the Elder and Magistrate also
Graced the scene with their presence, and stood like the Law
    and the Gospel,
One with the sanction of earth and one with the blessing of
    heaven.
Simple and brief was the wedding, as that of Ruth and of Boaz.
Softly the youth and the maiden repeated the words of betrothal,
Taking each other for husband and wife in the Magistrate's
    presence.

After the Puritan way, and the laudable custom of Holland.
Fervently then, and devoutly, the excellent Elder of Plymouth
Prayed for the hearth and the home, that were founded that day in affection,
Speaking of life and of death, and imploring divine benedictions.

Lo! when the service was ended, a form appeared on the threshold,
Clad in armour of steel, a sombre and sorrowful figure!
Why does the bridegroom start and stare at the strange apparition?
Why does the bride turn pale, and hide her face on his shoulder?
Is it a phantom of air, – a bodiless, spectral illusion?
Is it a ghost from the grave, that has come to forbid the betrothal?
Long had it stood there unseen, a guest uninvited, unwelcomed;
Over its clouded eyes there had passed at times an expression
Softening the gloom and revealing the warm heart hidden beneath them,
As when across the sky the driving rack of the rain-cloud
Grows for a moment thin, and betrays the sun by its brightness.
Once it had lifted its hand, and moved its lips, but was silent,
As if an iron will had mastered the fleeting intention.
But when were ended the troth and the prayer and the last benediction,
Into the room it strode, and the people beheld with amazement
Bodily there in his armour Miles Standish, the Captain of Plymouth!
Grasping the bridegroom's hand, he said with emotion, 'Forgive me!
I have been angry and hurt, – too long have I cherished the feeling;
I have been cruel and hard, but now, thank God! it is ended.
Mine is the same hot blood that leaped in the veins of Hugh Standish,
Sensitive, swift to resent, but as swift in atoning for error.
Never so much as now was Miles Standish the friend of John Alden.'
Thereupon answered the bridegroom: 'Let all be forgotten between us, –

All save the dear, old friendship, and that shall grow older and
    dearer !'
Then the Captain advanced, and, bowing, saluted Priscilla,
Gravely, and after the manner of old-fashioned gentry in
    England,
Something of camp and of court, of town and of country,
    commingled,
Wishing her joy of her wedding, and loudly lauding her
    husband.
Then he said with a smile : 'I should have remembered the
    adage, —
If you would be well served, you must serve yourself ; and
    moreover,
No man can gather cherries in Kent at the season of Christmas !'

  Great was the people's amazement, and greater yet their
    rejoicing,
Thus to behold once more the sun-burnt face of their Captain,
Whom they had mourned as dead ; and they gathered and
    crowded about him,
Eager to see him and hear him, forgetful of bride and of
    bridegroom,
Questioning, answering, laughing, and each interrupting the
    other,
Till the good Captain declared, being quite overpowered and
    bewildered,
He had rather by far break into an Indian encampment,
Than come again to a wedding to which he had not been invited.

  Meanwhile the bridegroom went forth and stood with the
    bride at the doorway,
Breathing the perfumed air of that warm and beautiful morning.
Touched with autumnal tints, but lonely and sad in the sunshine,
Lay extended before them the land of toil and privation ;
There were the graves of the dead, and the barren waste of the
    seashore,
There the familiar fields, the groves of pine, and the meadows ;
But to their eyes transfigured, it seemed as the Garden of Eden,
Filled with the presence of God, whose voice was the sound of
    the ocean.

Soon was their vision disturbed by the noise and stir of departure,
Friends coming forth from the house, and impatient of longer delaying,
Each with his plan for the day, and the work that was left uncompleted.
Then from a stall near at hand, amid exclamations of wonder,
Alden the thoughtful, the careful, so happy, so proud of Priscilla,
Brought out his snow-white steer, obeying the hand of its master,
Led by a cord that was tied to an iron ring in its nostrils,
Covered with crimson cloth, and a cushion placed for a saddle.
She should not walk, he said, through the dust and heat of the noon-day;
Nay, she should ride like a queen, not plod along like a peasant.
Somewhat alarmed at first, but reassured by the others,
Placing her hand on the cushion, her foot in the hand of her husband,
Gaily, with joyous laugh, Priscilla mounted her palfrey.
'Nothing is wanting now,' he said with a smile, 'but the distaff;
Then you would be in truth my queen, my beautiful Bertha!'

Onward the bridal procession now moved to their new habitation,
Happy husband and wife, and friends conversing together.
Pleasantly murmured the brook, as they crossed the ford in the forest,
Pleased with the image that passed, like a dream of love through its bosom,
Tremulous, floating in air, o'er the depths of the azure abysses.
Down through the golden leaves the sun was pouring his splendours,
Gleaming on purple grapes, that, from branches above them suspended,
Mingled their odorous breath with the balm of the pine and the fir-tree,
Wild and sweet as the clusters that grew in the valley of Eshcol.
Like a picture it seemed of the primitive, pastoral ages,
Fresh with the youth of the world, and recalling Rebecca and Isaac,

Old and yet ever new, and simple and beautiful always,
Love immortal and young in the endless succession of lovers.
So through the Plymouth woods passed onward the bridal
    procession.

The Song of Hiawatha

INTRODUCTION

Should you ask me, whence these stories?
Whence these legends and traditions,
With the odours of the forest,
With the dew and damp of meadows,
With the curling smoke of wigwams,
With the rushing of great rivers,
With their frequent repetitions,
And their wild reverberations,
As of thunder in the mountains?
  I should answer, I should tell you,
'From the forests and the prairies,
From the great lakes of the North-land,
From the land of the Ojibways,
From the land of the Dakotahs,
From the mountains, moors, and fen-lands,
Where the heron, and Shuh-shuh-gah,
Feeds among the reeds and rushes.
I repeat them as I heard them
From the lips of Nawadaha,
The musician, the sweet singer.'
  Should you ask where Nawadaha
Found these songs, so wild and wayward,
Found these legends and traditions,
I should answer, I should tell you,
'In the bird's-nests of the forest,
In the lodges of the beaver,
In the hoof-prints of the bison,
In the eyrie of the eagle!
'All the wild-fowl sang them to him,
In the moorlands and the fen-lands,
In the melancholy marshes;
Chetowaik, the plover, sang them,
Mahng, the loon, the wild-goose, Wawa,
The blue heron, the Shuh-shuh-gah,
And the grouse, the Mushkodasa!'

If still further you should ask me
Saying, 'Who was Nawadaha?
Tell us of this Nawadaha,'
I should answer your inquiries
Straightway in such words as follow:
    In the Vale of Tawasentha,
In the green and silent valley,
By the pleasant watercourses,
Dwelt the singer Nawadaha.
Round about the Indian village
Spread the meadows and the corn-fields,
And beyond them stood the forest,
Stood the groves of the singing pine-trees,
Green in Summer, white in Winter,
Ever sighing, ever singing.
    'And the pleasant watercourses,
You could trace them through the valley,
By the rushing in the Spring-time,
By the alders in the Summer,
By the white fog in the Autumn,
By the black line in the Winter;
And beside them dwelt the singer,
In the vale of Tawasentha,
In the green and silent valley.
    'There he sang of Hiawatha,
Sang the Song of Hiawatha,
Sang his wondrous birth and being,
How he prayed and how he fasted,
How he lived, and toiled, and suffered,
That the tribes of men might prosper,
That he might advance his people!'
    Ye who love the haunts of Nature,
Love the sunshine of the meadow,
Love the shadow of the forest,
Love the wind among the branches,
And the rain-shower and the snow-storm,
And the rushing of great rivers
Through their palisades of pine-trees,
And the thunder in the mountains,
Whose innumerable echoes
Flap like eagles in their eyries; –

Listen to these wild traditions,
To this Song of Hiawatha!
   Ye who love a nation's legends,
Love the ballads of a people,
That like voices from afar off
Waving like a hand that beckons,
Call to us to pause and listen,
Speak in tones so plain and child-like,
Scarcely can the ear distinguish
Whether they are sung or spoken; –
Listen to this Indian Legend,
To this Song of Hiawatha!
   Ye whose hearts are fresh and simple,
Who have faith in God and Nature,
Who believe, that in all ages
Every human heart is human,
That in even savage bosoms
There are longings, yearnings, strivings
For the good they comprehend not,
That the feeble hands and helpless,
Groping blindly in the darkness,
Touch God's right hand in that darkness
And are lifted up and strengthened; –
Listen to this simple story,
To this Song of Hiawatha!
   Ye, who sometimes in your rambles
Through the green lanes of the country,
Where the tangled barberry-bushes
Hang their tufts of crimson berries
Over stone walls gray with mosses,
Pause by some neglected grave-yard,
For a while to muse, and ponder
On a half-effaced inscription,
Written with little skill of song-craft,
Homely phrases, but each letter
Full of hope, and yet of heart-break,
Full of all the tender pathos
Of the Here and the Hereafter; –
Stay and read this rude inscription,
Read this Song of Hiawatha!

I

THE PEACE-PIPE

On the Mountains of the Prairie,
On the great Red Pipe-Stone Quarry,
Gitche Manito, the mighty,
He the Master of Life, descending,
On the red crags of the quarry
Stood erect, and called the nations,
Called the tribes of men together.

From his footprints flowed a river,
Leaped into the light of morning,
O'er the precipice plunging downward
Gleamed like Ishkoodah, the comet.
And the Spirit, stooping earthward,
With his finger on the meadow
Traced a winding pathway for it,
Saying to it, 'Run in this way!'

From the red stone of the quarry
With his hand he broke a fragment,
Moulded it into a pipe-head,
Shaped and fashioned it with figures;
From the margin of the river
Took a long reed for a pipe-stem,
With its dark green leaves upon it;
Filled the pipe with bark of willow,
With the bark of the red willow;
Breathed upon the neighbouring forest,
Made its great boughs chafe together,
Till in flame they burst and kindled;
And erect upon the mountains,
Gitche Manito, the mighty,
Smoked the calumet, the Peace-Pipe,
As a signal to the nations.

And the smoke rose slowly, slowly,
Through the tranquil air of morning.
First a single line of darkness,
Then a denser, bluer vapour,
Then a snow-white cloud unfolding,
Like the tree-tops of the forest,
Ever rising, rising, rising,

Till it touched the top of heaven,
Till it broke against the heaven,
And rolled outward all around it.
   From the Vale of Tawasentha,
From the Valley of Wyoming,
From the groves of Tuscaloosa,
From the far-off Rocky Mountains,
From the Northern lakes and rivers
All the tribes beheld the signal,
Saw the distant smoke ascending,
The Pukwana of the Peace-Pipe.
   And the Prophets of the nations
Said: 'Behold it, the Pukwana,
By this signal from afar off,
Bending like a wand of willow,
Gitche Manito, the mighty,
Calls the tribes of men together,
Calls the warriors to his council!'
   Down the rivers o'er the prairies,
Came the warriors of the nations,
Came the Delawares and Mohawks,
Came the Choctaws and Camanches,
Came the Shoshonies and Blackfeet,
Came the Pawnees and Omawhas,
Came the Mandans and Dacotahs,
Came the Hurons and Ojibways,
All the warriors drawn together
By the signal of the Peace-Pipe,
To the Mountains of the Prairie,
To the Great Red Pipe-Stone Quarry.
And they stood there on the meadow,
With their weapons and their wargear,
Painted like the leaves of Autumn,
Painted like the sky of morning,
Wildly glaring at each other;
In their faces stern defiance,
In their hearts the feuds of ages,
The hereditary hatred,
The ancestral thirst of vengeance.
   Gitche Manito, the mighty,
The creator of the nations,

Looked upon them with compassion,
With paternal love and pity;
Looked upon their wrath and wrangling
But as quarrels among children,
But as feuds and fights of children!
   Over them he stretched his right hand,
To subdue their stubborn natures,
To allay their thirst and fever,
By the shadow of his right hand;
Spake to them with voice majestic
As the sound of far-off waters,
Falling into deep abysses,
Warning, chiding, spake in this wise: —
   'O my children! my poor children!
Listen to the words of wisdom,
Listen to the words of warning,
From the lips of the Great Spirit,
From the Master of Life, who made you:
   'I have given you lands to hunt in,
I have given you streams to fish in,
I have given you bear and bison,
I have given you roe and reindeer,
I have given you brant and beaver,
Filled the marshes full of wild fowl,
Filled the rivers full of fishes;
Why then are you not contented?
Why then will you hunt each other?
   'I am weary of your quarrels,
Weary of your wars and bloodshed,
Weary of your prayers for vengeance,
Of your wranglings and dissensions;
All your strength is in your union,
All your danger is in discord;
Therefore be at peace henceforward,
And as brothers live together.
   'I will send a Prophet to you,
A Deliverer of the nations,
Who shall guide you and shall teach you,
Who shall toil and suffer with you.
If you listen to his counsels,
You will multiply and prosper;

If his warnings pass unheeded,
You will fade away and perish !
    'Bathe now in the stream before you,
Wash the war-paint from your faces,
Wash the blood-stains from your fingers,
Bury your war-clubs and your weapons,
Break the red stone from this quarry,
Mould and make it into Peace-Pipes,
Take the reeds that grow beside you,
Deck them with your brightest feathers,
Smoke the calumet together,
And as brothers live henceforward !'
    Then upon the ground the warriors
Threw their cloaks and shirts of deerskin,
Threw their weapons and their war-gear,
Leaped into the rushing river,
Washed the war-paint from their faces,
Clear above them flowed the water,
Clear and limpid from the footprints
Of the Master of Life descending ;
Dark below them flowed the water,
Soiled and stained with streaks of crimson,
As if blood were mingled with it !
    From the river came the warriors,
Clean and washed from all their war-paint ;
On the banks their clubs they buried,
Buried all their warlike weapons.
Gitche Manito, the mighty,
The Great Spirit, the creator,
Smiled upon his helpless children !
    And in silence all the warriors
Broke the red stone of the quarry.
Smoothed and formed it into Peace-Pipes,
Broke the long reeds by the river,
Decked them with their brightest feathers,
And departed each one homeward,
While the Master of Life, ascending,
Through the opening of cloud-curtains,
Through the doorway of the heaven,
Vanished from before their faces,

In the smoke that rolled around him,
The Pukwana of the Peace-Pipe !

II

THE FOUR WINDS

'Honour be to Mudjekeewis !'
Cried the warriors, cried the old men,
When he came in triumph homeward
With the sacred Belt of Wampum.
From the regions of the North-Wind,
From the kingdom of Wabasso,
From the land of the White Rabbit.

He had stolen the Belt of Wampum
From the neck of Mishe-Mokwa,
From the Great Bear of the mountains,
From the terror of the nations,
As he lay asleep and cumbrous
On the summit of the mountains,
Like a rock with mosses on it.
Spotted brown and gray with mosses.

Silently he stole upon him,
Till the red nails of the monster
Almost touched him, almost scared him,
Till the hot breath of his nostrils
Warmed the hands of Mudjekeewis,
As he drew the Belt of Wampum
Over the round ears, that heard not,
Over the small eyes, that saw not,
Over the long nose and nostrils,
The black muffle of the nostrils,
Out of which the heavy breathing
Warmed the hands of Mudjekeewis.

Then he swung aloft his war-club,
Shouted loud and long his war-cry,
Smote the mighty Mishe-Mokwa
In the middle of the forehead,
Right between the eyes he smote him.

With the heavy blow bewildered,
Rose the Great Bear of the mountains ;
But his knees beneath him trembled,

And he whimpered like a woman,
As he reeled and staggered forward,
As he sat upon his haunches;
And the mighty Mudjekeewis,
Standing fearlessly before him,
Taunted him in loud derision,
Spake disdainfully in this wise: —

  'Hark you, Bear! you are a coward,
And no Brave, as you pretended;
Else you would not cry and whimper
Like a miserable woman!
Bear! you know our tribes are hostile,
Long have been at war together;
Now you find that we are strongest,
You go sneaking in the forest,
You go hiding in the mountains!
Had you conquered me in battle
Not a groan would I have uttered;
But you, Bear! sit here and whimper,
And disgrace your tribe by crying,
Like a wretched Shaugodaya,
Like a cowardly old woman!'

  Then again he raised his war-club,
Smote again the Mishe-Mokwa
In the middle of his forehead,
Broke his skull, as ice is broken
When one goes to fish in Winter.
Thus was slain the Mishe-Mokwa,
He the Great Bear of the mountains,
He the terror of the nations.

  'Honour be to Mudjekeewis!'
With a shout exclaimed the people,
'Honour to be Mudjekeewis!'
Henceforth he shall be the West-Wind,
And hereafter and forever
Shall he hold supreme dominion
Over all the winds of heaven.
Call him no more Mudjekeewis,
Call him Kabeyun, the West-Wind!'

  Thus was Mudjekeewis chosen
Father of the Winds of Heaven.

For himself he kept the West-Wind,
Gave the others to his children;
Unto Wabun gave the East-Wind,
Gave the South to Shawondasee,
And the North-Wind, wild and cruel,
To the fierce Kabibonokka.

Young and beautiful was Wabun;
He it was who brought the morning,
He it was whose silver arrows
Chased the dark o'er hill and valley;
He it was whose cheeks were painted
With the brightest streaks of crimson,
And whose voice awoke the village,
Called the deer, and called the hunter.

Lonely in the sky was Wabun;
Though the birds sang gaily to him,
Though the wild-flowers of the meadow
Filled the air with odours for him,
Though the forests and the rivers
Sang and shouted at his coming.
Still his heart was sad within him,
For he was alone in heaven.

But one morning, gazing earthward,
While the village still was sleeping,
And the fog lay on the river,
Like a ghost, that goes at sunrise,
He beheld a maiden walking
All alone upon a meadow,
Gathering water-flags and rushes
By a river in the meadow.

Every morning, gazing earthward,
Still the first thing he beheld there
Was her blue eyes looking at him,
Two blue lakes among the rushes.
And he loved the lonely maiden,
Who thus waited for his coming;
For they both were solitary,
She on earth and he in heaven.

And he wooed her with caresses,
Wooed her with his smile of sunshine,
With his flattering words he wooed her,

With his sighing and his singing,
Gentlest whispers in the branches,
Softest music, sweetest odours,
Till he drew her to his bosom,
Folded in his robes of crimson,
Till into a star he changed her,
Trembling still upon his bosom;
And for ever in the heavens
They are seen together walking,
Wabun and the Wabun-Annung,
Wabun and the Star of Morning.

But the fierce Kabibonokka
Had his dwelling among icebergs,
In the everlasting snowdrifts,
In the kingdom of Wabasso,
In the land of the White Rabbit.
He it was whose hand in Autumn
Painted all the trees with scarlet,
Stained the leaves with red and yellow;
He it was who sent the snowflakes,
Sifting, hissing through the forest,
Froze the ponds, the lakes, the rivers,
Drove the loon and sea-gull southward,
Drove the cormorant and curlew
To their nests of sedge and sea-tang
In the realms of Shawondasee.

Once the fierce Kabibonokka
Issued from his lodge of snowdrifts,
From his home among the icebergs,
And his hair, with snow besprinkled,
Streamed behind him like a river,
Like a black and wintry river,
As he howled and hurried southward,
Over frozen lakes and moorlands.

There among the reeds and rushes
Found he Shingebis, the diver,
Trailing strings of fish behind him,
O'er the frozen fens and moorlands,
Lingering still among the moorlands,
Though his tribe had long departed
To the land of Shawondasee.

Cried the fierce Kabibonokka,
'Who is this that dares to brave me?
Dares to stay in my dominions,
When the Wawa has departed,
When the wild-goose has gone southward,
And the heron, the Shuh-shuh-gah,
Long ago departed southward?
I will go into his wigwam,
I will put his smouldering fire out!'

And at night Kabibonokka,
To the lodge came wild and wailing,
Heaped the snow in drifts about it,
Shouted down into the smoke-flue,
Shook the lodge-poles in his fury,
Flapped the curtain of the doorway.
Shingebis, the diver, feared not,
Shingebis, the diver, cared not;
Four great logs had he for firewood,
One for each moon of the winter,
And for food the fishes served him.
By his blazing fire he sat there,
Warm and merry, eating, laughing,
Singing 'O Kabibonokka,
You are but my fellow-mortal!'

Then Kabibonokka entered,
And though Shingebis, the diver,
Felt his presence by the coldness,
Felt his icy breath upon him,
Still he did not cease his singing,
Still he did not leave his laughing,
Only turned the log a little,
Only made the fire burn brighter,
Made the sparks fly up the smoke-flue.

From Kabibonokka's forehead,
From his snow-besprinkled tresses,
Drops of sweat fell fast and heavy,
Making dints upon the ashes,
As along the eaves of lodges,
As from drooping boughs of hemlock,
Drips the melting snow in springtime,
Making hollows in the snowdrifts.

Till at last he rose defeated,
Could not bear the heat and laughter,
Could not bear the merry singing,
But rushed headlong through the doorway,
Stamped upon the crusted snowdrifts,
Stamped upon the lakes and rivers,
Made the snow upon them harder,
Made the ice upon them thicker,
Challenged Shingebis, the diver,
To come forth and wrestle with him,
To come forth and wrestle naked
On the frozen fens and moorlands.

Forth went Shingebis, the diver,
Wrestled all night with the North-Wind,
Wrestled naked on the moorlands
With the fierce Kabibonokka,
Till his panting breath grew fainter,
Till his frozen grasp grew feebler,
Till he reeled and staggered backward,
And retreated, baffled, beaten,
To the kingdom of Wabasso,
To the land of the White Rabbit,
Hearing still the gusty laughter,
Hearing Shingebis, the diver,
Singing, 'O Kabibonokka,
You are but my fellow-mortal!'

Shawondasee, fat and lazy,
Had his dwelling far to southward,
In the drowsy, dreamy sunshine,
In the never-ending Summer.
He it was who sent the wood-birds,
Sent the Opechee, the robin,
Sent the blue-bird, the Owaissa,
Sent the Shawshaw, sent the swallow,
Sent the wild-goose, Wawa, northward,
Sent the melons and tobacco,
And the grapes in purple clusters.

From his pipe the smoke ascending
Filled the sky with haze and vapour,
Filled the air with dreamy softness,
Gave a twinkle to the water,

Touched the rugged hills with smoothness,
Brought the tender Indian Summer
To the melancholy North-land,
In the dreary Moon of Snow-shoes.

   Listless, careless, Shawondasee!
In his life he had one shadow,
In his heart one sorrow had he.
Once, as he was gazing northward,
Far away upon a prairie
He beheld a maiden standing,
Saw tall and slender maiden
All alone upon a prairie;
Brightest green were all her garments
And her hair was like the sunshine.

   Day by day he gazed upon her,
Day by day his heart within him
Grew more hot with love and longing
For the maid with yellow tresses.
But he was too fat and lazy
To bestir himself and woo her;
Yes, too indolent and easy
To pursue her and persuade her.
So he only gazed upon her,
Only sat and sighed with passion
For the maiden of the prairie.

   Till one morning, looking northward,
He beheld her yellow tresses
Changed and covered o'er with whiteness,
Covered as with whitest snowflakes.
'Ah! my brother from the North-land,
From the kingdom of Wabasso,
From the land of the White Rabbit!
You have stolen the maiden from me,
You have laid your hand upon her,
You have wooed and won my maiden,
With your stories of the North-land!'

   Thus the wretched Shawondasee
Breathed into the air his sorrow;
And the South-Wind o'er the prairie
Wandered warm with sighs of passion
With the sighs of Shawondasee,

Till the air seemed full of snowflakes,
Full of thistle-down the prairie,
And the maid with hair like sunshine
Vanished from his sight for ever;
Nevermore did Shawondasee
See the maid with yellow tresses!

Poor, deluded Shawondasee!
'Twas no woman that you gazed at,
'Twas no maiden that you sighed for,
'Twas the prairie dandelion
That through all the dreamy Summer
You had gazed at with such longing,
You had sighed for with such passion
And had puffed away for ever,
Blown into the air with sighing.
Ah! deluded Shawondasee!

Thus the Four Winds were divided;
Thus the sons of Mudjekeewis
Had their stations in the heavens,
At the corners of the heavens;
For himself the West-Wind only
Kept the mighty Mudjekeewis.

III

HIAWATHA'S CHILDHOOD

Downward through the evening twilight,
In the days that are forgotten,
In the unremembered ages,
From the full moon fell Nokomis,
Fell the beautiful Nokomis,
She a wife, but not a mother.

She was sporting with her women
Swinging in a swing of grape-vines,
When her rival, the rejected,
Full of jealousy and hatred,
Cut the leafy swing asunder,
Cut in twain the twisted grapevines,
And Nokomis fell affrighted
Downward through the evening twilight,
On the Muskoday, the meadow,

On the prairie full of blossoms.
'See ! a star falls !' said the people ;
'From the sky a star is falling !'
There among the ferns and mosses,
There among the prairie lilies,
On the Muskoday the meadow,
In the moonlight and the starlight,
Fair Nokomis bore a daughter.
And she called her name Wenonah,
As the first-born of her daughters.
And the daughter of Nokomis
Grew up like the prairie lilies,
Grew a tall and slender maiden,
With the beauty of the moonlight,
With the beauty of the starlight,

   And Nokomis warned her often,
Saying oft, and oft repeating,
'O, beware of Mudjekeewis,
Of the West-Wind, Mudjekeewis ;
Listen not to what he tells you ;
Lie not down upon the meadow,
Stoop not down among the lilies,
Lest the West-Wind come and harm you !'

   But she heeded not the warning,
Heeded not those words of wisdom,
And the West-Wind came at evening,
Walking lightly o'er the prairie,
Whispering to the leaves and blossoms,
Bending low the flowers and grasses,
Found the beautiful Wenonah,
Lying there among the lilies,
Wooed her with his words of sweetness,
Wooed her with his soft caresses,
Till she bore a son in sorrow,
Bore a son of love and sorrow.

   Thus was born my Hiawatha,
Thus was born the child of wonder ;
But the daughter of Nokomis,
Hiawatha's gentle mother,
In her anguish died deserted
By the West-Wind, false and faithless,

By the heartless Mudjekeewis.
    For her daughter, long and loudly
Wailed and wept the sad Nokomis;
'O that I were dead!' she murmured,
'O that I were dead, as thou art!
No more work, and no more weeping,
Wahonowin! Wahonowin!'
    By the shores of Gitche Gumee,
By the shining Big-Sea-Water,
Stood the wigwam of Nokomis,
Daughter of the Moon, Nokomis,
Dark behind it rose the forest,
Rose the black and gloomy pine-trees,
Rose the firs with cones upon them;
Bright before it beat the water,
Beat the clear and sunny water,
Beat the shining Big-Sea-Water.
    There the wrinkled, old Nokomis
Nursed the little Hiawatha,
Rocked him in his linden cradle,
Bedded soft in moss and rushes,
Safely bound with reindeer sinews;
Stilled his fretful wail by saying,
'Hush! the Naked Bear will get thee!'
Lulled him into slumber, singing,
'Ewa-yea! my little owlet!
Who is this, that lights the wig-wam?
With his great eyes lights the wig-wam?
Ewa-yea! my little owlet!'
    Many things Nokomis taught him
Of the stars that shine in heaven;
Showed him Ishkoodah, the comet,
Ishkoodah, with fiery tresses;
Showed the Death-Dance of the spirits,
Warriors with their plumes and war-clubs,
Flaring far away to northward
In the frosty nights of Winter;
Showed the broad, white road in heaven,
Pathway of the ghosts, the shadows,
Running straight across the heavens,
Crowded with the ghosts, the shadows.

At the door on Summer evenings
Sat the little Hiawatha ;
Heard the whispering of the pine-trees,
Heard the lapping of the water,
Sounds of music, words of wonder ;
'Minne-wawa !' said the pine-trees,
'Mudway-aushka !' said the water.
Saw the fire-fly, Wah-wah-taysee,
Flitting through the dusk of evening,
With the twinkle of its candle
Lighting up the brakes and bushes,
And he sang the song of children,
Sang the song Nokomis taught him :
'Wah-wah-taysee, little firefly,
Little, flitting, white-fire insect,
Little, dancing, white-fire creature,
Light me with your little cradle,
Ere upon my bed I lay me,
Ere in sleep I close my eyelids !'

Saw the moon rise from the water
Rippling, rounding from the water,
Saw the flecks and shadows on it,
Whispered, 'What is that, Nokomis ?'
And the good Nokomis answered :
'Once a warrior, very angry,
Seized his grandmother, and threw her
Up into the sky at midnight ;
Right against the moon he threw her ;
'Tis her body that you see there.'

Saw the rainbow in the heaven,
In the eastern sky, the rainbow,
Whispered, 'What is that, Nokomis ?'
And the good Nokomis answered :
''Tis the heaven of flowers you see there ;
All the wild-flowers of the forest,
All the lilies of the prairie,
When on earth they fade and perish,
Blossom in that heaven above us.'

When he heard the owls at midnight,
Hooting, laughing in the forest,
'What is that ?' he cried in terror.

'What is that ?' he said, 'Nokomis ?'
And the good Nokomis answered :
'That is but the owl and owlet,
Talking in their native language,
Talking, scolding at each other.'
   Then the little Hiawatha,
Learned of every bird its language,
Learned their names and all their secrets,
How they built their nests in Summer,
Where they hid themselves in Winter,
Talked with them whene'er he met them,
Called them 'Hiawatha's Chickens.'
   Of all beasts he learned the language,
Learned their names and all their secrets,
How the beavers built their lodges,
Where the squirrels hid their acorns,
How the reindeer ran so swiftly,
Why the rabbit was so timid,
Talked with them when'er he met them,
Called them 'Hiawatha's Brothers.'
   Then Iagoo, the great boaster,
He the marvellous story-teller,
He the traveller and the talker.
He the friend of old Nokomis,
Made a bow for Hiawatha :
From a branch of ash he made it,
From an oak-bough made the arrows,
Tipped with flint, and winged with feathers,
And the cord he made of deer-skin.
   Then he said to Hiawatha :
'Go, my son, into the forest,
Where the red deer herd together,
Kill for us a famous roebuck,
Kill for us a deer with antlers !'
   Forth into the forest straightway
All alone walked Hiawatha
Proudly, with his bow and arrows ;
And the birds sang round him, o'er him,
'Do not shoot us, Hiawatha !'
Sang the Opechee, the robin,
Sang the bluebird, the Owaissa,

'Do not shoot us, Hiawatha!'
Up the oak-tree, close beside him,
Sprang the squirrel, Adjidaumo,
In and out among the branches,
Coughed and chattered from the oak-tree,
Laughed, and said between his laughing,
'Do not shoot me, Hiawatha!'
And the rabbit from his pathway
Leaped aside, and at a distance
Sat erect upon his haunches,
Half in fear and half in frolic,
Saying to the little hunter,
'Do not shoot me, Hiawatha!'
But he heeded not, nor heard them,
For his thoughts were with the red deer;
On their tracks his eyes were fastened,
Leading downward to the river,
To the ford across the river,
And as one in slumber walked he.
Hidden in the alder bushes,
There he waited till the deer came,
Till he saw two antlers lifted,
Saw two eyes look from the thicket
Saw two nostrils point to wind-ward,
And a deer came down the pathway,
Flecked with leafy light and shadow,
And his heart within him fluttered,
Trembled like the leaves above him,
Like the birch-leaf palpitated,
As the deer came down the pathway.
Then upon one knee uprising,
Hiawatha aimed an arrow;
Scarce a twig moved with his motion,
Scarce a leaf was stirred or rustled,
But the wary roebuck started,
Stamped with all his hoofs together,
Listened with one foot uplifted,
Leaped as if to meet the arrow;
Ah! the singing, fatal arrow,
Like a wasp it buzzed and stung him!
Dead he lay there in the forest,

By the ford across the river;
Beat his timid heart no longer,
But the heart of Hiawatha
Throbbed and shouted and exulted,
As he bore the red deer homeward
And Iagoo and Nokomis
Hailed his coming with applauses.

From the red deer's hide Nokomis
Made a cloak for Hiawatha,
From the red deer's flesh Nokomis
Made a banquet in his honour.
All the village came and feasted,
All the guests praised Hiawatha,
Called him Strong-heart, Soan getaha!
Called him Loon-Heart, Mahn-go taysee!

IV

HIAWATHA AND MUDJEKEEWIS

Out of childhood into manhood
Now had grown my Hiawatha,
Skilled in all the craft of hunters,
Learned in all the lore of old men,
In all youthful sports and pastimes,
In all manly arts and labours.

Swift of foot was Hiawatha;
He could shoot an arrow from him,
And run forward with such fleetness,
That the arrow fell behind him!
Strong of arm was Hiawatha;
He could shoot ten arrows upward,
Shoot them with such strength and swiftness,
That the tenth had left the bowstring
Ere the first to earth had fallen!

He had mittens, Minjekahwun,
Magic mittens made of deer-skin;
When upon his hands he wore them,
He could smite the rocks asunder,
He could grind them into powder,
He had moccasins enchanted,
Magic moccasins of deer-skin;

When he bound them round his ankles,
When upon his feet he tied them,
At each stride a mile he measured !
  Much he questioned old Nokomis
Of his father Mudjekeewis ;
Learned from her the fatal secret
Of the beauty of his mother,
Of the falsehood of his father ;
And his heart was hot within him,
Like a living coal his heart was.
  Then he said to old Nokomis,
'I will go to Mudjekeewis,
See how fares it with my father,
At the doorways of the West-Wind,
At the portals of the Sunset !'
  From his lodge went Hiawatha,
Dressed for travel, armed for hunting ;
Dressed in deer-skin shirt and leggings,
Richly wrought with quills and wampum ;
On his head his eagle feathers,
Round his waist his belt of wampum,
In his hand his bow of ash-wood,
Strung with sinews of the reindeer ;
In his quiver oaken arrows,
Tipped with jasper, winged with feathers ;
With his mittens, Minjekahwun,
With his moccasins enchanted.
  Warning said the old Nokomis,
'Go not forth, O Hiawatha !
To the kingdom of the West-Wind,
To the realms of Mudjekeewis,
Lest he harm you with his magic,
Lest he kill you with his cunning !'
  But the fearless Hiawatha
Heeded not her woman's warning ;
Forth he strode into the forest,
At each stride a mile he measured ;
Lurid seemed the sky above him,
Lurid seemed the earth beneath him,
Hot and close the air around him,
Filled with smoke and fiery vapours,

As of burning woods and prairies,
For his heart was hot within him,
Like a living coal his heart was.

   So he journeyed westward, westward,
Left the fleetest deer behind him,
Left the antelope and bison;
Crossed the rushing Esconawbaw,
Crossed the mighty Mississippi,
Passed the Mountains of the Prairie,
Passed the land of Crows and Foxes,
Passed the dwellings of the Blackfeet,
Came unto the Rocky Mountains,
To the kingdom of the West-Wind,
Where upon the gusty summits
Sat the ancient Mudjekeewis,
Ruler of the winds of heaven.

   Filled with awe was Hiawatha
At the aspect of his father.
On the air about him wildly
Tossed and streamed his cloudy tresses,
Gleamed like drifting snow his tresses,
Glared like Ishkoodah, the comet,
Like the star with fiery tresses.

   Filled with joy was Mudjekeewis
When he looked on Hiawatha,
Saw his youth rise up before him
In the face of Hiawatha,
Saw the beauty of Wenonah
From the grave rise up before him.

   'Welcome!' said he, 'Hiawatha,
To the kingdom of the West-Wind!
Long have I been waiting for you!
Youth is lovely, age is lonely,
Youth is fiery, age is frosty;
You bring back the days departed,
You bring back my youth of passion,
And the beautiful Wenonah!'

   Many days they talked together,
Questioned, listened, waited, answered
Much the mighty Mudjekeewis
Boasted of his ancient prowess,

Of his perilous adventures,
His indomitable courage,
His invulnerable body.

Patiently sat Hiawatha,
Listening to his father's boasting;
With a smile he sat and listened,
Uttered neither threat nor menace,
Neither word nor look betrayed him,
But his heart was hot within him,
Like a living coal his heart was.

Then he said, 'O Mudjekeewis,
Is there nothing that can harm you?
Nothing that you are afraid of?'
And the mighty Mudjekeewis,
Grand and gracious in his boasting,
Answered, saying, 'There is nothing,
Nothing but the black rock yonder,
Nothing but the fatal Wawbeek!'

And he looked at Hiawatha
With a wise look and benignant,
With a countenance paternal,
Looked with pride upon the beauty
Of his tall and graceful figure,
Saying, 'O my Hiawatha!
Is there anything can harm you?
Anything you are afraid of?'

But the wary Hiawatha
Paused awhile, as if uncertain,
Held his peace, as if resolving,
And then answered, 'There is nothing,
Nothing but the bulrush yonder,
Nothing but the great Apukwa!'

And as Mudjekeewis, rising,
Stretched his hand to pluck the bulrush,
Hiawatha cried in terror,
Cried in well-dissembled terror,
'Kago! kago! do not touch it!'
'Ah, kaween!' said Mudjekeewis,
'No, indeed, I will not touch it!'

Then they talked of other matters;
First of Hiawatha's brothers,

First of Wabun, of the East-Wind,
Of the South-Wind, Shawondasee,
Of the North, Kabibonokka;
Then of Hiawatha's mother,
Of the beautiful Wenonah,
Of her birth upon the meadow,
Of her death, as old Nokomis
Had remembered and related.

And he cried, 'O Mudjekeewis,
It was you who killed Wenonah,
Took her young life and her beauty,
Broke the Lily of the Prairie,
Trampled it beneath your footsteps;
You confess it! you confess it!'
And the mighty Mudjekeewis
Tossed his gray hairs to the west wind,
Bowed his hoary head in anguish,
With a silent nod assented.

Then up started Hiawatha,
And with threatening look and gesture
Laid his hand upon the black rock,
On the fatal Wawbeek laid it.
With his mittens, Minjekahwun,
Rent the jutting crag asunder,
Smote and crushed it into fragments,
Hurled them madly at his father,
The remorseful Mudjekeewis,
For his heart was hot within him,
Like a living coal his heart was.

But the ruler of the West-Wind
Blew the fragments backwards from him,
With the breathing of his nostrils,
With the tempest of his anger,
Blew them back at his assailant;
Seized the bulrush, the Apukwa,
Dragged it with its roots and fibres
From the margin of the meadow,
From its ooze, the giant bulrush;
Long and loud laughed Hiawatha!

Then began the deadly conflict,
Hand to hand among the mountains;

From his eyrie screamed the eagle,
The Keneu, the great war-eagle,
Sat upon the crags around them,
Wheeling flapped his wings above them.

    Like a tall tree in the tempest
Bent and lashed the giant bulrush ;
And in masses huge and heavy
Crashing fell the fatal Wawbeek ;
Till the earth shook with the tumult
And confusion of the battle,
And the air was full of shoutings,
And the thunder of the mountains,
Starting, answered, 'Biam-wa-wa !'

    Back retreated Mudjekeewis,
Rushing westward o'er the mountains,
Stumbling westward down the mountains,
Three whole days retreated fighting,
Still pursued by Hiawatha
To the doorways of the West-Wind,
To the portals of the Sunset,
To the earth's remotest border,
Where into the empty spaces
Sinks the sun, as a flamingo
Drops into her nest at nightfall,
In the melancholy marshes.

    'Hold !' at length cried Mudjekeewis,
'Hold, my son, my Hiawatha !
'Tis impossible to kill me,
For you cannot kill the immortal.
I have put you to this trial,
But to know and prove your courage ;
Now receive the prize of valour !

    'Go back to your home and people,
Live among them, toil among them,
Cleanse the earth from all that harms it,
Clear the fishing-grounds and rivers,
Slay all monsters and magicians,
All the giants, the Wendigoes,
All the serpents, the Kenabeeks,
As I slew the Mishe-Mokwa,
Slew the Great Bear of the mountains.

'And at last when Death draws near you,
When the awful eyes of Pauguk
Glare upon you in the darkness,
I shall share my kingdom with you,
Ruler shall you be thenceforward
Of the Northwest-Wind, Keewaydin.
Of the home-wind, the Keewaydin.'

Thus was fought that famous battle
In the dreadful days of Shah-shah,
In the days long since departed,
In the kingdom of the West-Wind.
Still the hunter sees its traces
Scattered far o'er hill and valley;
Sees the giant bulrush growing
By the ponds and watercourses,
Sees the masses of the Wawbeek
Lying still in every valley.

Homeward now went Hiawatha;
Pleasant was the landscape round him,
Pleasant was the air above him,
For the bitterness of anger
Had departed wholly from him,
From his brain the thought of vengeance,
From his heart the burning fever.

Only once his pace he slackened,
Only once he paused or halted,
Paused to purchase heads of arrows
Of the ancient Arrow-maker,
In the land of the Dacotahs,
Where the Falls of Minnehaha
Flash and gleam among the oak trees,
Laugh and leap into the valley.

There the ancient Arrow-maker
Made his arrow-heads of sandstone,
Arrow-heads of chalcedony,
Arrow-heads of flint and jasper,
Smoothed and sharpened at the edges,
Hard and polished, keen and costly.

With him dwelt his dark-eyed daughter,
Wayward as the Minnehaha,
With her moods of shade and sunshine,

Eyes that smiled and frowned alternate,
Feet as rapid as the river,
Tresses flowing like the water,
And as musical a laughter;
And he named her from the river,
From the waterfall he named her,
Minnehaha, Laughing Water.

Was it then for heads of arrows,
Arrow-heads of chalcedony,
Arrow-heads of flint and jasper,
That my Hiawatha halted
In the land of the Dacotahs?
Was it not to see the maiden,
See the face of Laughing Water,
Peeping from behind the curtain,
Hear the rustling of her garments
From behind the waving curtain,
As one sees the Minnehaha
Gleaming, glancing through the branches,
As one hears the Laughing Water
From behind its screen of branches?
Who shall say what thoughts and visions
Fill the fiery brains of young men?
Who shall say that dreams of beauty
Filled the heart of Hiawatha?
All he told to old Nokomis,
When he reached the lodge at sunset,
Was the meeting with his father,
Was his fight with Mudjekeewis;
Not a word he said of arrows,
Not a word of Laughing Water.

V

HIAWATHA'S FASTING

You shall hear how Hiawatha
Prayed and fasted in the forest,
Not for greater skill in hunting,
Not for greater craft in fishing,
Not for triumphs in the battle,
And renown among the warriors,

But for profit of the people,
For advantage of the nations.
  First he built a lodge for fasting,
Built a wigwam in the forest,
By the shining Big-Sea-Water,
In the blithe and pleasant Springtime,
In the Moon of Leaves he built it,
And, with dreams and visions many,
Seven whole days and nights he fasted.
  On the first day of his fasting
Through the leafy woods he wandered ;
Saw the deer start from the thicket,
Saw the rabbit in his burrow,
Heard the pheasant, Bena, drumming,
Heard the squirrel, Adjidaumo,
Rattling in his hoard of acorns,
Saw the pigeon, the Omeme,
Building nests among the pinetrees,
And in flocks the wild goose, Wawa,
Flying to the fen-lands northward,
Whirring, wailing far above him.
'Master of Life !' he cried, desponding,
'Must our lives depend on these things ?'
  On the next day of his fasting
By the river's bank he wandered,
Through the Muskoday, the meadow,
Saw the wild rice, Mahnomonee,
Saw the blueberry, Meenahga,
And the strawberry, Odahmin,
And the gooseberry, Shahbomin,
And the grape-vine, the Bemahgut,
Trailing o'er the alder-branches,
Filling all the air with fragrance !
'Master of Life !' he cried, desponding,
'Must our lives depend on these things ?'
  On the third day of his fasting
By the lake he sat and pondered,
By the still, transparent water ;
Saw the sturgeon, Nahma, leaping,
Scattering drops like beads of wampum,
Saw the yellow perch, the Sahwa,

Like a sunbeam in the water,
Saw the pike, the Maskenozha,
And the herring, Okahahwis,
And the Shawgashee, the crawfish !
'Master of Life !' he cried desponding,
'Must our lives depend on these things ?'

On the fourth day of his fasting
In his lodge he lay exhausted ;
From his couch of leaves and branches
Gazing with half-open eyelids,
Full of shadowy dreams and visions,
On the dizzy, swimming landscape,
On the gleaming of the water,
On the splendour of the sunset.

And he saw a youth approaching,
Dressed in garments green and yellow
Coming through the purple twilight,
Through the splendour of the sunset ;
Plumes of green bent o'er his forehead,
And his hair was soft and golden.

Standing at the open doorway,
Long he looked at Hiawatha,
Looked with pity and compassion
On his wasted form and features,
And, in accents like the sighing
Of the South-Wind in the tree-tops,
Said he, 'O my Hiawatha !
All your prayers are heard in heaven,
For you pray not like the others ;
Not for greater skill in hunting,
Not for greater craft in fishing,
Not for triumph in the battle,
Nor renown among the warriors,
But for profit of the people,
For advantage of the nations.

'From the Master of Life descending,
I, the friend of man, Mondamin,
Come to warn you and instruct you,
How by struggle and by labour
You shall gain what you have prayed for.
Rise up from your bed of branches,

Rise, O youth, and wrestle with me !'
　　Faint with famine, Hiawatha
Started from his bed of branches,
From the twilight of his wigwam
Forth into the flush of sunset
Came, and wrestled with Mondamin ;
At his touch he felt new courage
Throbbing in his brain and bosom,
Felt new life and hope and vigour
Run through every nerve and fibre.
　　So they wrestled there together
In the glory of the sunset,
And the more they strove and struggled,
Stronger still grew Hiawatha ;
Till the darkness fell around them,
And the heron, the Shuh-shuh-gah,
From her haunts among the fen-lands,
Gave a cry of lamentation,
Gave a scream of pain and famine.
　　''Tis enough !' then said Mondamin,
Smiling upon Hiawatha,
'But to-morrow, when the sun sets,
I will come again to try you.'
And he vanished, and was seen not ;
Whether sinking as the rain sinks,
Whether rising as the mists rise,
Hiawatha saw not, knew not,
Only saw that he had vanished,
Leaving him alone and fainting,
With the misty lake below him,
And the reeling stars above him.
On the morrow and the next day,
When the sun through heaven descending,
Like a red and burning cinder
From the hearth of the Great Spirit,
Fell into the western waters,
Came Mondamin for the trial,
For the strife with Hiawatha ;
Came as silent as the dew comes,
From the empty air appearing,
Into empty air returning,

Taking shape when earth it touches,
But invisible to all men
In its coming and its going.
   Thrice they wrestled there together
In the glory of the sunset,
Till the darkness fell around them,
Till the heron, the Shuh-shuh-gah,
From her haunts among the fen-lands,
Uttered her loud cry of famine,
And Mondamin paused to listen.

   Tall and beautiful he stood there,
In his garments green and yellow;
To and fro his plumes above him
Waved and nodded with his breathing,
And the sweat of the encounter
Stood like drops of dew upon him.

   And he cried, 'O Hiawatha!
Bravely have you wrestled with me,
Thrice have wrestled stoutly with me,
And the Master of Life, who sees us,
He will give to you the triumph!'

   Then he smiled, and said: 'To-morrow
Is the last day of your conflict,
Is the last day of your fasting.
You will conquer and o'ercome me:
Make a bed for me to lie in,
Where the rain may fall upon me,
Where the sun may come and warm me;
Strip these garments, green and yellow,
Strip this nodding plumage from me,
Lay me in the earth, and make it
Soft and loose and light above me.

   'Let no hand disturb my slumber,
Let no weed nor worm molest me,
Let not Kahgahgee, the raven,
Come to haunt me and molest me,
Only come yourself to watch me,
Till I wake, and start, and quicken,
Till I leap into the sunshine.'

   And thus saying, he departed.
Peacefully slept Hiawatha,

But he heard the Wawonaissa,
Heard the whippoorwill complaining,
Perched upon his lonely wigwam;
Heard the rushing Sebowisha,
Heard the rivulet rippling near him,
Talking to the darksome forest;
Heard the sighing of the branches,
As they lifted and subsided
At the passing of the night-wind,
Heard them, as one hears in slumber
Far-off murmurs, dreamy whispers:
Peacefully slept Hiawatha.

On the morrow came Nokomis,
On the seventh day of his fasting,
Came with food for Hiawatha,
Came imploring and bewailing,
Lest his hunger should o'ercome him,
Lest his fasting should be fatal.

But he tasted not, and touched not,
Only said to her, 'Nokomis,
Wait until the sun is setting,
Till the darkness falls around us,
Till the heron, the Shuh-shuh-gah,
Crying from the desolate marshes,
Tells us that the day is ended.'

Homeward weeping went Nokomis,
Sorrowing for her Hiawatha,
Fearing lest his strength should fail him,
Lest his fasting should be fatal.
He meanwhile sat weary waiting
For the coming of Mondamin,
Till the shadows, pointing eastward,
Lengthened over field and forest,
Till the sun dropped from the heaven,
Floating on the waters westward,
As a red leaf in the Autumn
Falls and floats upon the water,
Falls and sinks into its bosom.

And behold! the young Mondamin,
With his soft and shining tresses,
With his garments green and yellow,

With his long and glossy plumage,
Stood and beckoned at the doorway.
And as one in slumber walking,
Pale and haggard, but undaunted,
From the wigwam Hiawatha
Came and wrestled with Mondamin.

Round about him spun the landscape,
Sky and forest reeled together,
And his strong heart leaped within him,
As the sturgeon leaps and struggles
In a net to break its meshes.
Like a ring of fire around him
Blazed and flared the red horizon,
And a hundred suns seemed looking
At the combat of the wrestlers.

Suddenly upon the greensward
All alone stood Hiawatha,
Panting with his wild exertion,
Palpitating with the struggle;
And before him, breathless, lifeless,
Lay the youth, with hair dishevelled,
Plumage torn, and garments tattered,
Dead he lay there in the sunset.

And victorious Hiawatha
Made the grave as he commanded,
Stripped the garments from Mondamin,
Stripped his tattered plumage from him,
Laid him in the earth, and made it
Soft and loose and light above him;
And the heron, the Shuh-shuh-gah,
From the melancholy moorlands,
Gave a cry of lamentation,
Gave a cry of pain and anguish!

Homeward then went Hiawatha
To the lodge of old Nokomis,
And the seven days of his fasting
Were accomplished and completed.
But the place was not forgotten
Where he wrestled with Mondamin;
Nor forgotten nor neglected
Was the grave where lay Mondamin,

Sleeping in the rain and sunshine,
Where his scattered plumes and garments
Faded in the rain and sunshine.

 Day by day did Hiawatha
Go to wait and watch beside it;
Kept the dark mould soft above it,
Kept it clean from weeds and insects,
Drove away, with scoffs and shoutings,
Kahgahgee, the king of ravens.

 Till at length a small green feather
From the earth shot slowly upward,
Then another and another,
And before the Summer ended
Stood the maize in all its beauty,
With its shining robes about it,
And its long, soft, yellow tresses;
And in rapture Hiawatha
Cried aloud, 'It is Mondamin!
Yes, the friend of man, Mondamin!'

 Then he called to old Nokomis
And Iagoo, the great boaster,
Showed them where the maize was growing,
Told them of his wondrous vision,
Of his wrestling and his triumph,
Of this new gift to the nations,
Which should be their food forever.

 And still later, when the Autumn
Changed the long, green leaves to yellow,
And the soft and juicy kernels
Grew like wampum hard and yellow,
Then the ripened ears he gathered,
Stripped the withered husks from off them,
As he once had stripped the wrestler,
Gave the first Feast of Mondamin,
And made known unto the people
This new gift of the Great Spirit.

VI

HIAWATHA'S FRIENDS

 Two good friends had Hiawatha,
Singled out from all the others,

Bound to him in closest union,
And to whom he gave the right hand
Of his heart, in joy and sorrow;
Chibiabos, the musician,
And the very strong man, Kwasind.

Straight between them ran the pathway,
Never grew the grass upon it;
Singing birds, that utter falsehoods,
Story-tellers, mischief-makers,
Found no eager ear to listen,
Could not breed ill-will between them,
For they kept each other's counsel,
Spake with naked hearts together,
Pondering much and much contriving
How the tribes of men might prosper.

Most beloved by Hiawatha
Was the gentle Chibiabos,
He the best of all musicians,
He the sweetest of all singers.
Beautiful and childlike was he,
Brave as man is, soft as woman,
Pliant as a wand of willow,
Stately as a deer with antlers.

When he sang, the village listened:
All the warriors gathered round him,
All the women came to hear him;
Now he stirred their souls to passion,
Now he melted them to pity.

From the hollow reeds he fashioned
Flutes so musical and mellow,
That the brook, the Sebowisha,
Ceased to murmur in the woodland,
That the wood-birds ceased from singing,
And the squirrel, Adjidaumo,
Ceased his chatter in the oak-tree,
And the rabbit, the Wabasso,
Sat upright to look and listen.

Yes, the brook, the Sebowisha,
Pausing, said, 'O Chibiabos,
Teach my waves to flow in music,
Softly as your words in singing!'

Yes, the bluebird, the Owaissa,
Envious, said, 'O Chibiabos,
Teach me tones as wild and wayward,
Teach me songs as full of frenzy!'
Yes, the Opechee, the robin,
Joyous, said, 'O Chibiabos,
Teach me tones as sweet and tender,
Teach me songs as full of gladness!'
And the whippoorwill, Wawonaissa,
Sobbing, said, 'O Chibiabos,
Teach me tones as melancholy,
Teach me songs as full of sadness!'
All the many sounds of nature
Borrowed sweetness from his singing;
All the hearts of men were softened
By the pathos of his music;
For he sang of peace and freedom,
Sang of beauty, love, and longing;
Sang of death, and life undying
In the Islands of the Blessed,
In the kingdom of Ponemah,
In the land of the Hereafter.
Very dear to Hiawatha
Was the gentle Chibiabos,
He the best of all musicians,
He the sweetest of all singers;
For his gentleness he loved him,
And the magic of his singing.
Dear, too, unto Hiawatha
Was the very strong man, Kwasind,
He the strongest of all mortals,
He the mightiest among many:
For his very strength he loved him,
For his strength allied to goodness.
Idle in his youth was Kwasind,
Very listless, dull, and dreamy,
Never played with other children,
Never fished and never hunted,
Not like other children was he;
But they saw that much he fasted,
Much his Manito entreated,

Much besought his Guardian Spirit.
    'Lazy Kwasind !' said his mother,
'In my work you never help me !
In the Summer you are roaming
Idly in the fields and forests ;
In the Winter you are cowering
O'er the firebrands in the wigwam !
In the coldest days of Winter
I must break the ice for fishing ;
With my nets you never help me ;
At the door my nets are hanging,
Dripping, freezing with the water ;
Go and wring them, Yenadizze !
Go and dry them in the sunshine !'
    Slowly, from the ashes, Kwasind
Rose, but made no angry answer ;
From the lodge went forth in silence,
Took the nets, that hung together,
Dripping, freezing at the doorway,
Like a wisp of straw he wrung them,
Like a wisp of straw he broke them,
Could not wring them without breaking,
Such the strength was in his fingers.
    'Lazy Kwasind !' said his father,
'In the hunt you never help me ;
Every bow you touch is broken,
Snapped asunder every arrow ;
Yet come with me to the forest,
You shall bring the hunting homeward.'
    Down a narrow pass they wandered,
Where a brooklet led them onward,
Where the trail of deer and bison
Marked the soft mud on the margin,
Till they found all further passage
Shut against them, barred securely
By the trunks of trees uprooted,
Lying lengthwise, lying crosswise,
And forbidding further passage.
    'We must go back,' said the old man,
'O'er these logs we cannot clamber ;
Not a woodchuck could get through them,

Not a squirrel clamber o'er them!'
And straightway his pipe he lighted,
And sat down to smoke and ponder.
But before his pipe was finished,
Lo! the path was cleared before him;
All the trunks had Kwasind lifted,
To the right hand, to the left hand,
Shot the pine-trees swift as arrows,
Hurled the cedars light as lances.

'Lazy Kwasind!' said the young men,
As they sported in the meadow:
'Why stand idly looking at us,
Leaning on the rock behind you?
Come and wrestle with the others,
Let us pitch the quoit together!'

Lazy Kwasind made no answer,
To their challenge made no answer,
Only rose, and, slowly turning,
Seized the huge rock in his fingers,
Tore it from its deep foundation,
Poised it in the air a moment,
Pitched it sheer into the river,
Sheer into the swift Pauwating,
Where it still is seen in Summer.

Once as down that foaming river,
Down the rapids of Pauwating,
Kwasind sailed with his companions,
In the stream he saw a beaver,
Saw Ahmeek, the King of Beavers,
Struggling with the rushing currents,
Rising, sinking in the water.

Without speaking, without pausing,
Kwasind leaped into the river,
Plunged beneath the bubbling surface,
Through the whirlpools chased the beaver,
Followed him among the islands,
Stayed so long beneath the water,
That his terrified companions
Cried, 'Alas! good-by to Kwasind!
We shall never more see Kwasind!'
But he reappeared triumphant,

And upon his shining shoulders
Brought the beaver, dead and dripping,
Brought the King of all the Beavers.
    And these two, as I have told you,
Were the friends of Hiawatha,
Chibiabos, the musician,
And the very strong man, Kwasind.
Long they lived in peace together,
Spake with naked hearts together,
Pondering much and much contriving
How the tribes of men might prosper.

VII

HIAWATHA'S SAILING

'Give me of your bark, O Birch-Tree !
Of your yellow bark, O Birth-Tree !
Growing by the rushing river,
Tall and stately in the valley !
I a light canoe will build me,
Build a swift Cheemaun for sailing,
That shall float upon the river,
Like a yellow leaf in Autumn,
Like a yellow water-lily !
    'Lay aside your cloak, O Birch-Tree !
Lay aside your white-skin wrapper,
For the Summer-time is coming,
And the sun is warm in heaven,
And you need no white-skin wrapper !'
    Thus aloud cried Hiawatha
In the solitary forest,
By the rushing Taquamenaw,
When the birds were singing gaily,
In the Moon of Leaves were singing,
And the sun, from sleep awaking,
Started up and said, 'Behold me !
Gheezis, the great Sun, behold me !'
    And the tree with all its branches
Rustled in the breeze of morning,
Saying, with a sigh of patience,
'Take my cloak, O Hiawatha !'

With his knife the tree he girdled;
Just beneath its lowest branches,
Just above the roots he cut it,
Till the sap came oozing outward;
Down the trunk, from top to bottom,
Sheer he cleft the bark asunder,
With a wooden wedge he raised it,
Stripped it from the trunk unbroken.
　'Give me of your boughs, O Cedar!
Of your strong and pliant branches,
My canoe to make more steady,
Make more strong and firm beneath me!'
　Through the summit of the cedar
Went a sound, a cry of horror,
Went a murmur of resistance;
But it whispered, bending downward,
'Take my boughs, O Hiawatha!'
　Down he hewed the boughs of cedar,
Shaped them straightway to a framework,
Like two bows he formed and shaped them,
Like two bended bows together.
'Give me of your roots, O Tamarack!
Of your fibrous roots, O Larch-Tree!
My canoe to bind together.
So to bind the ends together
That the water may not enter,
That the river may not wet me!'
　And the larch, with all its fibres,
Shivered in the air of morning,
Touched his forehead with its tassels,
Said, with one long sigh of sorrow,
'Take them all, O Hiawatha!'
　From the earth he tore the fibres,
Tore the tough roots of the Larch-Tree,
Closely sewed the bark together,
Bound it closely to the framework.
　'Give me of your balm, O Fir-Tree!
Of your balsam and your resin,
So to close the seams together
That the water may not enter,
That the river may not wet me!'

And the Fir-Tree, tall and sombre,
Sobbed through all its robes of darkness,
Rattled like a shore with pebbles,
Answered wailing, answered weeping,
'Take my balm, O Hiawatha!'
　　And he took the tears of balsam,
Took the resin of the Fir-Tree,
Smeared therewith each seam and fissure,
Made each crevice safe from water.
　　'Give me of your quills, O Hedge-hog!
All your quills, O Kagh, the Hedge-hog!
I will make a necklace of them,
Make a girdle for my beauty,
And two stars to deck her bosom!'
　　From a hollow tree the Hedge-hog
With his sleepy eyes looked at him,
Shot his shining quills, like arrows,
Saying, with a drowsy murmur,
Through the tangle of his whiskers,
'Take my quills, O Hiawatha!'
　　From the ground the quills he gathered,
All the little shining arrows,
Stained them red and blue and yellow,
With the juice of roots and berries;
Into his canoe he wrought them,
Round its waist a shining girdle,
Round its bows a gleaming necklace,
On its breast two stars resplendent.
　　Thus the Birch Canoe was builded
In the valley, by the river,
In the bosom of the forest;
And the forest's life was in it,
All its mystery and its magic,
All the lightness of the birch-tree,
All the toughness of the cedar,
All the larch's supple sinews;
And it floated on the river
Like a yellow leaf in Autumn,
Like a yellow water-lily.
　　Paddles none had Hiawatha,
Paddles none he had or needed,

For his thoughts as paddles served him,
And his wishes served to guide him ;
Swift or slow at will he glided,
Veered to right or left at pleasure.
　Then he called aloud to Kwasind,
To his friend, the strong man, Kwasind,
Saying, 'Help me clear this river
Of its sunken logs and sand-bars.'
　Straight into the river Kwasind
Plunged as if he were an otter,
Dived as if he were a beaver,
Stood up to his waist in water,
To his armpits in the river,
Swam and shouted in the river,
Tugged at sunken logs and branches,
With his hands he scooped the sand-bars,
With his feet the ooze and tangle.
　And thus sailed my Hiawatha
Down the rushing Taquamenaw,
Sailed through all its bends and windings,
Sailed through all its deeps and shallows,
While his friend, the strong man Kwasind,
Swam the deeps, the shallows waded.
　Up and down the river went they,
In and out among its islands,
Cleared its bed of root and sand-bar,
Dragged the dead trees from its channel,
Made its passage safe and certain,
Made a pathway for the people,
From its springs among the mountains,
To the water of Pauwating,
To the bay of Taquamenaw.

VIII

HIAWATHA'S FISHING

　Forth upon the Gitche Gumee,
On the shining Big-Sea-Water,
With his fishing line of cedar,
Of the twisted bark of cedar,
Forth to catch the sturgeon Nahma,

Mishe-Nahma, King of Fishes,
In his birch canoe exulting
All alone went Hiawatha.
    Through the clear, transparent water
He could see the fishes swimming
Far down in the depths below him;
See the yellow perch, the Sahwa,
Like a sunbeam in the water,
See the Shawgashee, the crawfish,
Like a spider on the bottom,
On the white and sandy bottom.
    At the stern sat Hiawatha,
With his fishing-line of cedar;
In his plumes the breeze of morning
Played as in the hemlock branches;
On the bows, with tail erected,
Sat the squirrel, Adjidaumo;
In his fur the breeze of morning
Played as in the prairie grasses.
    On the white sand of the bottom
Lay the monster Mishe-Nahma,
Lay the sturgeon, King of Fishes;
Through his gills he breathed the water,
With his fins he fanned and winnowed,
With his tail he swept the sand-floor.
    There he lay in all his armour;
On each side a shield to guard him,
Plates of bone upon his forehead.
Down his sides and back and shoulders
Plates of bone with spines projecting!
Painted was he with his war-paints,
Stripes of yellow, red, and azure,
Spots of brown and spots of sable;
And he lay there on the bottom,
Fanning with his fins of purple,
As above him Hiawatha
In his birch canoe came sailing,
With his fishing-line of cedar.
    'Take my bait,' cried Hiawatha,
Down into the depths beneath him,
    'Take my bait, O Sturgeon, Nahma!

Come up from below the water,
Let us see which is the stronger !'
And he dropped his line of cedar
Through the clear, transparent water,
Waited vainly for an answer,
Long sat waiting for an answer,
And repeating loud and louder,
'Take my bait, O King of Fishes !'
    Quiet lay the sturgeon, Nahma,
Fanning slowly in the water,
Looking up at Hiawatha,
Listening to his call and clamour,
His unnecessary tumult,
Till he wearied of the shouting;
And he said to the Kenozha,
To the pike, the Maskenozha,
'Take the bait of this rude fellow,
Break the line of Hiawatha !'
In his fingers Hiawatha
Felt the loose line jerk and tighten
As he drew it in, it tugged so
That the birch canoe stood end wise,
Like a birch log in the water,
With the squirrel, Adjidaumo,
Perched and frisking on the summit.
    Full of scorn was Hiawatha
When he saw the fish rise upward,
Saw the pike, the Maskenozha,
Coming nearer, nearer to him,
And he shouted through the water,
'Esa ! esa ! shame upon you !
You are but the pike, Kenozha,
You are not the fish I wanted,
You are not the King of Fishes !'
    Reeling downward to the bottom
Sank the pike in great confusion,
And the mighty sturgeon, Nahma,
Said to Ugudwash, the sun-fish,
'Take the bait of this great boaster,
Break the line of Hiawatha !'
    Slowly upward, wavering, gleaming,

Like a white moon in the water,
Rose the Ugudwash, the sun-fish,
Seized the line of Hiawatha,
Swung with all his weight upon it,
Made a whirlpool in the water,
Whirled the birch canoe in circles,
Round and round in gurgling eddies,
Till the circles in the water
Reached the far-off sandy beaches,
Till the water-flags and rushes
Nodded on the distant margins.

But when Hiawatha saw him
Slowly rising through the water,
Lifting his great disk of whiteness,
Loud he shouted in derision,
'Esa! esa! shame upon you!
You are Ugudwash, the sun-fish,
You are not the fish I wanted,
You are not the King of Fishes!'
Wavering downward, white and ghastly,
Sank the Ugudwash, the sun-fish,
And again the sturgeon, Nahma,
Heard the shout of Hiawatha,
Heard his challenge of defiance,
The unnecessary tumult,
Ringing far across the water.

From the white sand of the bottom
Up he rose with angry gesture,
Quivering in each nerve and fibre,
Clashing all his plates of armour,
Gleaming bright with all his war-paint;
In his wrath he darted upward,
Flashing leaped into the sunshine,
Opened his great jaws, and swallowed
Both canoe and Hiawatha.

Down into that darksome cavern
Plunged the headlong Hiawatha,
As a log on some black river
Shoots and plunges down the rapids,
Found himself in utter darkness,
Groped about in helpless wonder,

Till he felt a great heart beating,
Throbbing in that utter darkness.
  And he smote it in his anger,
With his fist, the heart of Nahma,
Felt the mighty King of Fishes
Shudder through each nerve and fibre,
Heard the water gurgle round him
As he leaped and staggered through it,
Sick at heart, and faint and weary.
  Crosswise then did Hiawatha
Drag his birch-canoe for safety,
Lest from out the jaws of Nahma,
In the turmoil and confusion,
Forth he might be hurled and perish.
  And the squirrel, Adjidaumo,
Frisked and chattered very gaily,
Toiled and tugged with Hiawatha
Till the labour was completed.
  Then said Hiawatha to him,
'O my little friend, the squirrel,
Bravely have you toiled to help me;
Take the thanks of Hiawatha,
And the name which now he gives you;
For hereafter and for ever
Boys shall call you Adjidaumo,
Tail-in-air the boys shall call you!'
  And again the sturgeon, Nahma,
Gasped and quivered in the water,
Then was still, and drifted landward
Till he grated on the pebbles,
Till the listening Hiawatha
Heard him grate upon the margin,
Felt him strand upon the pebbles,
Knew that Nahma, King of Fishes,
Lay there dead upon the margin.
  Then he heard a clang and flapping,
As of many wings assembling,
Heard a screaming and confusion,
As of birds of prey contending,
Saw a gleam of light above him,
Shining through the ribs of Nahma,

Saw the glittering eyes of sea-gulls,
Of Kayoshk, the sea-gulls, peering,
Gazing at him through the opening,
Heard them saying to each other,
''Tis our brother, Hiawatha!'
  And he shouted from below them,
Cried exulting from the caverns:
'O ye sea-gulls! O my brother!
I have slain the sturgeon, Nahma;
Make the rifts a little larger,
With your claws the openings widen,
Set me free from this dark prison,
And henceforward and for ever
Men shall speak of your achievements,
Calling you Kayoshk, the sea-gulls,
Yes, Kayoshk, the Noble Scratchers!'
  And the wild and clamorous sea-gulls
Toiled with beak and claws together,
Made the rifts and openings wider
In the mighty ribs of Nahma,
And from peril and from prison,
From the body of the sturgeon,
From the peril of the water,
Was released my Hiawatha.
  He was standing near his wigwam,
On the margin of the water,
And he called to old Nokomis,
Called and beckoned to Nokomis,
Pointed to the sturgeon, Nahma,
Lying lifeless on the pebbles,
With the sea-gulls feeding on him.
  'I have slain the Mishe-Nahma,
Slain the King of Fishes!' said he;
'Look! the sea-gulls feed upon him,
Yes, my friends Kayoshk, the sea-gulls;
Drive them not away, Nokomis,
They have saved me from great peril
In the body of the sturgeon,
Wait until their meal is ended,
Till their craws are full with feasting,
Till they homeward fly, at sunset,

To their nests among the marshes;
Then bring all your pots and kettles
And make oil for us in Winter.'
   And she waited till the sun set,
Till the pallid moon, the Night-sun,
Rose above the tranquil water,
Till Kayoshk, the sated sea-gulls,
From their banquet rose with clamour,
And across the fiery sunset
Winged their way to far-off islands,
To their nests among the rushes.
   To his sleep went Hiawatha,
And Nokomis to her labour,
Toiling patient in the moonlight,
Till the sun and moon changed places,
Till the sky was red with sunrise,
And Kayoshk, the hungry sea-gulls,
Came back from the reedy islands,
Clamorous for their morning banquet.
   Three whole days and nights alternate
Old Nokomis and the sea-gulls
Stripped the oily flesh of Nahma,
Till the waves washed through the rib-bones,
Till the sea-gulls came no longer,
And upon the sands lay nothing
But the skeleton of Nahma.

IX

HIAWATHA AND THE PEARL-FEATHER

   On the shores of Gitche Gumee,
Of the shining Big-Sea-Water,
Stood Nokomis, the old woman,
Pointing with her finger westward,
O'er the water pointing westward,
To the purple clouds of sunset.
   Fiercely the red sun descending
Burned his way along the heavens,
Set the sky on fire behind him,
As war-parties, when retreating,
Burn the prairies on their war-trail;

And the moon, the Night-sun, eastward,
Suddenly starting from his ambush,
Followed fast those bloody footprints,
Followed in that fiery war-trail,
With its glare upon his features.

    And Nokomis, the old woman,
Pointing with her finger westward,
Spake these words to Hiawatha :
'Yonder dwells the great Pearl-Feather,
Megissogwon, the Magician,
Manito of Wealth and Wampum,
Guarded by his fiery serpents,
Guarded by the black pitch-water.
You can see his fiery serpents,
The Kenabeek, the great serpents,
Coiling, playing in the water ;
You can see the black pitch-water
Stretching far away beyond them,
To the purple clouds of sunset !

    'He it was who slew my father,
By his wicked wiles and cunning,
When he from the moon descended,
When he came on earth to seek me.
He, the mightiest of Magicians,
Sends the fever from the marshes,
Sends the pestilential vapours,
Sends the poisonous exhalations,
Sends the white fog from the fen-lands,
Sends disease and death among us !

    'Take your bow, O Hiawatha,
Take your arrows, jasper-headed,
Take your war-club, Puggawaugun,
And your mittens, Minjekahwun,
And your birch-canoe for sailing,
And the oil of Mishe-Nahma,
So to smear its sides, that swiftly
You may pass the black pitch-water ;
Slay this merciless magician,
Save the people from the fever
That he breathes across the fen-lands,
And avenge my father's murder !'

Straightway then my Hiawatha
Armed himself with all his war-gear,
Launched his birch-canoe for sailing;
With his palm its sides he patted,
Said with glee, 'Cheemaun, my darling,
O my Birch-Canoe! leap forward,
Where you see the fiery serpents,
Where you see the black pitch-water!'

Forward leaped Cheemaun exulting,
And the noble Hiawatha
Sang his war-song wild and woeful,
And above him the war-eagle,
The Keneu, the great war-eagle,
Master of all fowls with feathers,
Screamed and hurtled through the heavens.

Soon he reached the fiery serpents,
The Kenabeek, the great serpents,
Lying huge upon the water,
Sparkling, rippling in the water,
Lying coiled across the passage,
With their blazing crests uplifted,
Breathing fiery fogs and vapours,
So that none could pass beyond them.

But the fearless Hiawatha
Cried aloud, and spake in this wise:
'Let me pass my way, Kenabeek,
Let me go upon my journey!'
And they answered, hissing fiercely,
With their fiery breath made answer:
'Back, go back! O Shaugodaya!
Back to old Nokomis, Faint-heart!'

Then the angry Hiawatha
Raised his mighty bow of ash-tree,
Seized his arrows, jasper-headed,
Shot them fast among the serpents;
Every twanging of the bowstring
Was a war-cry and a death-cry,
Every whizzing of an arrow
Was a death-song of Kenabeek.

Weltering in the bloody water,
Dead lay all the fiery serpents,

And among them Hiawatha
Harmless sailed, and cried exulting:
'Onward, O Cheemaun, my darling!
Onward to the black pitch-water!'
  Then he took the oil of Nahma,
And the bows and sides anointed,
Smeared them well with oil, that swiftly
He might pass the black pitch-water.
  All night long he sailed upon it,
Sailed upon that sluggish water,
Covered with its mould of ages,
Black with rotting water-rushes,
Rank with flags and leaves of lilies,
Stagnant, lifeless, dreary, dismal,
Lighted by the shimmering moonlight,
And by will-o'-the-wisps illumined,
Fires by ghosts of dead men kindled,
In their weary night-encampments.
  All the air was white with moonlight,
All the water black with shadow,
And around him the Suggema,
The mosquito, sang their war-song,
And the fireflies, Wah-wah-taysee,
Waved their torches to mislead him:
And the bullfrog, the Dahinda,
Thrust his head into the moonlight,
Fixed his yellow eyes upon him,
Sobbed and sank beneath the surface;
And anon a thousand whistles,
Answered over all the fen-lands,
And the heron, the Shuh-shuh-gah,
Far off on the reedy margin,
Heralded the hero's coming.
  Westward thus fared Hiawatha,
Toward the realm of Megissogwon,
Toward the land of the Pearl-Feather,
Till the level moon stared at him,
In his face stared pale and haggard,
Till the sun was hot behind him,
Till it burned upon his shoulders,
And before him on the upland

He could see the Shining Wigwam
Of the Manito of Wampum,
Of the mightiest of Magicians.
　　Then once more Cheemaun he patted,
To his birch-canoe said, 'Onward!'
And it stirred in all its fibres,
And with one great bound of triumph
Leaped across the water-lilies,
Leaped through tangled flags and rushes,
And upon the beach beyond them
Dry-shod landed Hiawatha.
　　Straight he took his bow of ash-tree,
One end on the sand he rested,
With his knee he pressed the middle,
Stretched the faithful bowstring tighter,
Took an arrow, jasper-headed,
Shot it at the Shining Wigwam,
Sent it singing as a herald,
As a bearer of his message,
Of his challenge loud and lofty:
'Come forth from your lodge, Pearl-Feather!
Hiawatha waits your coming!'
　　Straightway from the Shining Wigwam
Came the mighty Megissogwon,
Tall of stature, broad of shoulder,
Dark and terrible in aspect,
Clad from head to foot in wampum,
Armed with all his warlike weapons,
Painted like the sky of morning,
Streaked with crimson, blue, and yellow,
Crested with great eagle-feathers,
Streaming upward, streaming outward,
　　'Well I know you, Hiawatha!'
Cried he in a voice of thunder,
In a tone of loud derision.
'Hasten back, O Shaugodaya!
Hasten back, among the women,
Back to old Nokomis, Faint-heart,
I will slay you as you stand there,
As of old I slew her father!'
　　But my Hiawatha answered,

Nothing daunted, fearing nothing:
'Big words do not smite like war-clubs,
Boastful breath is not a bowstring,
Taunts are not so sharp as arrows,
Deeds are better things than words are,
Actions mightier than boastings!'

Then began the greatest battle
That the sun had ever looked on,
That the war-birds ever witnessed.
All a Summer's day it lasted,
From the sunrise to the sunset;
For the shafts of Hiawatha
Harmless hit the shirt of wampum,
Harmless fell the blows he dealt it
With his mittens, Minjekahwun,
Harmless fell the heavy war-club;
It could dash the rocks asunder,
But it could not break the meshes
Of that magic shirt of wampum.

Till at sunset Hiawatha,
Leaning on his bow of ash-tree,
Wounded, weary, and desponding,
With his mighty war-club broken,
With his mittens torn and tattered,
And three useless arrows only,
Paused to rest beneath a pine-tree,
From whose branches trailed the mosses,
And whose trunk was coated over
With the Dead-man's Moccasin-leather,
With the fungus white and yellow.

Suddenly from the boughs above him
Sang the Mama, the woodpecker:
'Aim your arrows, Hiawatha,
At the head of Megissogwon,
Strike the tuft of hair upon it,
At their roots the long black tresses;
There alone can he be wounded!'

Winged with feathers, tipped with jasper,
Swift flew Hiawatha's arrow,
Just as Megissogwon, stooping,
Raised a heavy stone to throw it.

Full upon the crown it struck him,
At the roots of his long tresses,
And he reeled and staggered forward,
Plunging like a wounded bison,
Yes, like Pezhekee, the bison,
When the snow is on the prairie.
  Swifter flew the second arrow.
In the pathway of the other,
Piercing deeper than the other,
Wounding sorer than the other,
And the knees of Megissogwon
Shook like windy reeds beneath him,
Bent and trembled like the rushes.
  But the third and latest arrow
Swiftest flew, and wounded sorest,
And the mighty Megissogwon
Saw the fiery eyes of Pauguk,
Saw the eyes of Death glare at him,
Heard his voice call in the darkness;
At the feet of Hiawatha
Lifeless lay the great Pearl-Feather,
Lay the mightiest of Magicians.
  Then the grateful Hiawatha
Called the Mama, the woodpecker,
From his perch among the branches
Of the melancholy pine-tree,
And in honour of his service,
Stained with blood the tuft of feathers
On the little head of Mama;
Even to this day he wears it,
Wears the tuft of crimson feathers,
As a symbol of his service.
  Then he stripped the shirt of wampum
From the back of Megissogwon,
As a trophy of the battle,
As a signal of his conquest.
On the shore he left the body,
Half on land and half in water,
In the sand his feet were buried,
And his face was in the water,
And above him, wheeled and clamoured

The Keneu, the great war-eagle,
Sailing round in narrow circles,
Hovering nearer, nearer, nearer.
   From the wigwam Hiawatha
Bore the wealth of Megissogwon
All his wealth of skins and wampum,
Furs of bison and of beaver,
Furs of sable and of ermine,
Wampum belts and strings and pouches,
Quivers wrought with beads of wampum,
Filled with arrows, silver-headed.
   Homeward then he sailed exulting,
Homeward through the black pitch-water,
Homeward through the weltering serpents,
With the trophies of the battle,
With a shout and song of triumph.
   On the shore stood Chibiabos,
And the very strong man, Kwasind,
Waiting for the hero's coming,
Listening to his song of triumph.
And the people of the village
Welcomed him with songs and dances,
Made a joyous feast, and shouted !
'Honour be to Hiawatha !
He has slain the great Pearl-Feather,
Slain the mightiest of Magicians,
Him, who sent the fiery fever,
Sent the white fog from the fen-lands,
Sent disease and death among us !'
   Ever dear to Hiawatha
Was the memory of Mama !
And in token of his friendship,
As a mark of his remembrance,
He adorned and decked his pipestem
With the crimson tuft of feathers,
With the blood-red crest of Mama.
But the wealth of Megissogwon,
All the trophies of the battle,
He divided with his people,
Shared it equally among them.

X

HIAWATHA'S WOOING

'As unto the bow the cord is,
So unto the man is woman,
Though she bends him, she obeys him,
Though she draws him, yet she follows,
Useless each without the other!'
   Thus the youthful Hiawatha
Said within himself and pondered,
Much perplexed by various feelings,
Listless, longing, hoping, fearing,
Dreaming still of Minnehaha,
Of the lovely Laughing Water,
In the land of the Dacotahs.
'Wed a maiden of your people,'
Warning said the old Nokomis;
'Go not eastward, go not westward,
For a stranger, whom we know not!
Like a fire upon the hearthstone
Is a neighbour's homely daughter,
Like the starlight or the moonlight
Is the handsomest of strangers!'
   Thus dissuading spake Nokomis,
And my Hiawatha answered
Only this: 'Dear old Nokomis,
Very pleasant is the firelight,
But I like the starlight better,
Better do I like the moonlight!'
   Gravely then said old Nokomis:
'Bring not here an idle maiden,
Bring not here a useless woman,
Hands unskilful, feet unwilling;
Bring a wife with nimble fingers,
Heart and hand that move together,
Feet that run on willing errands!'
   Smiling answered Hiawatha;
'In the land of the Dacotahs
Lives the Arrow-maker's daughter,
Minnehaha, Laughing Water,
Handsomest of all the women.

I will bring her to your wigwam,
She shall run upon your errands,
Be your starlight, moonlight, firelight,
Be the sunlight of my people !'
   Still dissuading said Nokomis :
'Bring not to my lodge a stranger
From the land of the Dacotahs !
Very fierce are the Dacotahs,
Often is there war between us,
There are feuds yet unforgotten,
Wounds that ache and still may open !'
   Laughing answered Hiawatha :
'For that reason, if no other,
Would I wed the fair Dacotah,
That our tribes might be united,
That old feuds might be forgotten,
And old wounds be healed for ever !'
   Thus departed Hiawatha
To the land of the Dacotahs,
To the land of handsome women ;
Striding over moor and meadow,
Through interminable forests,
Through uninterrupted silence.

   With his moccasins of magic,
At each stride a mile he measured ;
Yet the way seemed long before him,
And his heart outrun his footsteps ;
And he journeyed without resting,
Till he heard the cataract's thunder,
Heard the Falls of Minnehaha,
Calling to him through the silence.
'Pleasant is the sound !' he murmured,
'Pleasant is the voice that calls me !'
   On the outskirts of the forest,
'Twixt the shadow and the sunshine,
Herds of fallow deer were feeding,
But they saw not Hiawatha ;
To his bow he whispered, 'Fail not !'
To his arrow whispered, 'Swerve not !'
Sent it singing on its errand,
To the red heart of the roebuck ;

Threw the deer across his shoulder,
And sped forward without pausing.
   At the doorway of his wigwam
Sat the ancient Arrow-maker,
In the land of the Dacotahs,
Making arrow-heads of jasper,
Arrow-heads of chalcedony.
At his side, in all her beauty,
Sat the lovely Minnehaha,
Sat his daughter, Laughing Water,
Plaiting mats of flags and rushes;
Of the past the old man's thoughts were,
And the maiden's of the future.
   He was thinking, as he sat there,
Of the days when with such arrows
He had struck the deer and bison,
On the Muskoday, the meadow;
Shot the wild goose, flying southward,
On the wing, the clamorous Wawa;
Thinking of the great war-parties,
How they came to buy his arrows,
Could not fight without his arrows.
Ah, no more such noble warriors
Could be found on earth as they were!
Now the men were all like women,
Only used their tongues for weapons!
   She was thinking of a hunter,
From another tribe and country,
Young and tall and very handsome,
Who one morning, in the Springtime,
Came to buy her father's arrows,
Sat and rested in the wigwam,
Lingered long about the doorway,
Looking back as he departed.
She had heard her father praise him,
Praise his courage and his wisdom;
Would he come again for arrows
To the Falls of Minnehaha?
On the mat her hands lay idle,
And her eyes were very dreamy.
   Through their thoughts they heard a footstep,

Heard a rustling in the branches,
And with glowing cheek and forehead,
With the deer upon his shoulders,
Suddenly from out the woodlands
Hiawatha stood before them.

Straight the ancient Arrowmaker
Looked up gravely from his labour,
Laid aside the unfinished arrow,
Bade him enter at the doorway,
Saying, as he rose to meet him,
'Hiawatha, you are welcome!'

At the feet of Laughing Water
Hiawatha laid his burden,
Threw the red deer from his shoulders;
And the maiden looked up at him,
Looked up from her mat of rushes,
Said with gentle look and accent,
'You are welcome, Hiawatha!'

Very spacious was the wigwam,
Made of deerskin dressed and whitened,
With the Gods of the Dacotahs
Drawn and painted on its curtains,
And so tall the doorway, hardly
Hiawatha stooped to enter,
Hardly touched his eagle-feathers
As he entered at the doorway.

Then uprose the Laughing Water,
From the ground fair Minnehaha,
Lay aside her mat unfinished,
Brought forth food and set before them,
Water brought them from the brooklet,
Gave them food in earthen vessels,
Gave them drink in bowls of basswood,
Listened while the guest was speaking,
Listened while her father answered,
But not once her lips she opened,
Not a single word she uttered.

Yes, as in a dream she listened
To the words of Hiawatha,
As he talked of old Nokomis,
Who had nursed him in his childhood,

As he told of his companions,
Chibiabos, the musician,
And the very strong man, Kwasind,
And of happiness and plenty
In the land of the Ojibways,
In the pleasant land and peaceful.
   'After many years of warfare,
Many years of strife and bloodshed,
There is peace between the Ojibways
And the tribe of the Dacotahs.'
Thus continued Hiawatha,
And then added, speaking slowly,
'That this peace may last for ever,
And our hands be clasped more closely,
And our hearts be more united,
Give me as my wife this maiden,
Minnehaha, Laughing Water,
Loveliest of Dacotah women!'
   And the ancient Arrow-maker
Paused a moment ere he answered,
Smoked a little while in silence,
Looked at Hiawatha proudly,
Fondly looked at Laughing Water,
And made answer very gravely:
'Yes, if Minnehaha wishes;
Let your heart speak, Minnehaha!'
   And the lovely Laughing Water
Seemed more lovely, as she stood there,
Neither willing nor reluctant,
As she went to Hiawatha,
Softly took the seat beside him,
While she said, and blushed to say it,
'I will follow you, my husband!'
   This was Hiawatha's wooing!
Thus it was he won the daughter
Of the ancient Arrow-maker,
In the land of the Dacotahs!
   From the wigwam he departed,
Leading with him Laughing Water;
Hand in hand they went together,
Through the woodland and the meadow,

Left the old man standing lonely
At the doorway of his wigwam,
Heard the Falls of Minnehaha
Calling to them from the distance,
Crying to them from afar off,
'Fare thee well, O Minnehaha !'

And the ancient Arrow-maker
Turned again unto his labour,
Sat down by his sunny doorway,
Murmuring to himself, and saying:
'Thus it is our daughters leave us,
Those we love, and those who love us !
Just when they have learned to help us,
When we are old and lean upon them,
Comes a youth with flaunting feathers,
With his flute of reeds, a stranger
Wanders piping through the village,
Beckons to the fairest maiden,
As she follows where he leads her,
Leaving all things for the stranger !'

Pleasant was the journey homeward,
Through interminable forests,
Over meadow, over mountain,
Over river, hill, and hollow.
Short it seemed to Hiawatha,
Though they journeyed very slowly,
Though his pace he checked and slackened
To the steps of Laughing Water.

Over wide and rushing rivers
In his arms he bore the maiden;
Light he thought her as a feather,
As the plume upon his headgear;
Cleared the tangled pathway for her,
Bent aside the swaying branches,
Made at night a lodge of branches,
And a bed with boughs of hemlock,
And a fire before the doorway
With the dry cones of the pine tree.

All the travelling winds went with them,
O'er the meadow, through the forest;
All the stars of night looked at them,

Watched with sleepless eyes their slumber;
From his ambush in the oak tree
Peeped the squirrel, Adjidaumo,
Watched with eager eyes the lovers;
And the rabbit, the Wabasso,
Scampered from the path before them,
Peering, peeping from his burrow,
Sat erect upon his haunches,
Watched with curious eyes the lovers.

Pleasant was the journey homeward!
All the birds sang loud and sweetly
Songs of happiness and heart's-ease;
Sang the bluebird, the Owaissa,
'Happy are you, Hiawatha,
Having such a wife to love you!'
Sang the Opechee, the robin,
'Happy are you, Laughing Water,
Having such a noble husband!'

From the sky the sun benignant
Looked upon them through the branches,
Saying to them, 'O my children,
Love is sunshine, hate is shadow,
Life is checkered shade and sunshine,
Rule by love, O Hiawatha!'

From the sky the moon looked at them,
Filled the lodge with mystic splendours,
Whispered to them, 'O my children,
Day is restless, night is quiet,
Man imperious, woman feeble;
Half is mine, although I follow;
Rule by patience, Laughing Water!'

Thus it was they journeyed homeward;
Thus it was that Hiawatha
To the lodge of old Nokomis
Brought the moonlight, starlight, firelight,
Brought the sunshine of his people,
Minnehaha, Laughing Water,
Handsomest of all the women
In the land of the Dacotahs,
In the land of handsome women.

XI
HIAWATHA'S WEDDING-FEAST

You shall hear how Pau-Puk-Keewis,
How the handsome Yenadizze
Danced at Hiawatha's wedding;
How the gentle Chibiabos,
He the sweetest of musicians,
Sang his songs of love and longing;
How Iagoo, the great boaster,
He the marvellous story-teller,
Told his tales of strange adventure,
That the feast might be more joyous,
That the time might pass more gaily,
And the guests be more contented.

Sumptuous was the feast Nokomis
Made at Hiawatha's wedding;
All the bowls were made of basswood,
White and polished very smoothly,
All the spoons of horn and bison,
Black and polished very smoothly.

She had sent through all the village
Messengers with wands of willow,
As a sign of invitation,
As a token of the feasting;
And the wedding guests assembled,
Clad in all their richest raiment,
Robes of fur and belts of wampum,
Splendid with their paint and plumage,
Beautiful with beads and tassels.

First they ate the sturgeon, Nahma,
And the pike, the Maskenozha,
Caught and cooked by old Nokomis;
Then on pemican they feasted,
Pemican and buffalo marrow,
Haunch of deer and hump of bison,
Yellow cakes of the Mondamin,
And the wild rice of the river.

But the gracious Hiawatha,
And the lovely Laughing Water,
And the careful old Nokomis,

Tasted not the food before them,
Only waited on the others,
Only served their guests in silence.
    And when all the guests had finished,
Old Nokomis, brisk and busy,
From an ample pouch of otter,
Filled the redstone pipes for smoking
With tobacco from the South-land,
Mixed with bark of the red willow,
And with herbs and leaves of fragrance.
    Then she said, 'O Pau-Puk-Keewis,
Dance for us your merry dances,
Dance the Beggar's Dance to please us,
That the feast may be more joyous,
That the time may pass more gaily,
And our guests be more contented!'
    Then the handsome Pau-Puk-Keewis,
He the idle Yenadizze,
He the merry mischief-maker,
Whom the people called the Storm-Fool,
Rose among the guests assembled.
Skilled was he in sports and pastimes,
In the merry dance of snowshoes,
In the play of quoits and ball-play;
Skilled was he in games of hazard,
In all games of skill and hazard,
Pugasaing, the Bowl and Counters,
Kuntassoo, the Game of Plumstones.
    Though the warriors called him Faint-Heart,
Called him coward, Shaugodaya,
Idler, gambler, Yenadizze,
Little heeded he their jesting,
Little cared he for their insults,
For the women and the maidens
Loved the handsome Pau-Puk-Keewis.
    He was dressed in shirt of doeskin,
White and soft, and fringed with ermine,
All inwrought with beads of wampum;
He was dressed in deerskin leggings,
Fringed with hedgehog quills and ermine,
And in moccasins of buckskin,

Thick with quills and beads embroidered.
On his head were plumes of swan's down,
On his heels were tails of foxes,
In one hand a fan of feathers,
And a pipe was in the other.
　　Barred with streaks of red and yellow,
Streaks of blue and bright vermilion,
Shone the face of Pau-Puk-Keewis.
From his forehead fell his tresses,
Smooth, and parted like a woman's,
Shining bright with oil, and plaited,
Hung with braids of scented grasses,
As among the guests assembled.
To the sound of flutes and singing,
To the sound of drums and voices,
Rose the handsome Pau-Puk-Keewis,
And began his mystic dances.
　　First he danced a solemn measure,
Very slow in step and gesture,
In and out among the pine trees,
Through the shadows and the sunshine,
Treading softly like a panther,
Then more swiftly and still swifter,
Whirling, spinning round in circles,
Leaping o'er the guests assembled,
Eddying round and round the wigwam,
Till the leaves went whirling with him,
Till the dust and wind together
Swept in eddies round about him.
　　Then along the sandy margin
Of the lake, the Big-Sea-Water,
On he sped with frenzied gestures,
Stamped upon the sand, and tossed it
Wildly in the air around him;
Till the wind became a whirlwind,
Till the sand was blown and sifted
Like great snowdrifts o'er the landscape,
Heaping all the shores with Sand Dunes,
Sand Hills of the Nagow Wudjoo!
　　Thus the merry Pau-Puk-Keewis
Danced his Beggar's Dance to please them,

And, returning, sat down laughing
There among the guests assembled,
Sat and fanned himself serenely
With his fan of turkey-feathers.

   Then they said to Chibiabos,
To the friend of Hiawatha,
To the sweetest of all singers,
To the best of all musicians,
'Sing to us, O Chibiabos !
Songs of love and songs of longing,
That the feast may be more joyous,
That the time may pass more gaily,
And our guests be more contented !'

   And the gentle Chibiabos
Sang in accents sweet and tender,
Sang in tones of deep emotion,
Songs of love and songs of longing ;
Looking still at Hiawatha,
Looking at fair Laughing Water,
Sang he softly, sang in this wise.

   'Onaway ! Awake, beloved !
Thou the wild flower of the forest !
Thou the wild bird of the prairie !
Thou with eyes so soft and fawnlike !

   'If thou only lookest on me,
I am happy, I am happy,
As the lilies of the prairie,
When they feel the dew upon them !

   'Sweet thy breath is as the fragrance
Of the wild flowers in the morning,
As their fragrance is at evening,
In the Moon when leaves are falling.

   'Does not all the blood within me,
Leap to meet thee, leap to meet thee,
As the springs to meet the sunshine,
In the Moon when nights are brightest ?

   'Onaway ! my heart sings to thee,
Sings with joy when thou art near me,
As the sighing, singing branches
In the pleasant Moon of Strawberries !

   'When thou art not pleased, beloved,

Then my heart is sad and darkened,
As the shining river darkens
When the clouds drop shadows on it !
    'When thou smilest, my beloved,
Then my troubled heart is brightened,
As in sunshine gleam the ripples
That the cold wind makes in rivers.
    'Smiles the earth, and smile the waters,
Smile the cloudless skies above us,
But I lose the way of smiling
When thou art no longer near me !
    'I myself, myself ! behold me !
Blood of my beating heart, behold me !
O awake, awake, beloved !
Onaway ! awake, beloved !'
    Thus the gentle Chibiabos
Sang his song of love and longing ;
And Iagoo, the great boaster,
He the marvellous story-teller,
He the friend of old Nokomis,
Jealous of the sweet musician,
Jealous of the applause they gave him,
Saw in all the eyes around him,
Saw in all their looks and gestures,
That the wedding guests assembled
Longed to hear his pleasant stories,
His immeasurable falsehoods.
    Very boastful was Iagoo ;
Never heard he an adventure
But himself had met a greater ;
Never any deed of daring
But himself had done a bolder ;
Never any marvellous story
But himself could tell a stranger.
    Would you listen to his boasting,
Would you only give him credence,
No one ever shot an arrow
Half so far and high as he had ;
Ever caught so many fishes,
Ever killed so many reindeer,
Ever trapped so many beaver !

None could run so fast as he could,
None could dive so deep as he could,
None could swim as far as he could;
None had made so many journeys,
None had seen so many wonders,
As this wonderful Iagoo,
As this marvellous story-teller!

Thus his name became a by-word
And a jest among the people;
And whene'er a boastful hunter
Praised his own address too highly,
Or a warrior, home returning,
Talked too much of his achievements,
All his hearers cried, 'Iagoo!
Here's Iagoo come among us!'

He it was who carved the cradle
Of the little Hiawatha,
Carved its framework out of linden,
Bound it strong with reindeer sinews;
He it was who taught him later
How to make his bows and arrows,
How to make the bows of ash tree,
And the arrows of the oak tree,
So among the guests assembled
At my Hiawatha's wedding
Sat Iagoo, old and ugly,
Sat the marvellous story-teller.

And they said, 'O good Iagoo,
Tell us now a tale of wonder,
Tell us of some strange adventure,
That the feast may be more joyous,
That the time may pass more gaily,
And our guests be more contented!'

And Iagoo answered straightway,
'You shall hear a tale of wonder.
You shall hear the strange adventures
Of Osseo, the magician,
From the Evening Star descended.'

XII

THE SUN OF THE EVENING STAR

Can it be the sun descending
O'er the level plain of water?
Or the Red Swan floating, flying,
Wounded by the magic arrow,
Staining all the waves with crimson,
With the crimson of its life-blood,
Filling all the air with splendour,
With the splendour of its plumage?
Yes; it is the sun descending,
Sinking down into the water;
All the sky is stained with purple,
All the water flushed with crimson!
No; it is the Red Swan floating,
Diving down beneath the water;
To the sky its wings are lifted,
With its blood the waves are reddened!
Over it the Star of Evening
Melts and trembles through the purple,
Hangs suspended in the twilight.
No; it is a bead of wampum
On the robes of the Great Spirit,
As he passes through the twilight,
Walks in silence through the heavens.
This with joy beheld Iagoo
And he said in haste: 'Behold it!
See the sacred Star of Evening!
You shall hear a tale of wonder,
Hear the story of Osseo,
Son of the Evening Star, Osseo!
'Once, in days no more remembered,
Ages nearer the beginning,
When the heavens were closer to us,
And the Gods were more familiar,
In the North-land lived a hunter,
With ten young and comely daughters,
Tall and lithe as wands of willow;
Only Oweenee, the youngest,
She the wilful and the wayward,

She the silent, dreamy maiden,
Was the fairest of the sisters.
  'All these women married warriors,
Married brave and haughty husbands;
Only Oweenee, the youngest,
Laughed and flouted all her lovers,
All her young and handsome suitors,
And then married old Osseo,
Old Osseo, poor and ugly,
Broken with age and weak from coughing,
Always coughing like a squirrel.
  'Ah, but beautiful within him
Was the spirit of Osseo,
From the Evening Star descended,
Star of Evening, Star of Woman,
Star of tenderness and passion!
All its fire was in his bosom,
All its beauty in his spirit,
All its mystery in his being,
All its splendour in his language!
  'And her lovers, the rejected,
Handsome men with belts of wampum,
Handsome men with paint and feathers,
Pointed at her in derision,
Followed her with jest and laughter.
But she said: "I care not for you,
Care not for your paint and feathers,
Care not for your jests and laughter;
I am happy with Osseo!"
  'Once to some great feast invited,
Through the damp and dusk of evening
Walked together the ten sisters,
Walked together with their husbands;
Slowly followed old Osseo,
With fair Oweenee beside him;
All the others chatted gaily,
These two only walked in silence.
  'At the western sky Osseo
Gazed intent, as if imploring,
Often stopped and gazed imploring
At the trembling Star of Evening,

At the tender Star of Woman;
And they heard him murmur softly,
"*Ah, showain nemeshin, Nosa!*
Pity, pity me, my father!"
    '"Listen!" said the eldest sister,
"He is praying to his father!
What a pity that the old man
Does not stumble in the pathway,
Does not break his neck by falling!"
And they laughed till all the forest
Rang with their unseemly laughter.

    'On their pathway through the woodlands
Lay an oak, by storms uprooted,
Lay the great trunk of an oak tree,
Buried half in leaves and mosses,
Mouldering, crumbling, huge and hollow
And Osseo, when he saw it,
Gave a shout, a cry of anguish,
Leaped into its yawning cavern,
At one end went in an old man,
Wasted, wrinkled, old, and ugly;
From the other came a young man,
Tall and straight and strong and handsome.

    'Thus Osseo was transfigured,
Thus restored to youth and beauty;
But alas for good Osseo,
And for Oweenee, the faithful!
Strangely, too, was she transfigured.
Changed into a weak old woman,
With a staff she tottered onward,
Wasted, wrinkled, old, and ugly!
And the sisters and their husbands
Laughed until the echoing forest
Rang with their unseemly laughter.

    'But Osseo turned not from her,
Walked with slower step beside her,
Took her hand, as brown and withered
As an oak-leaf is in Winter,
Called her sweetheart, Nenomoosha,
Soothed her with soft words of kindness,
Till they reached the lodge of feasting,

Till they sat down in the wigwam,
Sacred to the Star of Evening,
To the tender Star of Woman.
  'Wrapt in visions, lost in dreaming,
At the banquet sat Osseo;
All were merry, all were happy,
All were joyous but Osseo,
Neither food nor drink he tasted,
Neither did he speak nor listen,
But as one bewildered sat he,
Looking dreamily and sadly,
First at Oweenee, then upward
At the gleaming sky above them.
  'Then a voice was heard, a whisper,
Coming from the starry distance.
Coming from the empty vastness,
Low, and musical, and tender;
And the voice said: "O Osseo!
O my son, my best beloved!
Broken are the spells that bound you,
All the charms of the magicians,
All the magic powers of evil;
Come to me; ascend, Osseo!
  '"Taste the food that stands before you;
It is blessed and enchanted,
It has magic virtues in it,
It will change you to a spirit.
All your bowls and all your kettles
Shall be wood and clay no longer;
But the bowls be changed to wampum,
And the kettles shall be silver;
They shall shine like shells of scarlet,
Like the fire shall gleam and glimmer.
  '"And the women shall no longer
Bear the dreary doom of labour,
But be changed to birds, and glisten
With the beauty of the starlight,
Painted with the dusky splendours
Of the skies and clouds of evening!"
  'What Osseo heard as whispers,
What as words he comprehended,

Was but music to the others,
Music as of birds afar off,
Of the whippoorwill afar off,
Of the lonely Wawonaissa
Singing in the darksome forest.
  'Then the lodge began to tremble,
Straight began to shake and tremble,
And they felt it rising, rising,
Slowly through the air ascending,
From the darkness of the tree-tops
Forth into the dewy starlight,
Till it passed the topmost branches;
And behold! the wooden dishes
All were changed to shells of scarlet!
And behold! the earthen kettles
All were changed to bowls of silver!
And the roof-poles of the wigwam
Were as glittering rods of silver,
And the roof of bark upon them
As the shining shards of beetles.
  'Then Osseo gazed around him,
And he saw the nine fair sisters,
All the sisters and their husbands,
Changed to birds of various plumage.
Some were jays and some were magpies,
Others thrushes, others blackbirds;
And they hopped, and sang, and twittered,
Pecked and fluttered all their feathers,
Strutted in their shining plumage,
And their tails like fans unfolded.
  'Only Oweenee, the youngest,
Was not changed, but sat in silence,
Wasted, wrinkled, old, and ugly,
Looking sadly at the others;
Till Osseo, gazing upward,
Gave another cry of anguish,
Such a cry as he had uttered
By the oak tree in the forest.
  'Then returned her youth and beauty
And her soiled and tattered garments
Were transformed to robes of ermine,

And her staff became a feather,
Yes, a shining silver feather!
  'And again the wigwam trembled,
Swayed and rushed through airy currents,
Through transparent cloud and vapour,
And amid celestial splendours
On the Evening Star alighted,
As a snowflake falls on snowflake,
As a leaf drops on a river,
As the thistledown on water.
  'Forth with cheerful words of welcome
Came the father of Osseo,
He with radiant locks of silver,
He with eyes serene and tender,
And he said: "My son, Osseo,
Hang the cage of birds you bring there,
Hang the cage with rods of silver,
And the birds with glistening feathers,
At the doorway of my wigwam."
  'At the door he hung the birdcage,
And they entered in and gladly
Listened to Osseo's father,
Ruler of the Star of Evening,
As he said: "O my Osseo!
I have had compassion on you,
Given you back your youth and beauty,
Into birds of various plumage
Changed your sisters and their husbands;
Changed them thus because they mocked you
In the figure of the old man,
In that aspect sad and wrinkled,
Could not see your heart of passion,
Could not see your youth immortal;
Only Oweenee, the faithful,
Saw your naked heart and loved you.
  '" In the lodge that glimmers yonder,
In the little star that twinkles
Through the vapours, on the left hand,
Lives the envious Evil Spirit,
The Wabeno, the magician,
Who transformed you to an old man.

Take heed lest his beams fall on you,
For the rays he darts around him
Are the power of his enchantment,
Are the arrows that he uses."

'Many years, in peace and quiet,
On the peaceful Star of Evening
Dwelt Osseo with his father;
Many years, in song and flutter,
At the doorway of the wigwam,
Hung the cage with rods of silver,
And fair Oweenee, the faithful,
Bore a son unto Osseo,
With the beauty of his mother,
With the courage of his father.

'And the boy grew up and prospered,
And Osseo, to delight him,
Made him little bows and arrows,
Opened the great cage of silver,
And let loose his aunts and uncles,
All those birds with glossy feathers,
For his little son to shoot at.

'Round and round they wheeled and darted,
Filled the Evening Star with music,
With their songs of joy and freedom;
Filled the Evening Star with splendour,
With the fluttering of their plumage;
Till the boy, the little hunter,
Bent his bow and shot an arrow,
Shot a swift and fatal arrow,
And a bird, with shining feathers,
At his feet fell wounded sorely.

'But, O wondrous transformation!
'Twas no bird he saw before him,
'Twas a beautiful young woman,
With the arrow in her bosom!

'When her blood fell on the planet,
On the sacred Star of Evening,
Broken was the spell of magic,
Powerless was the strange enchantment,
And the youth, the fearless bowman,
Suddenly felt himself descending,

Held by unseen hands, but sinking
Downward through the empty spaces,
Downward through the clouds and vapours,
Till he rested on an island,
On an island, green and grassy,
Yonder in the Big-Sea-Water.

'After him he saw descending
All the birds with shining feathers,
Fluttering, falling, wafted downward,
Like the painted leaves of Autumn;
And the lodge with poles of silver,
With its roof like wings of beetles,
Like the shining shards of beetles,
By the winds of heaven uplifted,
Slowly sank upon the island,
Bringing back the good Osseo,
Bringing Oweenee, the faithful.

'Then the birds again transfigured,
Reassumed the shape of mortals,
Took their shape but not their stature;
They remained as Little People,
Like the pygmies, the Puk-Wudjies,
And on pleasant nights of Summer
When the Evening Star was shining,
Hand in hand they danced together
On the island's craggy headlands,
On the sand-beach low and level.

'Still their glittering lodge is seen there,
On the tranquil Summer evenings,
And upon the shore the fisher,
Sometimes hears their happy voices,
Sees them dancing in the starlight!'

When the story was completed,
When the wondrous tale was ended,
Looking round upon his listeners,
Solemnly Iagoo added:
'There are great men, I have known such,
Whom their people understand not,
Whom they even make a jest of,
Scoff and jeer at in derision.
From the story of Osseo

Let them learn the fate of jesters!'
   All the wedding guests delighted
Listened to the marvellous story,
Listened laughing and applauding,
And they whispered to each other:
'Does he mean himself, I wonder?
And are we the aunts and uncles?'
   Then again sang Chibiabos,
Sang a song of love and longing,
In those accents sweet and tender,
In those tones of pensive sadness,
Sang a maiden's lamentation
For her lover her Algonquin.
   'When I think of my beloved,
Ah me! think of my beloved,
When my heart is thinking of him,
O my sweetheart, my Algonquin!
   'Ah me! when I parted from him,
Round my neck he hung the wampum,
As a pledge, the snow-white wampum,
O my sweetheart, my Algonquin!
   'I will go with you, he whispered,
Ah me! to your native country;
Let me go with you, he whispered,
O my sweetheart, my Algonquin!
   'Far away, away, I answered,
Very far away, I answered,
Ah me! is my native country,
O my sweetheart, my Algonquin!
   'When I looked back to behold him,
Where we parted, to behold him,
After me he still was gazing,
O my sweetheart, my Algonquin!
   'By the tree he still was standing,
By the fallen tree was standing,
That had dropped into the water,
O my sweetheart, my Algonquin!
   'When I think of my beloved,
Ah me! think of my beloved,
When my heart is thinking of him
O my sweetheart, my Algonquin!'

Such was Hiawatha's Wedding,
Such the dance of Pau-Puk-Keewis,
Such the story of Iagoo,
Such the songs of Chibiabos;
Thus the wedding banquet ended,
And the wedding guests departed,
Leaving Hiawatha happy
With the night and Minnehaha.

XIII

BLESSING THE CORNFIELDS

Sing, O Song of Hiawatha,
Of the happy days that followed,
In the land of the Ojibways,
In the pleasant land and peaceful
Sing the mysteries of Mondamin,
Sing the Blessing of the Cornfields!
Buried was the bloody hatchet,
Buried was the dreadful war-club,
Buried were all warlike weapons,
And the war-cry was forgotten.
There was peace among the nations;
Unmolested roved the hunters,
Built the birch canoe for sailing,
Caught the fish in lake and river,
Shot the deer and trapped the beaver;
Unmolested worked the women,
Made their sugar from the maple,
Gathered wild rice in the meadows,
Dressed the skins of deer and beaver.
All around the happy village,
Stood the maize fields, green and shining,
Waved the green plumes of Mondamin,
Waved his soft and sunny tresses,
Filling all the land with plenty.
'Twas the women who in Springtime
Planted the broad fields and fruitful,
Buried in the earth Mondamin;
'Twas the women who in Autumn
Stripped the yellow husks of harvest,
Stripped the garments from Mondamin,

Even as Hiawatha taught them.
　Once, when all the maize was planted,
Hiawatha, wise and thoughtful,
Spake and said to Minnehaha,
To his wife, the Laughing Water:
'You shall bless to-night the cornfields,
Draw a magic circle round them,
To protect them from destruction,
Blast of mildew, blight of insect,
Wagemin, the thief of cornfields,
Paimosaid, who steals the maize-ear!
　'In the night, when all is silence,
In the night, when all is darkness,
When the Spirit of Sleep, Nepahwin,
Shuts the doors of all the wigwams,
So that not an ear can hear you,
So that not an eye can see you,
Rise up from your bed in silence,
Lay aside your garments wholly,
Walk around the fields you planted,
Round the borders of the cornfields,
Covered by your tresses only,
Robed with darkness as a garment.
　'Thus the fields shall be more fruitful,
And the passing of your footsteps
Draw a magic circle round them,
So that neither blight nor mildew,
Neither burrowing word nor insect,
Shall pass o'er the magic circle;
Not the dragon fly, Kwo-ne-she,
Nor the Spider, Subbekashe,
Nor the grasshopper, Paw-Puk-keena,
Nor the mighty caterpillar,
Way-muk-kwana, with the bearskin,
King of all the caterpillars!'
　On the tree-tops near the cornfields
Sat the hungry crows and ravens,
Kahgahgee, the King of Ravens,
With his band of black marauders.
And they laughed at Hiawatha,
Till the tree-tops shook with laughter,

With their melancholy laughter,
At the words of Hiawatha.
'Hear him !' said they ; 'hear the Wise Man,
Hear the plots of Hiawatha !'

When the noiseless night descended
Broad and dark o'er field and forest,
When the mournful Wawonaissa,
Sorrowing sang among the hemlocks,
And the Spirit of Sleep, Nepahwin,
Shut the doors of all the wigwams,
From her bed rose Laughing Water,
Laid aside her garments wholly,
And with darkness clothed and guarded,
Unashamed and unaffrighted,
Walked securely round the cornfields,
Drew the sacred, magic circle,
Of her footprints round the cornfields.

No one but the Midnight only
Saw her beauty in the darkness,
No one but the Wawonaissa
Heard the panting of her bosom ;
Guskewau, the darkness, wrapped her
Closely in his sacred mantle,
So that none might see her beauty,
So that none might boast, 'I saw her !'

On the morrow, as the day dawned,
Kahgahgee, the King of Ravens,
Gathered all his black marauders,
Crows and blackbirds, jays, and ravens,
Clamorous on the dusky tree-tops,
And descended, fast and fearless,
On the fields of Hiawatha,
On the grave of the Mondamin.

'We will drag Mondamin,' said they,
'From the grave where he is buried,
Spite of all the magic circles
Laughing Water draws around it,
Spite of all the sacred footprints
Minnehaha stamps upon it !'

But the wary Hiawatha,
Ever thoughtful, careful, watchful,

Had o'erheard the scornful laughter
When they mocked him from the tree-tops.
'Kaw!' he said, 'my friends the ravens!
Kahgahgee, my King of Ravens!
I will teach you all a lesson
That shall not be soon forgotten!'

He had risen before the day-break,
He had spread o'er all the cornfields
Snares to catch the black marauders,
And was lying now in ambush
In the neighbouring grove of pine trees,
Waiting for the crows and blackbirds,
Waiting for the jays and ravens.

Soon they came with caw and clamour,
Rush of wings and cry of voices,
To their work of devastation,
Settling down upon the cornfields,
Delving deep with beak and talon,
For the body of Mondamin.
And with all their craft and cunning,
All their skill in wiles of warfare,
They perceived no danger near them.
Till their claws became entangled,
Till they found themselves imprisoned
In the snares of Hiawatha.

From his place of ambush came he,
Striding terrible among them,
And so awful was his aspect
That the bravest quailed with terror.
Without mercy he destroyed them
Right and left, by tens and twenties,
And their wretched, lifeless bodies
Hung aloft on poles for scarecrows
Round the consecrated cornfields,
As a signal of his vengeance,
As a warning to marauders.

Only Kahgahgee, the leader,
Kahgahgee, the King of Ravens,
He alone was spared among them
As a hostage for his people.
With his prisoner-string he bound him,

Led him captive to his wigwam,
Tied him fast with cords of elm bark
To the ridgepole of his wigwam.

'Kahgahgee, my raven !' said he,
'You the leader of the robbers,
You the plotter of this mischief,
The contriver of this outrage,
I will keep you, I will hold you,
As a hostage for your people,
As a pledge of good behaviour !'

And he left him, grim and sulky,
Sitting in the morning sunshine
On the summit of the wigwam,
Croaking fiercely his displeasure,
Flapping his great sable pinions,
Vainly struggling for his freedom,
Vainly calling on his people !

Summer passed, and Shawondasee
Breathed his sighs o'er all the landscape,
From the Southland sent his ardours,
Wafted kisses warm and tender ;
And the maize field grew and ripened,
Till it stood in all the splendour,
Of its garments green and yellow,
Of its tassels and its plumage,
And the maize ears full and shining
Gleamed from bursting sheaths of verdure.

Then Nokomis, the old woman,
Spake, and said to Minnehaha :
''Tis the Moon when leaves are falling ;
All the wild rice has been gathered,
And the maize is ripe and ready ;
Let us gather in the harvest,
Let us wrestle with Mondamin,
Strip him of his plumes and tassels,
Of his garments green and yellow !'

And the merry Laughing Water
Went rejoicing from the wigwam,
With Nokomis old and wrinkled,
And they called the women round them,
Called the young men and the maidens,

To the harvest of the cornfields,
To the husking of the maize ear.
  On the border of the forest,
Underneath the fragrant pine trees,
Sat the old man and the warriors
Smoking in the pleasant shadow.
In uninterrupted silence
Looked they at the gamesome labour
Of the young men and the women;
Listened to their noisy talking,
To their laughter and their singing,
Heard them chattering like the magpies,
Heard them laughing like the blue-jays,
Heard them singing like the robins.
  And whene'er some lucky maiden
Found a red ear in the husking,
Found a maize ear red as blood is,
'Nushka!' cried they all together,
'Nushka! you shall have a sweetheart,
You shall have a handsome husband!'
'Ugh!' the old men all responded
From their seats beneath the pine trees.
  And whene'er a youth or maiden
Found a crooked ear in husking,
Found a maize ear in the husking
Blighted, mildewed, or misshapen,
Then they laughed and sang together,
Crept and limped about the cornfields,
Mimicked in their gait and gestures
Some old man bent almost double,
Singing singly or together:
'Wagemin, the thief of cornfields!
Paimosaid, the skulking robber!'
  Till the cornfields rang with laughter,
Till from Hiawatha's wigwam
Kahgahgee, the King of Ravens,
Screamed and quivered in his anger,
And from all the neighbouring tree-tops
Cawed and croaked the black marauders.
'Ugh!' the old men all responded,
From their seats beneath the pine trees!

XIV
PICTURE-WRITING

In those days said Hiawatha,
'Lo ! how all things fade and perish !
From the memory of the old men
Fade away the great traditions,
The achievements of the warriors,
The adventures of the hunters,
All the wisdom of the Medas,
All the craft of the Wabenos,
All the marvellous dreams and visions
Of the Jossakeeds, the Prophets !

'Great men die and are forgotten,
Wise men speak ; their words of wisdom
Perish in the ears that hear them,
Do not reach the generations
That, as yet unborn, are waiting
In the great, mysterious darkness
Of the speechless days that shall be !

'On the grave-posts of our fathers
Are no signs, no figures painted ;
Who are in those graves we know not,
Only know they are our fathers.
Of what kith they are and kindred,
From what old, ancestral Totem,
Be it Eagle, Bear, or Beaver,
They descended, this we know not,
Only know they are our fathers.

'Face to face we speak together,
But we cannot speak when absent,
Cannot send our voices from us
To the friends that dwell afar off ;
Cannot send a secret message,
But the bearer learns our secret,
May pervert it, may betray it,
May reveal it unto others.'

Thus said Hiawatha, walking
In the solitary forest,
Pondering, musing in the forest,
On the welfare of his people.

From his pouch he took his colours,
Took his paints of different colours,
On the smooth bark of a birch tree
Painted many shapes and figures,
Wonderful and mystic figures,
And each figure had a meaning,
Each some word or thought suggested.

Gitche Manito the Mighty,
He, the Master of Life, was painted
As an egg, with points projecting
To the four winds of the heavens.
Everywhere is the Great Spirit,
Was the meaning of this symbol.

Mitche Manito the Mighty,
He the dreadful Spirit of Evil,
As a serpent was depicted,
As Kenabeek, the great serpent.
Very crafty, very cunning,
Is the creeping Spirit of Evil,
Was the meaning of this symbol.

Life and Death he drew as circles,
Life was white, but Death was darkness;
Sun and moon and stars he painted,
Man and beast, and fish and reptile,
Forests, mountains, lakes, and rivers.

For the earth he drew a straight line,
For the sky a bow above it;
White the space between for day-time,
Filled with little stars for night-time;
On the left a point for sunrise,
On the right a point for sunset,
On the top a point for noontide,
And for rain and cloudy weather
Waving lines descending from it.

Footprints pointing toward a wigwam
Were a sign of invitation,
Were a sign of guests assembling;
Bloody hands with palms uplifted
Were a symbol of destruction,
Were a hostile sign and symbol.

All these things did Hiawatha

Show unto his wondering people,
And interpreted their meaning,
And he said: 'Behold, your grave-posts
Have no mark, no sign, nor symbol.
Go and paint them all with figures;
Each one with its household symbol,
With its own ancestral Totem;
So that those who follow after
May distinguish them and know them.'
    And they painted on the grave-posts
Of the graves yet unforgotten,
Each his own ancestral Totem,
Each the symbol of his household;
Figures of the Bear and Reindeer,
Of the Turtle, Crane, and Beaver,
Each inverted as a token
That the owner was departed,
That the chief who bore the symbol
Lay beneath in dust and ashes.
    And the Jossakeeds, the Prophets,
The Wabenos, the Magicians,
And the Medicine-men, the Medas,
Painted upon bark and deerskin
Figures for the songs they chaunted,
For each song a separate symbol,
Figures mystical and awful,
Figures strange and brightly coloured;
And each figure had its meaning,
Each some magic song suggested.
    The Great Spirit, the Creator,
Flashing light through all the heaven;
The Great Serpent, the Kenabeek,
With his bloody crest erected,
Creeping, looking into heaven;
In the sky the sun, that listens,
And the moon eclipsed and dying;
Owl and eagle, crane and henhawk,
And the cormorant, bird of magic;
Headless men, that walk the heavens,
Bodies lying pierced with arrows
Bloody hands of death uplifted,

Flags on graves, and great war captains
Grasping both the earth and heaven !
  Such as these the shapes they painted
On the birchbark and the deerskin ;
Songs of war and songs of hunting,
Songs of medicine and of magic,
All were written in these figures,
For each figure had its meaning,
Each its separate song recorded.
  Nor forgotten was the Love-Song,
The most subtle of all medicines,
The most potent spell of magic,
Dangerous more than war or hunting !
Thus the Love-Song was recorded,
Symbol and interpretation.
  First a human figure standing,
Painted in the brightest scarlet ;
'Tis the lover, the musician,
And the meaning is, 'My painting
Makes me powerful over others.'
  Then the figure seated, singing,
Playing on a drum of magic,
And the interpretation, 'Listen !
'Tis my voice you hear, my singing !'
  Then the same red figure seated
In the shelter of a wigwam,
And the meaning of the symbol,
  'I will come and sit beside you
In the mystery of my passion !'
  Then two figures, man and woman,
Standing hand in hand together
With their hands so clasped together
That they seem in one united,
And the words thus represented
Are, 'I see your heart within you,
And your cheeks are red with blushes !'
  Next the maiden on an island,
In the centre of an island ;
And the song this shape suggested
Was, 'Though you were at a distance,
Were upon some far-off island,

Such the spell I cast upon you,
Such the magic power of passion,
I could straightway draw you to me !'
   Then the figure of the maiden
Sleeping, and the lover near her,
Whispering to her in her slumbers,
Saying, 'Though you were far from me
In the land of Sleep and Silence,
Still the voice of love would reach you !'
   And the last of all the figures
Was a heart within a circle,
Drawn within a magic circle,
And the image had this meaning :
'Naked lies your heart before me,
To your naked heart I whisper !'
   Thus it was that Hiawatha,
In his wisdom, taught the people
All the mysteries of painting,
All the art of Picture-Writing,
On the smooth bark of the birch tree,
On the white skin of the reindeer,
On the grave-posts of the village.

XV

HIAWATHA'S LAMENTATION

   In those days the Evil Spirits,
All the Manitos of mischief,
Fearing Hiawatha's wisdom,
And his love for Chibiabos,
Jealous of their faithful friendship,
And their noble words and actions,
Made at length a league against them,
To molest them and destroy them.
   Hiawatha, wise and wary,
Often said to Chibiabos,
'O my brother ! do not leave me,
Lest the Evil Spirits harm you !'
Chibiabos, young and heedless,
Laughing shook his coal-black tresses,
Answered ever sweet and childlike.

'Do not fear for me, O brother !
Harm and evil come not near me !'
　　Once when Peboan, the Winter,
Roofed with ice the Big-Sea-Water,
When the snowflakes whirling downward,
Hissed among the withered oak leaves,
Changed the pine trees into wigwams,
Covered all the earth with silence, –
Armed with arrows, shod with snowshoes,
Heeding not his brother's warning,
Fearing not the Evil Spirits,
Forth to hunt the deer with antlers
All alone went Chibiabos.
　　Right across the Big-Sea-Water
Sprang with speed the deer before him,
With the wind and snow he followed,
O'er the treacherous ice he followed,
Wild with all the fierce commotion
And the rapture of the hunting.
　　But beneath, the Evil Spirits
Lay in ambush, waiting for him,
Broke the treacherous ice beneath him,
Dragged him downward to the bottom,
Buried in the sand his body,
Unktahee, the god of water,
He the god of the Dacotahs,
Drowned him in the deep abysses
Of the lake of Gitche Gumee.
　　From the headlands Hiawatha
Sent forth such a wail of anguish,
Such a fearful lamentation,
That the bison paused to listen,
And the wolves howled from the prairies,
And the thunder in the distance
Woke and answered 'Baimwawa !'
　　Then his face with black he painted,
With his robe his head he covered,
In his wigwam sat lamenting,
Seven long weeks he sat lamenting,
Uttering still this moan of sorrow :
　　'He is dead, the sweet musician !

He the sweetest of all singers !
He has gone from us for ever,
He has moved a little nearer
To the Master of all music,
To the Master of all singing !
O my brother, Chibiabos !'
   And the melancholy fir trees
Waved their dark-green fans above him,
Waved their purple cones above him,
Sighing with him to console him,
Mingling with his lamentation
Their complaining, their lamenting.
   Came the Spring, and all the forest
Looked in vain for Chibiabos ;
Sighed the rivulet, Sebowisha,
Sighed the rushes in the meadow.
   From the tree-tops sang the bluebird,
Sang the bluebird, the Owaissa,
'Chibiabos ! Chibiabos !
He is dead, the sweet musician !'
   From the wigwam sang the robin,
Sang the Opechee, the robin,
'Chibiabos ! Chibiabos !
He is dead, the sweetest singer !'
   And at night through all the forest
Went the whippoorwill complaining,
Wailing went the Wawonaissa,
'Chibiabos ! Chibiabos !
He is dead, the sweet musician !
He the sweetest of all singers !'
   Then the Medicine-men, the Medas,
The magicians, the Wabenos,
And the Jossakeeds, the prophets,
Came to visit Hiawatha ;
Built a Sacred Lodge beside him,
To appease him, to console him,
Walked in silent, grave procession,
Bearing each a pouch of healing,
Skin of beaver, lynx, or otter,
Filled with magic roots and simples,
Filled with very potent medicines.

When he heard their steps approaching,
Hiawatha ceased lamenting,
Called no more on Chibiabos;
Naught he questioned, naught he answered
But his mournful head uncovered,
From his face the mourning colours
Washed he slowly and in silence,
Slowly and in silence followed
Onward to the Sacred Wigwam.

There a magic drink they gave him,
Made of Nahma-wusk, the spearmint,
And Wabeno-wusk, the yarrow,
Roots of power, and herbs of healing;
Beat their drums, and shook their rattles;
Chaunted singly and in chorus,
Mystic songs like these, they chaunted.
    'I myself, myself! behold me!
'Tis the great Gray Eagle talking;
Come, ye white crows, come and hear him!
The loud-speaking thunder helps me;
All the unseen spirits help me;
I can hear their voices calling,
All around the sky I hear them!
I can blow you strong, my brother,
I can heal you, Hiawatha!'
    'Hi-au-ha!' replied the chorus,
'Way-ha-way!' the mystic chorus,
    'Friends of mine are all the serpents!
Hear me shake my skin of hen-hawk!
Mahng, the white loon, I can kill him;
I can shoot your heart and kill it!
I can blow you strong, my brother,
I can heal you, Hiawatha!'
    'Hi-au-ha!' replied the chorus,
'Way-ha-way!' the mystic chorus.
    'I myself, myself! the prophet!
When I speak the wigwam trembles,
Shakes the Sacred Lodge with terror,
Hands unseen begin to shake it!
When I walk, the sky I tread on
Bends and makes a noise beneath me!

I can blow you strong, my brother!
Rise and speak, O Hiawatha!'
  'Hi-au-ha!' replied the chorus,
'Way-ha-way!' the mystic chorus.
Then they shook their medicine-pouches
O'er the head of Hiawatha,
Danced their medicine-dance around him;
And upstarting wild and haggard,
Like a man from dreams awakened,
He was healed of all his madness.
As the clouds are swept from heaven,
Straightway from his brain departed
All his moody melancholy;
As the ice is swept from rivers,
Straightway from his heart departed
All his sorrow and affliction.
  Then they summoned Chibiabos
From his grave beneath the waters,
From the sands of Gitche Gumee
Summoned Hiawatha's brother.
And so mighty was the magic
Of that cry and invocation,
That he heard it as he lay there
Underneath the Big-Sea-Water;
From the sand he rose and listened,
Heard the music and the singing,
Came, obedient to the summons,
To the doorway of the wigwam,
But to enter they forbade him.
Through a chink a coal they gave him,
Through the door a burning fire-brand;
Ruler in the Land of Spirits,
Ruler o'er the dead, they made him,
Telling him a fire to kindle
For all those that died thereafter,
Camp-fires for their night encampments
On their solitary journey
To the kingdom of Ponemah,
To the land of the Hereafter.
  From the village of his childhood,
From the homes of those who knew him,

Passing silent through the forest,
Like a smoke-wreath wafted sideways,
Slowly vanished Chibiabos !
Where he passed, the branches moved not,
Where he trod the grasses bent not,
And the fallen leaves of last year
Made no sound beneath his footsteps.

    Four whole days he journeyed onward
Down the pathway of the dead men ;
On the dead man's strawberry feasted,
Crossed the melancholy river,
On the swinging log he crossed it,
Came unto the Lake of Silver,
In the Stone Canoe was carried
To the Islands of the Blessed,
To the land of ghosts and shadows.

    On that journey, moving slowly,
Many weary spirits saw he,
Panting under heavy burdens,
Laden with war-clubs, bows and arrows,
Robes of fur, and pots and kettles,
And with food that friends had given
For that solitary journey.

    'Ay ! why do the living,' said they,
'Lay such heavy burdens on us !
Better were it to go naked,
Better were it to go fasting,
Than to bear such heavy burdens
On our long and weary journey !'

    Forth then issued Hiawatha,
Wandered eastward, wandered westward,
Teaching men the use of simples
And the antidotes for poisons,
And the cure of all diseases.
Thus was first made known to mortals
All the mystery of Medamin,
All the sacred art of healing.

XVI

PAU-PUK-KEEWIS

You shall hear how Pau-Puk-Keewis,
He, the handsome Yenadizze,
Whom the people called the Storm Fool,
Vexed the village with disturbance;
You shall hear of all his mischief,
And his flight from Hiawatha,
And his wondrous transmigrations,
At the end of his adventures.

On the shores of Gitche Gumee,
On the dunes of Nagow Wudjoo,
By the shining Big-Sea-Water,
Stood the lodge of Pau-Puk-Keewis.
It was he who in his frenzy
Whirled these drifting sands together,
On the dunes of Nagow Wudjoo,
When, among the guests assembled,
He so merrily and madly
Danced at Hiawatha's wedding,
Danced the Beggar's Dance to please them.

Now, in search of new adventures,
From his lodge went Pau-Puk-Keewis,
Came with speed into the village,
Found the young men all assembled
In the lodge of old Iagoo,
Listening to his monstrous stories,
To his wonderful adventures.

He was telling them the story
Of Ojeeg, the Summer-Maker,
How he made a hole in heaven,
How he climbed up into heaven,
And let out the summer weather,
The perpetual, pleasant Summer;
How the Otter first essayed it;
How the Beaver, Lynx, and Badger,
Tried in turn the great achievement,
From the summit of the mountain
Smote their fists against the heavens,
Smote against the sky their foreheads,

Cracked the sky, but could not break it,
How the Wolverine, uprising,
Made him ready for the encounter,
Bent his knees down, like a squirrel,
Drew his arms back, like a cricket.

'Once he leaped,' said Old Iagoo,
'Once he leaped, and lo ! above him
Bent the sky, as ice in rivers
When the waters rise beneath it ;
Twice he leaped, and lo ! above him
Cracked the sky, as ice in rivers
When the freshet is at highest !
Thrice he leaped, and lo ! above him
Broke the shattered sky asunder,
And he disappeared within it,
And Ojeeg, the Fisher Weasel,
With a bound went in behind him !'

'Hark you !' shouted Pau-Puk-Keewis
As he entered at the doorway :
'I am tired of all this talking,
Tired of old Iagoo's stories,
Tired of Hiawatha's wisdom.
Here is something to amuse you,
Better than this endless talking.'

Then from out his pouch of wolf-skin
Forth he drew, with solemn manner,
All the game of Bowl and Counters,
Pugasaing, with thirteen pieces.
White on one side were they painted,
And vermilion on the other ;
Two Kenabeeks or great serpents,
Two Ininewug or wedge-men,
One great war-club, Pugamaugun,
And one slender fish, the Keego,
Four round pieces, Ozawabeeks,
And three Sheshebwug or ducklings,
All were made of bone and painted,
All except the Ozawabeeks ;
These were brass, on one side burnished,
And were black upon the other.

In a wooden bowl he placed them,

Shook and jostled them together,
Threw them on the ground before him.
Thus exclaiming and explaining:
  'Red side up are all the pieces,
And one great Kenabeek standing
On the bright side of a brass piece,
On a burnished Ozawabeek;
Thirteen tens and eight are counted.'

  Then again he shook the pieces,
Shook and jostled them together,
Threw them on the ground before him,
Still exclaiming and explaining:
'White are both the great Kenabeeks,
White the Ininewug, the wedgemen,
Red are all the other pieces;
Five tens and an eight are counted.'

  Thus he taught the game of hazard,
Thus displayed it and explained it,
Running through its various chances,
Various changes, various meanings;
Twenty curious eyes stared at him,
Full of eagerness stared at him.

  'Many games,' said old Iagoo,
'Many games of skill and hazard
Have I seen in different nations,
Have I played in different countries.
He who plays with old Iagoo
Must have very nimble fingers;
Though you think yourself so skilful
I can beat you, Pau-Puk-Keewis,
I can even give you lessons
In your game of Bowl and Counters!'

  So they sat and played together,
All the old men and the young men
Played for dresses, weapons, wampum,
Played till midnight, played till morning,
Played until the Yenadizze,
Till the cunning Pau-Puk-Keewis
Of their treasures had despoiled them,
Of the best of all their dresses,
Shirts of deerskin, robes of ermine,

Belts of wampum, crests of feathers,
Warlike weapons, pipes and pouches.
Twenty eyes glared wildly at him,
Like the eyes of wolves glared at him.
    Said the lucky Pau-Puk-Keewis:
'In my wigwam I am lonely,
In my wanderings and adventures
I have need of a companion,
Fain would have a Meshinauwa,
An attendant and pipe-bearer.
I will venture all these winnings,
All these garments heaped about me,
All this wampum, all these feathers,
On a single throw will venture
All against the young man yonder!'
'Twas a youth of sixteen summers,
'Twas a nephew of Iagoo;
Face-in-a-Mist the people called him.

    As the fire burns in a pipe-head
Dusky red beneath the ashes,
So beneath his shaggy eyebrows
Glowed the eyes of old Iagoo.
'Ugh!' he answered very fiercely;
'Ugh!' they answered all and each one.
    Seized the wooden bowl the old man,
Closely in his bony fingers
Clutched the fatal bowl, Onagon,
Shook it fiercely and with fury,
Made the pieces ring together
As he threw them down before him.
    Red were both the great Kenabeeks,
Red the Ininewug, the wedge-men,
Red the Sheshebwug, the ducklings,
Black the four brass Ozawabeeks,
White alone the fish, the Keego;
Only five the pieces counted!
    Then the smiling Pau-Puk-Keewis
Shook the bowl and threw the pieces;
Lightly in the air he tossed them,
And they fell about him scattered;
Dark and bright the Ozawabeeks,

Red and white the other pieces,
And upright among the others
One Ininewug was standing,
Even as crafty Pau-Puk-Keewis
Stood alone among the players,
Saying, 'Five tens! mine the game is!'

   Twenty eyes glared at him fiercely,
Like the eyes of wolves glared at him,
As he turned and left the wigwam,
Followed by his Meshinauwa,
By the nephew of Iagoo,
By the tall and graceful stripling,
Bearing in his arms the winnings,
Shirts of deerskin, robes of ermine,
Belts of wampum, pipes and weapons.

   'Carry them,' said Pau-Puk-Keewis,
Pointing with his fan of feathers,
'To my wigwam far to eastward,
On the dunes of Nagow Wudjoo!'

   Hot and red with smoke and gambling
Were the eyes of Pau-Puk-Keewis
As he came forth to the freshness
Of the pleasant summer morning.
All the birds were singing gaily,
All the streamlets flowing swiftly,
And the heart of Pau-Puk-Keewis
Sang with pleasure as the birds sing,
Beat with triumph like the streamlets,
As he wandered through the village,
In the early gray of morning,
With his fan of turkey-feathers,
With his plumes and tufts of swan's-down,
Till he reached the farthest wigwam,
Reached the lodge of Hiawatha.

   Silent was it and deserted;
No one met him at the doorway,
No one came to bid him welcome;
But the birds were singing round it,
In and out and round the doorway,
Hopping, singing, fluttering, feeding,
And aloft upon the ridge-pole

Kahgahgee, the King of Ravens,
Sat with fiery eyes, and, screaming,
Flapped his wings at Pau-Puk-Keewis,
  'All are gone ! the lodge is empty !'
Thus it was spake Pau-Puk-Keewis,
In his heart resolving mischief; —
'Gone is wary Hiawatha,
Gone the silly Laughing Water,
Gone Nokomis, the old woman,
And the lodge is left unguarded !'
  By the neck he seized the raven,
Whirled it round him like a rattle,
Like a medicine-pouch he shook it,
Strangled Kahgahgee, the raven,
From the ridge-pole of the wigwam
Left its lifeless body hanging,
As an insult to its master,
As a taunt to Hiawatha.
  With a stealthy step he entered,
Round the lodge in wild disorder
Threw the household things about him,
Piled together in confusion
Bowls of wood and earthen kettles,
Robes of buffalo and beaver,
Skins of otter, lynx, and ermine,
As an insult to Nokomis,
As a taunt to Minnehaha.
  Then departed Pau-Puk-Keewis,
Whistling, singing through the forest,
Whistling gaily to the squirrels,
Who from hollow boughs above him
Dropped their acorn-shells upon him,
Singing gaily to the wood birds,
Who from out the leafy darkness
Answered with a song as merry.
  Then he climbed the rocky headlands,
Looking o'er the Gitche Gumee,
Perched himself upon the summit,
Waiting full of mirth and mischief
The return of Hiawatha.
  Stretched upon his back he lay there ;

Far below him plashed the waters,
Plashed and washed the dreamy waters;
Far above him swam the heavens,
Swam the dizzy, dreamy heavens;
Round him hovered, fluttered, rustled,
Hiawatha's mountain chickens,
Flock-wise swept and wheeled about him,
Almost brushed him with their pinions.

And he killed them as he lay there,
Slaughtered them by tens and twenties,
Threw their bodies down the headland,
Threw them on the beach below him,
Till at length Kayoshk, the seagull,
Perched upon a crag above them,
Shouted: 'It is Pau-Puk-Keewis!
He is slaying us by hundreds!
Send a message to our brother,
Tidings send to Hiawatha!'

XVII

THE HUNTING OF PAU-PUK-KEEWIS

Full of wrath was Hiawatha,
When he came into the village,
Found the people in confusion,
Heard of all the misdemeanours,
All the malice and the mischief
Of the cunning Pau-Puk-Keewis.

Hard his breath came through his nostrils,
Through his teeth he buzzed and muttered
Words of anger and resentment,
Hot and humming like a hornet.
'I will slay this Pau-Puk-Keewis,
Slay this mischief-maker!' said he.
'Not so long and wide the world is,
Not so rude and rough the way is,
That my wrath shall not attain him,
That my vengeance shall not reach him!'

Then in swift pursuit departed,
Hiawatha and the hunters
On the trail of Pau-Puk-Keewis,

Through the forest, where he passed,
To the headlands where he rested;
But they found not Pau-Puk-Keewis,
Only in the trampled grasses,
In the whortleberry bushes,
Found the couch where he had rested,
Found the impress of his body.
From the lowlands far beneath them,
From the Muskoday, the meadow,
Pau-Puk-Keewis, turning backward,
Made a gesture of defiance,
Made a gesture of derision;
And aloud cried Hiawatha,
From the summit of the mountain:
'Not so long and wide the world is,
Not so rude and rough the way is,
But my wrath shall overtake you,
And my vengeance shall attain you!'
    Over rock and over river,
Through bush, and brake, and forest,
Ran the cunning Pau-Puk-Keewis;
Like an antelope he bounded,
Till he came unto a streamlet
In the middle of the forest,
To a streamlet still and tranquil,
That had overflowed its margin,
To a dam made by the beavers,
To a pond of quiet water,
Where knee-deep the trees were standing,
Where the water-lilies floated,
Where the rushes waved and whispered.
    On the dam stood Pau-Puk-Keewis,
On the dam of trunks and branches,
Through whose chinks the water spouted,
O'er whose summit flowed the streamlet.
From the bottom rose the beaver,
Looked with two great eyes of wonder,
Eyes that seemed to ask a question,
At the stranger, Pau-Puk-Keewis.
    On the dam stood Pau-Puk-Keewis,
O'er his ankles flowed the streamlet,

Flowed the bright and silvery water,
And he spake unto the beaver,
With a smile he spake in this wise:
  'O my friend Ahmeek, the beaver,
Cool and pleasant is the water;
Let me dive into the water,
Let me rest there in your lodges;
Change me, too, into a beaver!'
  Cautiously replied the beaver,
With reserve he thus made answer:
'Let me first consult the others,
Let me ask the other beavers.'
Down he sank into the water,
Heavily sank he, as a stone sinks,
Down among the leaves and branches,
Brown and matted at the bottom.
  On the dam stood Pau-Puk-Keewis,
O'er his ankles flowed the streamlet,
Spouted through the chinks below him,
Dashed upon the stones beneath him,
Spread serene and calm before him,
And the sunshine and the shadows
Fell in flecks and gleams upon him,
Fell in little shining patches,
Through the waving, rustling branches.
  From the bottom rose the beavers,
Silently above the surface
Rose one head and then another,
Till the pond seemed full of beavers,
Full of black and shining faces.
  To the beavers Pau-Puk-Keewis
Spake entreating, said in this wise:
'Very pleasant is your dwelling,
O my friends! and safe from danger;
Can you not with all your cunning,
All your wisdom and contrivance,
Change me, too, into a beaver?'
  'Yes!' replied Ahmeek, the beaver,
He the King of all the beavers,
'Let yourself slide down among us,
Down into the tranquil water.'

Down into the pond among them
Silently sank Pau-Puk-Keewis;
Black became his shirt of deerskin,
Black his moccasins and leggings,
In a broad black tail behind him
Spread his foxtails and his fringes;
He was changed into a beaver.

'Make me large,' said Pau-Puk-Keewis,
'Make me large and make me larger,
Larger than the other beavers.'
'Yes,' the beaver chief responded,
'When our lodge below you enter,
In our wigwam we will make you
Ten times larger than the others.'

Thus into the clear, brown water
Silently sank Pau-Puk-Keewis;
Found the bottom covered over
With the trunks of trees and branches,
Hoards of food against the winter,
Piles and heaps against the famine;
Found the lodge with arching doorway,
Leading into spacious chambers.

Here they made him large and larger,
Made him largest of the beavers,
Ten times larger than the others.
'You shall be our ruler,' said they;
'Chief and King of all the beavers.'

But not long had Pau-Puk-Keewis
Sat in state among the beavers,
When there came a voice of warning
From the watchman at his station
In the water-flags and lilies,
Saying, 'Here is Hiawatha!
Hiawatha with his hunters!'

Then they heard a cry above them,
Heard a shouting and a tramping,
Heard a crashing and a rushing,
And the water round and o'er them
Sank and sucked away in eddies,
And they knew their dam was broken.

On the lodge's roof the hunters

Leaped, and broke it all asunder;
Streamed the sunshine through the crevice,
Sprang the beavers through the doorway,
Hid themselves in deeper water,
In the channel of the streamlet;
But the mighty Pau-Puk-Keewis
Could not pass beneath the doorway;
He was puffed with pride and feeding,
He was swollen like a bladder.

Through the roof looked Hiawatha,
Cried aloud, 'O Pau-Puk-Keewis!
Vain are all your craft and cunning,
Vain your manifold disguises!
Well I know you, Pau-Puk-Keewis!'

With their clubs they beat and bruised him,
Beat to death poor Pau-Puk-Keewis,
Pounded him as maize is pounded,
Till his skull was crushed to pieces.

Six tall hunters, lithe and limber,
Bore him home on poles and branches,
Bore the body of the beaver;
But the ghost, the Jeebi in him,
Thought and felt as Pau-Puk-Keewis,
Still lived on as Pau-Puk-Keewis.

And it fluttered, strove, and struggled,
Waving hither, waving thither,
As the curtains of a wigwam
Struggle with their thongs of deerskin,
When the wintry wind is blowing;
Till it drew itself together,
Till it rose up from the body,
Till it took the form and features
Of the cunning Pau-Puk-Keewis,
Vanishing into the forest.

But the wary Hiawatha
Saw the figure ere it vanished,
Saw the form of Pau-Puk-Keewis
Glide into the soft blue Shadow
Of the pine-trees of the forest;
Toward the squares of white beyond it,
Toward an opening in the forest,

Like a wind it rushed and panted,
Bending all the boughs before it,
And behind it, as the rain comes,
Came the steps of Hiawatha.

To a lake with many islands
Came the breathless Pau-Puk-Keewis,
Where among the water-lilies
Pishnekuh, the brant, was sailing;
Through the tufts of rushes floating,
Steering through the reedy islands,
Now their broad black beaks they lifted,
Now they plunged beneath the water,
Now they darkened in the shadow,
Now they brightened in the sunshine.

'Pishnekuh!' cried Pau-Puk-Keewis,
'Pishnekuh! my brothers!' said he,
'Change me to a brant with plumage,
With a shining neck and feathers,
Make me large, and make me larger,
Ten times larger than the others.'

Straightway to a brant they changed him,
With two huge and dusky pinions,
With a bosom smooth and rounded,
With a bill like two great paddles,
Made him larger than the others,
Ten times larger than the largest,
Just as, shouting from the forest,
On the shore stood Hiawatha.

Up they rose with cry and clamour,
With a whir and beat of pinions,
Rose up from the reedy islands,
From the water-flags and lilies.
And they said to Pau-Puk-Keewis:
'In your flying, look not downward,
Take good heed and look not downward,
Lest some strange mischance should happen,
Lest some great mishap befall you!'
Fast and far they fled to northward,
Fast and far through mist and sunshine,
Fed among the moors and fenlands,
Slept among the reeds and rushes.

On the morrow as they journeyed,
Buoyed and lifted by the South-wind,
Wafted onward by the South-wind,
Blowing fresh and strong behind them,
Rose a sound of human voices,
Rose a clamour from beneath them,
From the lodges of a village,
From the people miles beneath them.

   For the people of the village
Saw the flock of brant with wonder,
Saw the wings of Pau-Puk-Keewis
Flapping far up in the ether,
Broader than two doorway curtains.

   Pau-Puk-Keewis heard the shouting,
Knew the voice of Hiawatha,
Knew the outcry of Iagoo,
And, forgetful of the warning,
Drew his neck in, and looked downward,
And the wind that blew behind him
Caught his mighty fan of feathers.
Sent him wheeling, whirling downward!

   All in vain did Pau-Puk-Keewis
Struggle to regain his balance!
Whirling round and round and downward,
He beheld in turn the village
And in turn the flock above him,
Saw the village coming nearer,
And the flock receding farther,
Heard the voices growing louder,
Heard the shouting and the laughter;
Saw no more the flock above him,
Only saw the earth beneath him;
Dead out of the empty heaven,
Dead among the shouting people,
With a heavy sound and sullen,
Fell the brant with broken pinions.

   But his soul, his ghost, his shadow,
Still survived as Pau-Puk-Keewis,
Took again the form and features
Of the handsome Yenadizze,
And again went rushing onward,

Followed fast by Hiawatha,
Crying : 'Not so wide the world is,
Not so long and rough the way is,
But my wrath shall overtake you,
But my vengeance shall attain you !'
   And so near he came, so near him,
That his hand was stretched to seize him,
His right hand to seize and hold him,
When the cunning Pau-Puk-Keewis
Whirled and spun about in circles,
Fanned the air into a whirlwind,
Danced the dust and leaves about him,
And amid the whirling eddies
Sprang into a hollow oak-tree,
Changed himself into a serpent,
Gliding out through root and rubbish.
   With his right hand Hiawatha
Smote amain the hollow oak-tree,
Rent it into shreds and splinters,
Left it lying there in fragments.
But in vain ; for Pau-Puk-Keewis,
Once again in human figure,
Full in sight ran on before him,
Sped away in gust and whirlwind,
On the shores of Gitche Gumee,
Westward by the Big-Sea-Water,
Came unto the rocky headlands,
To the Pictured Rocks of sandstone,
Looking over lake and landscape.
And the Old Man of the Mountain,
He the Manito of Mountains,
Opened wide his rocky doorways,
Opened wide his deep abysses,
Giving Pau-Puk-Keewis shelter
In his caverns dark and dreary,
Bidding Pau-Puk-Keewis welcome
To his gloomy lodge of sandstone.
   There without stood Hiawatha,
Found the doorways closed against him,
With his mittens, Minjekahwun,
Smote great caverns in the sandstone,

Cried aloud in tones of thunder,
'Open! I am Hiawatha!'
But the Old Man of the Mountain
Opened not, and made no answer
From the silent crags of sandstone,
From the gloomy rock abysses.

    Then he raised his hands to heaven,
Called imploring on the tempest,
Called Waywassimo, the lightning,
And the thunder, Annemeekee;
And they came with night and darkness,
Sweeping down the Big-Sea-Water
From the distant Thunder Mountains;
And the trembling Pau-Puk-Keewis
Heard the footsteps of the thunder,
Saw the red eyes of the lightning,
Was afraid, and crouched and trembled.

    Then Waywassimo, the lightning,
Smote the doorways of the caverns,
With his war club smote the doorways,
Smote the jutting crags of sandstone,
And the thunder, Annemeekee,
Shouted down into the caverns,
Saying, 'Where is Pau-Puk-Keewis!'
And the crags fell, and beneath them
Dead among the rocky ruins
Lay the cunning Pau-Puk-Keewis,
Lay the handsome Yenadizze,
Slain in his own human figure.

    Ended were his wild adventures,
Ended were his tricks and gambols,
Ended all his craft and cunning,
Ended all his mischief-making,
All his gambling and his dancing,
All his wooing of the maidens.

    Then the noble Hiawatha
Took his soul, his ghost, his shadow,
Spake and said: 'O Pau-Puk-Keewis,
Never more in human figure
Shall you search for new adventures;
Never more with jest and laughter

Dance the dust and leaves in whirlwinds;
But above there in the heavens
You shall soar and sail in circles:
I will change you to an eagle,
To Keneu, the great war-eagle,
Chief of all the fowls with feathers,
Chief of Hiawatha's chickens.'
    And the name of Pau-Puk-Keewis
Lingers still among the people,
Lingers still among the singers,
And among the story-tellers;
And in Winter, when the snowflakes
Whirl in eddies round the lodges,
When the wind in gusty tumult
O'er the smoke-flue pipes and whistles,
'There,' they cry, 'comes Pau-Puk-Keewis;
He is dancing through the village,
He is gathering in his harvest!'

XVIII

THE DEATH OF KWASIND

    Far and wide among the nations
Spread the name and fame of Kwasind;
No man dared to strive with Kwasind,
No man could compete with Kwasind.
But the mischievous Puk-Wudjies,
They the envious Little People,
They the fairies and the pygmies,
Plotted and conspired against him.
    'If this hateful Kwasind,' said they,
'If this great, outrageous fellow
Goes on thus a little longer,
Tearing everything he touches,
Rending everything to pieces,
Filling all the world with wonder,
What becomes of the Puk-Wudjies!
Who will care for the Puk-Wudjies?
He will tread us down like mushrooms,
Drive us all into the water,
Give our bodies to be eaten

By the wicked Nee-ba-naw-baigs,
By the Spirits of the water !'
  So the angry Little People
All conspired against the Strong Men,
All conspired to murder Kwasind,
Yes, to rid the world of Kwasind,
The audacious, overbearing,
Heartless, haughty, dangerous Kwasind !
  Now this wondrous strength of Kwasind
In his crown alone was seated ;
In his crown, too, was his weakness ;
There alone could he be wounded,
Nowhere else could weapon pierce him,
Nowhere else could weapon harm him.
  Even there the only weapon
That could wound him, that could slay him,
Was the seed-cone of the pine-tree,
Was the blue cone of the fir-tree.
This was Kwasind's fatal secret,
Known to no man among mortals ;
But the cunning Little People,
The Puk-Wudjies, knew the secret,
Knew the only way to kill him.
  So they gathered cones together,
Gathered seed-cones of the pine-tree,
Gathered blue cones of the fir-tree,
In the woods by Taquamenaw,
Brought them to the river's margin,
Heaped them in great piles together,
Where the red rocks from the margin
Jutting overhang the river.
There they lay in wait for Kwasind,
The malicious Little People.
  'Twas an afternoon in Summer ;
Very hot and still the air was,
Very smooth the gliding river,
Motionless the sleeping shadows ;
Insects glistened in the sunshine,
Insects skated on the water,
Filled the drowsy air with buzzing,
With a far resounding war-cry.

Down the river came the Strong Man,
In his birch canoe came Kwasind,
Floating slowly down the current
Of the sluggish Taquamenaw,
Very languid with the weather,
Very sleepy with the silence.

From the overhanging branches,
From the tassels of the birch-trees,
Soft the Spirit of Sleep descended;
By his airy hosts surrounded,
His invisible attendants,
Came the Spirit of Sleep, Nepahwin;
Like the burnished Dush-kwo-ne-she,
Like a dragon-fly he hovered
O'er the drowsy head of Kwasind.

To his ear there came a murmur
As of waves upon a seashore,
As of far-off tumbling waters,
As of wind among the pine-trees;
As he felt upon his forehead
Blows of little airy war-clubs,
Wielded by the slumbrous legions
Of the Spirit of Sleep, Nepahwin,
As of some one breathing on him.

At the first blow of their war-clubs,
Fell a drowsiness on Kwasind;
At the second blow they smote him,
Motionless his paddle rested;
At the third, before his vision
Reeled the landscape into darkness,
Very sound asleep was Kwasind.

So he floated down the river,
Like a blind man seated upright,
Floated down the Taquamenaw,
Underneath the trembling birch-trees,
Underneath the wooded headlands.
Underneath the war encampment
Of the pygmies, the Puk-Wudjies.

There they stood, all armed and waiting,
Hurled the pine-cones down upon him,
Struck him on his brawny shoulders,

On his crown defenceless struck him.
'Death to Kwasind!' was the sudden
War-cry of the Little People.

    And he sideways swayed and tumbled,
Sideways fell into the river,
Plunged beneath the sluggish water
Headlong, as an otter plunges;
And the birch-canoe, abandoned,
Drifted empty down the river,
Bottom upward swerved and drifted;
Nothing more was seen of Kwasind.

    But the memory of the Strong Man
Lingered long among the people,
And whenever through the forest
Raged and roared the wintry tempest,
And the branches, tossed and troubled,
Creaked and groaned and split asunder,
'Kwasind!' cried they; 'that is Kwasind!
He is gathering in his firewood!'

XIX

THE GHOSTS

    Never stoops the soaring vulture
On his quarry in the desert,
On the sick or wounded bison,
But another vulture, watching
From his high aerial lookout,
Sees the downward plunge, and follows;
And a third pursues the second,
Coming from the invisible ether,
First a speck, and then a vulture,
Till the air is dark with pinions.

    So disasters come not singly;
But as if they watched and waited,
Scanning one another's motions,
When the first descends, the others
Follow, follow, gathering flockwise
Round their victim, sick and wounded,
First a shadow, then a sorrow,
Till the air is dark with anguish.

    Now o'er all the dreary Northland,

Mighty Peboan, the Winter,
Breathing on the lakes and rivers,
Into stone had changed their waters.
From his hair he shook the snowflakes,
Till the plains were strewn with whiteness,
One uninterrupted level,
As if, stooping, the Creator
With his hands had smoothed them over.
  Through the forest, wide and wailing,
Roamed the hunter on his snowshoes;
In the village worked the women,
Pounded maize, or dressed the deer-skin;
And the young men played together
On the ice the noisy ball-play,
On the plain the dance of snowshoes.
  One dark evening, after sundown,
In her wigwam Laughing Water
Sat with old Nokomis, waiting
For the steps of Hiawatha
Homeward from the hunt returning.
  On their faces gleamed the firelight,
Painting them with streaks of crimson,
In the eyes of old Nokomis
Glimmered like the watery moonlight,
In the eyes of Laughing Water
Glistened like the sun in water;
And behind them crouched their shadows
In the corners of the wigwam,
And the smoke in wreaths above them
Climbed and crowded through the smoke-flue.
  Then the curtain of the doorway
From without was slowly lifted;
Brighter glowed the fire a moment,
And a moment swerved the smoke-wreath,
As two women entered softly,
Passed the doorway uninvited,
Without word of salutation,
Without sign of recognition,
Sat down in the farthest corner,
Crouching low among the shadows.
  From their aspect and their garments,

Strangers seemed they in the village;
Very pale and haggard were they,
As they sat there sad and silent,
Trembling, cowering with the shadows.

Was it the wind above the smoke-flue,
Muttering down into the wigwam?
Was it the owl, the Koko-koho,
Hooting from the dismal forest?
Sure a voice said in the silence:
'These are corpses clad in garments,
These are ghosts that come to haunt you,
From the kingdom of Ponemah,
From the land of the Hereafter!'

Homeward now came Hiawatha
From his hunting in the forest,
With the snow upon his tresses,
And the red deer on his shoulders.
At the feet of Laughing Water
Down he threw his lifeless burden;
Nobler, handsomer she thought him,
Than when first he came to woo her,
First threw down the deer before her,
As a token of his wishes,
As a promise of the future.

Then he turned and saw the strangers,
Cowering, crouching with the shadows,
Said within himself, 'Who are they?
What strange guests has Minnehaha?'
But he questioned not the strangers,
Only spake to bid them welcome
To his lodge, his food, his fireside.

When the evening meal was ready,
And the deer had been divided,
Both the pallid guests, the strangers,
Springing from among the shadows,
Seized upon the choicest portions,
Seized the white fat of the roebuck,
Set apart for Laughing Water,
For the wife of Hiawatha;
Without asking, without thanking,
Eagerly devoured the morsels,

Flitted back among the shadows
In the corner of the wigwam.
　Not a word spake Hiawatha,
Not a motion made Nokomis,
Not a gesture Laughing Water;
Not a change came o'er their features,
Only Minnehaha softly
Whispered, saying, 'They are famished;
Let them do what best delights them;
Let them eat, for they are famished.'
　Many a daylight dawned and darkened,
Many a night shook off the daylight
As the pine shakes off the snowflakes
From the midnight of its branches;
Day by day the guests unmoving
Sat there silent in the wigwam;
But by night, in storm or starlight,
Forth they went into the forest,
Bringing firewood to the wigwam,
Bringing pine cones for the burning,
Always sad and always silent.
And whenever Hiawatha
Came from fishing or from hunting,
When the evening meal was ready,
And the food had been divided,
Gliding from their darksome corner,
Came the pallid guests, the strangers,
Seized upon the choicest portions
Set aside for Laughing Water,
And without rebuke or question
Flitted back among the shadows.
　Never once had Hiawatha
By a word or look reproved them;
Never once had old Nokomis
Made a gesture of impatience;
Never once had Laughing Water
Shown resentment at the outrage.
All had they endured in silence,
That the rights of guest and stranger,
That the virtue of free-giving,
By a look might not be lessened,

By a word might not be broken.
    Once at midnight Hiawatha,
Ever wakeful, ever watchful,
In the wigwam, dimly lighted
By the brands that still were burning,
By the glimmering, flickering firelight,
Heard a sighing, oft repeated,
Heard a sobbing, as of sorrow.
    From his couch rose Hiawatha,
From his shaggy hides of bison,
Pushed aside the deerskin curtain,
Saw the pallid guests, the shadows,
Sitting upright on their couches,
Weeping in the silent midnight.
    And he said: 'O guests! why is it
That your hearts are so afflicted,
That you sob so in the midnight?
Has perchance the old Nokomis,
Has my wife, my Minnehaha,
Wronged or grieved you by unkindness,
Failed in hospitable duties?'
    Then the shadows ceased from weeping,
Ceased from sobbing and lamenting,
And they said, with gentle voices,
'We are ghosts of the departed,
Souls of those who once were with you.
From the realm of Chibiabos
Hither have we come to try you,
Hither have we come to warn you:
    'Cries of grief and lamentation
Reach us in the Blessed Islands;
Cries of anguish from the living,
Calling back their friends departed,
Sadden us with useless sorrow.
Therefore have we come to try you:
No one knows us, no one heeds us.
We are but a burden to you,
And we see that the departed
Have no place among the living.
    'Think of this, O Hiawatha!
Speak of it to all the people,

That henceforward and for ever
They no more with lamentations
Sadden the souls of the departed
In the Islands of the Blessed.

   'Do not lay such heavy burdens
In the graves of those you bury,
Not such weight of furs and wampum,
Not such weight of pots and kettles,
For the spirits faint beneath them.
Only give them food to carry,
Only give them fire to light them.

   'Four days is the spirit's journey
To the land of ghosts and shadows,
Four its lonely night encampments;
Four times must their fires be lighted.
Therefore, when the dead are buried,
Let a fire, as night approaches,
Four times on the grave be kindled,
That the soul upon its journey
May not lack the cheerful firelight,
May not grope about in darkness.

   'Farewell, noble Hiawatha!
We have put you to the trial,
To the proof have put your patience,
By the insult of our presence,
By the outrage of our actions.
We have found you great and noble,
Fail not in the greater trial,
Faint not in the harder struggle.'

   When they ceased, a sudden darkness
Fell and filled the silent wigwam.
Hiawatha heard a rustle
As of garments trailing by him,
Heard the curtain of the doorway
Lifted by a hand he saw not,
Felt the cold breath of the night air,
For a moment saw the starlight;
But he saw the ghosts no longer,
Saw no more the wandering spirits
From the kingdom of Ponemah,
From the land of the Hereafter.

XX

THE FAMINE

O the long and dreary Winter!
O the cold and cruel Winter!
Ever thicker, thicker, thicker
Froze the ice on lake and river,
Ever deeper, deeper, deeper
Fell the snow o'er all the landscape,
Fell the covering snow, and drifted
Through the forest, round the village.

Hardly from his buried wigwam
Could the hunter force a passage;
With his mittens and his snowshoes
Vainly walked he through the forest,
Sought for bird or beast and found none,
Saw no track of deer or rabbit,
In the snow beheld no footprints,
In the ghastly, gleaming forest
Fell, and could not rise from weakness,
Perished there from cold and hunger.

O the famine and the fever!
O the wasting of the famine!
O the blasting of the fever!
O the wailing of the children!
O the anguish of the women!

All the earth was sick and famished;
Hungry was the air around them,
Hungry was the sky above them,
And the hungry stars in heaven
Like the eyes of wolves glared at them!

Into Hiawatha's wigwam
Came two other guests, as silent
As the ghosts were, and as gloomy,
Waited not to be invited,
Did not parley at the doorway,
Sat there without word of welcome
In the seat of Laughing Water;
Looked with haggard eyes and hollow
At the face of Laughing Water.

And the foremost said: 'Behold me!

I am Famine, Bukadawin!'
And the other said: 'Behold me!
I am Fever, Ahkosewin!'
  And the lovely Minnehaha
Shuddered as they looked upon her,
Shuddered at the words they uttered,
Lay down on her bed in silence,
Hid her face, but made no answer;
Lay there trembling, freezing, burning
At the looks they cast upon her,
At the fearful words they uttered.

  Forth into the empty forest
Rushed the maddened Hiawatha;
In his heart was deadly sorrow,
In his face a stony firmness;
On his brow the sweat of anguish
Started, but it froze and fell not.

  Wrapped in furs and armed for hunting,
With his mighty bow of ash-tree,
With his quiver full of arrows,
With his mittens, Minjekahwun,
Into the vast and vacant forest
On his snow-shoes strode he forward.

  'Gitche Manito, the Mighty!'
Cried he with his face uplifted
In that bitter hour of anguish,
'Give your children food, O father!
Give us food, or we must perish!
Give me food for Minnehaha,
For my dying Minnehaha!'

  Through the far-resounding forest,
Through the forest vast and vacant
Rang that cry of desolation.
But there came no other answer
Than the echo of his crying,
Than the echo of the woodlands,
'Minnehaha! Minnehaha!'

  All day long roved Hiawatha
In that melancholy forest,
Through the shadow of whose thickets,
In the pleasant days of Summer,

Of that ne'er forgotten Summer,
He had brought his young wife homeward
From the land of the Dacotahs;
When the birds sang in the thickets,
And the streamlets laughed and glistened,
And the air was full of fragrance,
And the lovely Laughing Water
Said with voice that did not tremble,
'I will follow you, my husband!'
In the wigwam with Nokomis,
With those gloomy guests, that watched her,
With the Famine and the Fever,
She was lying, the Beloved,
She the dying Minnehaha.

'Hark!' she said; 'I hear a rushing,
Hear a roaring and a rushing,
Hear the Falls of Minnehaha
Calling to me from a distance!'
'No, my child!' said old Nokomis
''Tis the night-wind in the pine-trees!'
'Look!' she said; 'I see my father
Standing lonely at his doorway,
Beckoning to me from his wigwam
In the land of the Dacotahs!'
'No, my child!' said old Nokomis,
''Tis the smoke, that waves and beckons!'

'Ah!' said she, 'the eyes of Pauguk
Glare upon me in the darkness,
I can feel his icy fingers
Clasping mine amid the darkness!
Hiawatha! Hiawatha!'

And the desolate Hiawatha,
Far away amid the forest,
Miles away among the mountains,
Heard that sudden cry of anguish,
Heard the voice of Minnehaha
Calling to him in the darkness,
'Hiawatha! Hiawatha!'

Over snowfields waste and pathless
Under snow-encumbered branches,
Homeward hurried Hiawatha,

Empty-handed, heavy-hearted,
Heard Nokomis moaning, wailing:
'Wahonowin! Wahonowin!
Would that I had perished for you,
Would that I were dead as you are!
Wahonowin! Wahonowin!'

And he rushed into the wigwam,
Saw the old Nokomis slowly
Rocking to and fro and moaning,
Saw his lovely Minnehaha
Lying dead and cold before him,
And his bursting heart within him
Uttered such a cry of anguish,
That the forest moaned and shuddered,
That the very stars in heaven
Shook and trembled with his anguish.

Then he sat down, still and speechless,
On the bed of Minnehaha,
At the feet of Laughing Water,
At those willing feet, that never
More would lightly run to meet him,
Never more would lightly follow.

With both hands his face he covered,
Seven long days and nights he sat there,
As if in a swoon he sat there,
Speechless, motionless, unconscious
Of the daylight or the darkness.

Then they buried Minnehaha;
In the snow a grave they made her,
In the forest deep and darksome,
Underneath the moaning hemlocks;
Clothed in her richest garments,
Wrapped in her robes of ermine;
Covered her with snow, like ermine,
Thus they buried Minnehaha.

And at night a fire was lighted,
On her grave four times was kindled,
For her soul upon its journey
To the Islands of the Blessed.
From his doorway Hiawatha
Saw it burning in the forest,

Lighting up the gloomy hemlocks;
From his sleepless bed uprising,
From the bed of Minnehaha,
Stood and watched it at the doorway,
That it might not be extinguished,
Might not leave her in the darkness.

'Farewell!' said he, 'Minnehaha!
Farewell, O my Laughing Water!
All my heart is buried with you,
All my thoughts go onward with you!
Come not back again to labour,
Come not back again to suffer,
Where the Famine and the Fever
Wear the heart and waste the body.
Soon my task will be completed,
Soon your footsteps I shall follow
To the Islands of the Blessed,
To the Kingdom of Ponemah,
To the Land of the Hereafter!'

XXI

THE WHITE MAN'S FOOT

In his lodge beside a river,
Close beside a frozen river,
Sat an old man, sad and lonely.
White his hair was as a snowdrift;
Dull and low his fire was burning,
And the old man shook and trembled,
Folded in his Waubewyon,
In his tattered white skin wrapper,
Hearing nothing but the tempest
As it roared along the forest,
Seeing nothing but the snowstorm,
As it whirled and hissed and drifted.

All the coals were white with ashes,
And the fire was slowly dying,
As a young man, walking lightly,
At the open doorway entered.
Red with blood of youth his cheeks were,
Soft his eyes, as stars in Spring-time,

Bound his forehead was with grasses,
Bound and plumed with scented grasses;
On his lips a smile of beauty,
Filling all the lodge with sunshine,
In his hand a bunch of blossoms
Filling all the lodge with sweetness.

   'Ah, my son!' exclaimed the old man,
'Happy are my eyes to see you.
Sit here on the mat beside me,
Sit here by the dying embers,
Let us pass the night together.
Tell me of your strange adventures,
Of the lands where you have travelled;
I will tell you of my prowess,
Of my many deeds of wonder.'

   From his pouch he drew his peace-pipe,
Very old and strangely fashioned;
Made of red stone was the pipe-head,
And the stem a reed with feathers,
Filled the pipe with bark of willow,
Placed a burning coal upon it,
Gave it to his guest, the stranger,
And began to speak in this wise:

   'When I blow my breath about me,
When I breathe upon the landscape,
Motionless are all the rivers,
Hard as stones become the water!'

   And the young man answered, smiling:
'When I blow my breath about me,
When I breathe upon the landscape,
Flowers spring up o'er all the meadows,
Singing, onward rush the rivers!'

   'When I shake my hoary tresses,'
Said the old man darkly frowning,
'All the land with snow is covered;
All the leaves from all the branches
Fall and fade and die and wither,
For I breathe, and lo! they are not.
From the waters and the marshes
Rise the wild goose and the heron,
Fly away to distant regions,

For I speak, and lo ! they are not.
And where'er my footsteps wander,
All the wild beasts of the forest
Hide themselves in holes and caverns,
And the earth becomes as flint-stone !'
   'When I shake my flowing ringlets,'
Said the young man, softly laughing,
'Showers of rain fall warm and welcome,
Plants lift up their heads rejoicing,
Back unto their lakes and marshes
Come the wild goose and the heron,
Homeward shoots the arrowy swallows,
Sing the bluebird and the robin,
And where'er my footsteps wander,
All the meadows wave with blossoms,
All the woodlands ring with music,
All the trees are dark with foliage !'
   While they spake, the night departed :
From the distant realms of Wabun,
From his shining lodge of silver,
Like a warrior robed and painted,
Came the sun, and said, 'Behold me !
Gheezis, the great sun, behold me !'
   Then the old man's tongue was speechless.
And the air grew warm and pleasant,
And upon the wigwam sweetly
Sang the bluebird and the robin,
And the stream began to murmur,
And a scent of growing grasses
Through the lodge was gently wafted.
   And Segwun, the youthful stranger,
More distinctly in the daylight
Saw the icy face before him ;
It was Peboan, the Winter !
   From his eyes the tears were flowing,
As from melting lakes the streamlets,
And his body shrunk and dwindled
As the shouting sun ascended,
Till into the air it faded,
Till into the ground it vanished,
And the young man saw before him,

On the hearth-stone of the wigwam,
Where the fire had smoked and smouldered,
Saw the earliest flower of Spring-time,
Saw the beauty of the Spring-time,
Saw the Miskodeed in blossom.

Thus it was that in the Northland
After that unheard-of coldness,
That intolerable Winter,
Came the Spring with all its splendour,
All its birds and all its blossoms,
All its flowers and leaves and grasses.

Sailing on the wind to northward,
Flying in great flocks, like arrows,
Like huge arrows shot through heaven,
Passed the swan, the Mahnahbezee,
Speaking almost as a man speaks;
And in long lines waving, bending
Like a bow-string snapped asunder,
Came the white goose, Wawbewawa;
And the pairs or singly flying,
Mahng the loon, with clangorous pinions,
The blue heron, the Shuh-shuh-gah,
And the grouse, the Mushkodasa.

In the thickets and the meadows
Piped the bluebird, the Owaissa,
On the summit of the lodges
Sang the Opechee, the robin,
In the covert of the pine-trees
Cooed the pigeon, the Omemee,
And the sorrowing Hiawatha,
Speechless in his infinite sorrow,
Heard their voices calling to him,
Went forth from his gloomy doorway,
Stood and gazed into the heaven,
Gazed upon the earth and waters.

From his wanderings far to eastward,
From the regions of the morning,
From the shining land of Wabun,
Homeward now returned Iagoo,
The great traveller, the great boaster,
Full of new and strange adventures,

Marvels many and many wonders.
   And the people of the village
Listened to him as he told them
Of his marvellous adventures,
Laughing answered him in this wise:
'Ugh! it is indeed Iagoo!
No one else beholds such wonders!'
   He had seen, he said, a water,
Bigger than the Big-Sea-Water,
Broader than the Gitche Gumee,
Bitter so that none could drink it!
At each other looked the warriors,
Looked the women at each other,
Smiled and said, 'It cannot be so!
Kaw!' they said, 'It cannot be so!'
   O'er it, said he, o'er this water
Came a great canoe with pinions,
A canoe with wings came flying,
Bigger than a grove of pine-trees,
Taller than the tallest tree-tops!
And the old men and the women
Looked and tittered at each other;
'Kaw!' they said, 'we don't believe it!'
   From its mouth, he said, to greet him,
Came Waywassimo, the lightning,
Came the thunder, Annemeekee!
And the warriors and the women
Laughed aloud at poor Iagoo;
'Kaw!' they said, 'what tales you tell us!'
   In it, said he, came a people,
In the great canoe with pinions
Came, he said, a hundred warriors;
Painted white were all their faces
And with hair their chins were covered!
And the warriors and the women
Laughed and shouted in derision,
Like the ravens on the tree-tops,
Like the crows upon the hemlocks.
'Kaw!' they said, 'what lies you tell us!
Do not think that we believe them!'
   Only Hiawatha laughed not,

But he gravely spake and answered
To their jeering and their jesting:
'True is all Iagoo tells us;
I have seen it in a vision,
Seen the great canoe with pinions,
Seen the people with white faces,
Seen the coming of this bearded
People of the wooden vessel
From the regions of the morning,
From the shining land of Wabun.

'Gitche Manito, the Mighty,
The Great Spirit, the Creator,
Sends them hither on his errand,
Sends them to us with his message.
Wheresoe'er they move, before them
Swarms the stinging fly, the Ahmo,
Swarms the bee, the honey-maker;
Wheresoe'er they tread, beneath them
Springs a flower unknown among us,
Springs the White-man's Foot in blossom.

'Let us welcome, then, the strangers,
Hail them as our friends and brothers,
And the heart's right hand of friendship
Give them when they come to see us.
Gitche Manito, the Mighty,
Said this to me in my vision.

'I beheld, too, in that vision,
All the secrets of the future,
Of the distant days that shall be.
I beheld the westward marches
Of the unknown, crowded nations.
All the land was full of people,
Restless, struggling, toiling, striving,
Speaking many tongues, yet feeling
But one heart-beat in their bosoms.
In the woodlands rang their axes,
Smoked their towns in all the valleys,
Over all the lakes and rivers
Rushed their great canoes of thunder.

'Then a darker, drearier vision
Passed before me, vague and cloud-like

I beheld our nation scattered,
All forgetful of my counsels,
Weakened, warring with each other;
Saw the remnants of our people
Sweeping westward, wild and woeful,
Like the cloud-rack of a tempest,
Like the withered leaves of Autumn!'

XXII

HIAWATHA'S DEPARTURE

By the shore of Gitche Gumee,
By the shining Big-Sea-Water,
At the doorway of his wigwam,
In the pleasant Summer morning,
Hiawatha stood and waited.
All the air was full of freshness,
All the earth was bright and joyous,
And before him through the sunshine,
Westward toward the neighbouring forest
Passed in golden swarms the Ahmo,
Passed the bees, the honey-makers,
Burning, singing in the sunshine.
Bright above him shone the heavens,
Level spread the lake before him;
From its bosom leaped the sturgeon,
Sparkling, flashing in the sunshine;
On its margin the great forest
Stood reflected in the water,
Every tree-top had its shadow,
Motionless beneath the water.
From the brow of Hiawatha
Gone was every trace of sorrow,
As the fog from off the water,
As the mist from off the meadow.
With a smile of joy and triumph,
With a look of exultation.
As of one who in a vision
Sees what is to be, but is not,
Stood and waited Hiawatha.
Toward the sun his hands were lifted,

Both the palms spread out against it,
And between the parted fingers
Fell the sunshine on his features,
Flecked with light his naked shoulders,
As it falls and flecks an oak tree
Through the rifted leaves and branches.

O'er the water floating, flying,
Something in the hazy distance,
Something in the mists of morning,
Loomed and lifted from the water,
Now seemed floating, now seemed flying,
Coming nearer, nearer, nearer.

Was it Shingebis, the diver?
Was it the pelican, the Shada?
Or the heron, the Shuh-shuh-gah?
Or the white goose, Waw-be-wawa,
With the water dripping, flashing,
From its glossy neck and feathers?

It was neither goose nor diver,
Neither pelican nor heron,
O'er the water floating, flying,
Through the shining mist of morning,
But a birch canoe with paddles,
Rising, sinking on the water,
Dripping, flashing in the sunshine;
And within it came a people
From the distant land of Wabun,
From the farthest realms of morning
Came the Black-Robe chief, the Prophet,
He the Priest of Prayer, the Pale-face,
With his guides and his companions.

And the noble Hiawatha,
With his hands aloft extended,
Held aloft in sign of welcome,
Waited, full of exultation,
Till the birch canoe with paddles
Grated on the shining pebbles,
Stranded on the sandy margin,
Till the Black-Robe chief, the Pale-face,
With the cross upon his bosom,
Landed on the sandy margin.

Then the joyous Hiawatha
Cried aloud and spake in this wise:
'Beautiful is the sun, O strangers,
When you come so far to see us!
All our town in peace awaits you,
All our doors stand open for you;
You shall enter all our wigwams,
For the heart's right hand we give you.

'Never bloomed the earth so gaily,
Never shone the sun so brightly,
As to-day they shine and blossom
When you come so far to see us!
Never was our lake so tranquil.
Nor so free from rocks and sand-bars;
For our birch canoe in passing
Has removed both rock and sand-bar.

'Never before had our tobacco
Such a sweet and pleasant flavour,
Never the broad leaves of our cornfields
Were so beautiful to look on,
As they seem to us this morning,
When you come so far to see us!'

And the Black-Robe chief made answer,
Stammered in his speech a little,
Speaking words yet unfamiliar:
'Peace be with you, Hiawatha,
Peace be with you and your people,
Peace of prayer, and peace of pardon,
Peace of Christ, and joy of Mary!'

Then the generous Hiawatha
Led the strangers to his wigwam,
Seated them on skins of bison,
Seated them on skins of ermine,
And the careful, old Nokomis
Brought them food in bowls of bass-wood,
Water brought in birchen dippers,
And the calumet, the peace-pipe,
Filled and lighted for their smoking.

All the old men of the village,
All the warriors of the nation,
All the Jossakeeds, the prophets,

The magicians, the Wabenos,
And the medicine-men, the Medas,
Came to bid the strangers welcome;
'It is well,' they said, 'O brothers,
That you come so far to see us!'
    In a circle round the doorway,
With their pipes they sat in silence,
Waiting to behold the strangers,
Waiting to receive their message;
Till the Black-Robe chief, the Pale-face,
From the wigwam came to greet them,
Stammering in his speech a little,
Speaking words yet unfamiliar;
'It is well,' they said, 'O brother,
That you come so far to see us!'
    Then the Black-Robe chief, the prophet,
Told his message to the people,
Told the purport of his mission,
Told them of the Virgin Mary,
And her blessed Son, the Saviour,
How in distant lands and ages
He had lived on earth as we do;
How he fasted, prayed, and laboured;
How the Jews, the tribe accursed,
Mocked him, scourged him, crucified him;
How he rose from where they laid him,
Walked again with his disciples,
And ascended into heaven.
    And the chiefs made answer, saying:
'We have listened to your message,
We have heard your words of wisdom,
We will think on what you tell us.
It is well for us, O brothers,
That you come so far to see us!'
    Then they rose up and departed
Each one homeward to his wigwam,
To the young men and the women
Told the story of the strangers
Whom the Master of Life had sent them
From the shining land of Wabun.
    Heavy with the heat and silence

Grew the afternoon of Summer;
With a drowsy sound the forest
Whispered round the sultry wigwam.
With a sound of sleep the water
Rippled on the beach below it;
From the cornfields shrill and ceaseless
Sang the grasshopper, Pah-puk-keena;
And the guests of Hiawatha,
Weary with the heat of Summer,
Slumbered in the sultry wigwam.

Slowly o'er the simmering landscape
Fell the evening's dusk and coolness,
And the long and level sunbeams
Shot their spears into the forest,
Breaking through its shields of shadow,
Rushed into each secret ambush,
Searched each thicket, dingle, hollow;
Still the guests of Hiawatha
Slumbered in the silent wigwam.

From his place rose Hiawatha,
Bade farewell to old Nokomis,
Spake in whispers, spake in this wise,
Did not wake the guests, that slumbered:
'I am going, O Nokomis,
On a long and distant journey,
To the portals of the Sunset,
To the regions of the home-wind,
Of the Northwest wind, Keewaydin.
But these guests I leave behind me,
In your watch and ward I leave them;
See that never harm comes near them,
See that never fear molests them,
Never danger nor suspicion,
Never want of food or shelter,
In the lodge of Hiawatha!'

Forth into the village went he,
Bade farewell to all the warriors,
Bade farewell to all the young men,
Spake persuading, spake in this wise:
'I am going, O my people,
On a long and distant journey;

Many moons and many winters
Will have come, and will have vanished,
Ere I come again to see you.
But my guests I leave behind me;
Listen to their words of wisdom,
Listen to the truth they tell you,
For the Master of Life has sent them
From the land of light and morning!'

On the shore stood Hiawatha,
Turned and waved his hands at parting;
On the clear and luminous water
Launched his birch canoe for sailing,
From the pebbles of the margin
Shoved it forth into the water;
Whispered to it, 'Westward! westward!'
And with speed it darted forward.

And the evening sun descending
Set the clouds on fire with redness,
Burned the broad sky, like a prairie,
Left upon the level water
One long track and trail of splendour,
Down whose stream, as down a river,
Westward, westward Hiawatha
Sailed into the fiery sunset,
Sailed into the purple vapours,
Sailed into the dusk of evening.

And the people from the margin
Watched him floating, rising, sinking,
Till the birch canoe seemed lifted
High into that sea of splendour,
Till it sank into the vapours
Like the new moon slowly, slowly
Sinking in the purple distance.

And they said, 'Farewell for ever!'
Said, 'Farewell, O Hiawatha!'
And the forests, dark and lonely,
Moved through all their depths of darkness,
Sighed, 'Farewell, O Hiawatha!'
And the waves upon the margin
Rising, rippling on the pebbles,
Sobbed, 'Farewell, O Hiawatha!'

And the heron, the Shuh-shuh-gah,
From her haunts among the fen-lands
Screamed, 'Farewell, O Hiawatha!'
   Thus departed Hiawatha!
Hiawatha the Beloved,
In the glory of the sunset,
In the purple mists of evening,
To the regions of the home-wind,
Of the Northwest wind, Keewaydin,
To the Islands of the Blessed,
To the Kingdom of Ponemah,
To the land of the Hereafter!

The Village Blacksmith

Under a spreading chestnut tree
　　The village smithy stands;
The smith, a mighty man is he,
　　With large and sinewy hands;
And the muscles of his brawny arms
　　Are strong as iron bands.

His hair is crisp, and black, and long,
　　His face is like the tan;
His brow is wet with honest sweat,
　　He earns whate'er he can,
And looks the whole world in the face,
　　For he owes not any man.

Week in, week out, from morn till night,
　　You can hear his bellows blow;
You can hear him swing his heavy sledge,
　　With measured beat and slow,
Like a sexton ringing the village bell,
　　When the evening sun is low.

And children coming home from school
　　Look in at the open door;
They love to see the flaming forge,
　　And hear the bellows roar,
And catch the burning sparks that fly
　　Like chaff from a threshing floor.

He goes on Sunday to the church,
　　And sits among his boys;
He hears the parson pray and preach,
　　He hears his daughter's voice,
Singing in the village choir,
　　And it makes his heart rejoice.

It sounds to him like her mother's voice,
　　Singing in Paradise!
He needs must think of her once more,

How in the grave she lies;
And with his hard, rough hand he wipes
  A tear out of his eyes.

Toiling, – rejoicing, – sorrowing,
  Onward through life he goes;
Each morning sees some task begin,
  Each evening sees it close;
Something attempted, something done,
  Has earned a night's repose.

Thanks, thanks to thee, my worthy friend,
  For the lesson thou hast taught!
Thus at the flaming forge of life
  Our fortunes must be wrought;
Thus on its sounding anvil shaped
  Each burning deed and thought!

The Rainy Day

The day is cold, and dark, and dreary;
It rains, and the wind is never weary;
The vine still clings to the mouldering wall,
But at every gust the dead leaves fall,
　And the day is dark and dreary.

My life is cold, and dark, and dreary;
It rains, and the wind is never weary;
My thoughts still cling to the mouldering Past,
But the hopes of youth fall thick in the blast,
　And the days are dark and dreary.

Be still, sad heart ! and cease repining;
Behind the clouds is the sun still shining;
Thy fate is the common fate of all,
Into each life some rain must fall,
　Some days must be dark and dreary.

God's-Acre

I like that ancient Saxon phrase which calls
  The burial-ground God's-Acre ! It is just ;
It consecrates each grave within its walls,
  And breathes a benison o'er the sleeping dust.

God's-Acre ! Yes, that blessèd name imparts
  Comfort to those, who in the grave have sown
The seed, that they had garnered in their hearts,
  Their bread of life, alas ! no more their own.

Into its furrows shall we all be cast,
  In the sure faith, that we shall rise again
At the great harvest, when the arch-angel's blast
  Shall winnow, like a fan, the chaff and grain.

Then shall the good stand in immortal bloom,
  In the fair gardens of that second birth ;
And each bright blossom, mingle its perfume
  With that of flowers, which never bloomed on earth.

With thy rude ploughshare, Death, turn up the sod,
  And spread the furrow for the seed we sow ;
This is the field and Acre of our God,
  This is the place, where human harvests grow !

Excelsior

The shades of night were falling fast,
As through an Alpine village passed
A youth, who bore, 'mid snow and ice,
A banner with the strange device,
   Excelsior!

His brow was sad; his eye beneath
Flashed like a falchion from its sheath,
And like a silver clarion rung
The accents of that unknown tongue,
   Excelsior!

In happy homes he saw the light
Of household fires gleam warm and bright;
Above, the spectral glaciers shone,
And from his lips escaped a groan,
   Excelsior!

'Try not the Pass!' the old man said;
'Dark lowers the tempest overhead,
The roaring torrent is deep and wide!
And loud that clarion voice replied,
   Excelsior!

'O stay,' the maiden said, 'and rest
Thy weary head upon this breast!'
A tear stood in his bright blue eye,
But still he answered, with a sigh,
   Excelsior!

'Beware the pine-tree's withered branch!
Beware the awful avalanche!'
This was the peasant's last Good-night,
A voice replied, far up the height,
   Excelsior!

At break of day, as heavenward
The pious monks of Saint Bernard

Uttered the oft-repeated prayer,
A voice cried through the startled air,
    Excelsior!

A traveller, by the faithful hound,
Half-buried in the snow was found,
Still grasping in his hand of ice
That banner with the strange device,
    Excelsior!

There in the twilight cold and gray,
Lifeless, but beautiful, he lay,
And from the sky, serene and far,
A voice fell, like a falling star,
    Excelsior!

The Arsenal at Springfield

This is the Arsenal. From floor to ceiling,
   Like a huge organ, rise the burnished arms;
But from their silent pipes no anthem pealing
   Startles the villages with strange alarms.

Ah! what a sound will rise, how wild and dreary,
   When the death-angel touches those swift keys!
What loud lament and dismal Miserere
   Will mingle with their awful symphonies!

I hear even now the infinite fierce chorus,
   The cries of agony, the endless groan,
Which, through the ages that have gone before us,
   In long reverberations reach our own.

On helm and harness rings the Saxon hammer,
   Through Cimbric forest roars the Norseman's song,
And loud, amid the universal clamour,
   O'er distant deserts sounds the Tartar gong.

I hear the Florentine, who from his palace
   Wheels out his battle-bell with dreadful din,
And Aztec priests upon their teocallis
   Beat the wild war-drums made of serpent's skin;

The tumult of each sacked and burning village;
   The shout that every prayer for mercy drowns;
The soldiers' revels in the midst of pillage;
   The wail of famine in beleaguered towns;

The bursting shell, the gateway wrenched asunder,
   The rattling musketry, the clashing blade;
And ever and anon, in tones of thunder,
   The diapason of the cannonade.

Is it, O man, with such discordant noises,
   With such accursed instruments as these,

Thou drownest Nature's sweet and kindly voices,
   And jarrest the celestial harmonies?

Were half the power, that fills the world with terror,
   Were half the wealth, bestowed on camps and courts,
Given to redeem the human mind from error,
   There were no need of arsenals nor forts:

The warrior's name would be a name abhorred!
   And every nation, that should lift again
Its hand against a brother, on its forehead
   Would wear for evermore the curse of Cain!

Down the dark future, through long generations,
   The echoing sounds grow fainter and then cease;
And like a bell, with solemn, sweet vibrations,
   I hear once more the voice of Christ say, 'Peace!'

Peace! and no longer from its brazen portals
   The blast of War's great organ shakes the skies!
But beautiful as songs of the immortals,
   The holy melodies of love arise.

The Bridge

I stood on the bridge at midnight,
  As the clocks were striking the hour,
And the moon rose o'er the city,
  Behind the dark church-tower.

I saw her bright reflection
  In the waters under me,
Like a golden goblet falling
  And sinking into the sea.

And far in the hazy distance
  Of that lovely night in June,
The blaze of the flaming furnace
  Gleamed redder than the moon.

Among the long, black rafters
  The waving shadows lay,
And the current that came from the ocean
  Seemed to lift and bear them away;

As, sweeping and eddying through them,
  Rose the belated tide,
And, streaming into the moonlight,
  The seaweed floated wide.

And like those waters rushing
  Among the wooden piers,
A flood of thoughts came o'er me
  That filled my eyes with tears.

How often, O, how often,
  In the days that had gone by,
I had stood on that bridge at midnight,
  And gazed on that wave and sky !

How often, O, how often,
  I had wished that the ebbing tide

Would bear me away on its bosom
  O'er the ocean wild and wide !

For my heart was hot and restless,
  And my life was full of care,
And the burden laid upon me
  Seemed greater than I could bear.

But now it has fallen from me,
  It is buried in the sea ;
And only the sorrow of others
  Throws its shadow over me.

Yet whenever I cross the river
  On its bridge with wooden piers,
Like the odour of brine from the ocean
  Comes the thought of other years.

And I think how many thousands
  Of care-encumbered men,
Each bearing his burden of sorrow,
  Have crossed the bridge since then.

I see the long procession
  Still passing to and fro,
The young heart hot and restless,
  And the old subdued and slow !

And for ever and for ever,
  As long as the river flows,
As long as the heart has passions,
  As long as life has woes ;

The moon and its broken reflection
  And its shadows shall appear,
As the symbol of love in heaven,
  · And its waving image here.

Seaweed

When descends on the Atlantic
   The gigantic
Storm-wind of the equinox,
Landward in his wrath he scourges
   The toiling surges,
Laden with seaweed from the rocks :

From Bermuda's reefs ; from edges
   Of sunken ledges,
In some far-off, bright Azore ;
From Bahama, and the dashing,
   Silver-flashing
Surges of San Salvador ;

From the tumbling surf, that buries
   The Orkneyan skerries,
Answering the hoarse Hebrides ;
And from wrecks of ships, and drifting
   Spars, uplifting
On the desolate, rainy seas ; –

Ever drifting, drifting, drifting
   On the shifting
Currents of the restless main ;
Till in sheltered coves, and reaches
   Of sandy beaches,
All have found repose again.

So when storms of wild emotion
   Strike the ocean
Of the poet's soul, ere long
From each cave and rocky fastness
   In its vastness,
Floats some fragment of a song :

From the far-off isles enchanted,
   Heaven has planted
With the golden fruit of Truth ;

From the flashing surf, whose vision
   Gleams Elysian
In the tropic clime of Youth;

From the strong Will, and the Endeavour
   That for ever
Wrestles with the tides of Fate;
From the wreck of Hopes far-scattered,
   Tempest-shattered,
Floating waste and desolate; –

Ever drifting, drifting, drifting
   On the shifting
Currents of the restless heart;
Till at length in books recorded,
   They, like hoarded
Household words, no more depart.

The Day is Done

The day is done, and the darkness
　Falls from the wings of Night,
As a feather is wafted downward
　From an eagle in his flight.

I see the lights of the village
　Gleam through the rain and the mist,
And a feeling of sadness comes o'er me,
　That my soul cannot resist:

A feeling of sadness and longing,
　That is not akin to pain,
And resembles sorrow only
　As the mist resembles the rain.

Come, read to me some poem,
　Some simple and heartfelt lay,
That shall soothe this restless feeling,
　And banish the thoughts of day.

Not from the grand old masters,
　Not from the bards sublime,
Whose distant footsteps echo
　Through the corridors of Time.

For, like strains of martial music,
　Their mighty thoughts suggest
Life's endless toil and endeavour;
　And to-night I long for rest.

Read from some humbler poet,
　Whose songs gushed from his heart,
As showers from the clouds of summer,
　Or tears from the eyelids start;

Who, through long days of labour,
　And nights devoid of ease,

Still heard in his soul the music
  Of wonderful melodies.

Such songs have power to quiet
  The restless pulse of care,
And come like the benediction
  That follows after prayer.

Then read from the treasured volume
  The poem of thy choice,
And lend to the rhyme of the poet
  The beauty of thy voice.

And the night shall be filled with music,
  And the cares that infest the day,
Shall fold their tents, like the Arabs,
  And as silently, steal away.

Afternoon in February

The day is ending,
The night is descending;
The marsh is frozen,
    The river dead.

Through clouds like ashes
The red sun flashes
On village windows
    That glimmer red.

The snow recommences;
The buried fences
Mark no longer
    The road o'er the plain;

While through the meadows,
Like fearful shadows,
Slowly passes
    A funeral train.

The bell is pealing,
And every feeling
Within me responds
    To the dismal knell;

Shadows are trailing,
My heart is bewailing
And toiling within
    Like a funeral bell.

The Arrow and the Song

I shot an arrow into the air,
It fell to earth, I knew not where;
For, so swiftly it flew, the sight
Could not follow it in its flight.

I breathed a song into the air,
It fell to earth, I knew not where;
For who has sight so keen and strong,
That it can follow the flight of song?

Long, long afterward, in an oak
I found the arrow, still unbroke;
And the song, from beginning to end,
I found again in the heart of a friend.

The Building of the Ship

'Build me straight, O worthy Master !
  Staunch and strong, a goodly vessel,
That shall laugh at all disaster,
  And with wave and whirlwind wrestle !'

The merchant's word
Delighted the Master heard ;
For his heart was in his work, and the heart
Giveth grace unto every Art.
A quiet smile played round his lips,
As the eddies and dimples of the tide
Play round the bows of ships,
That steadily at anchor ride.
And with a voice that was full of glee,
He answered, 'Ere long we will launch
A vessel as goodly, and strong, and staunch,
As ever weathered a wintry sea !'

And first with nicest skill and art,
Perfect and finished in every part,
A little model the Master wrought,
Which should be to the larger plan
What the child is to the man,
Its counterpart in miniature ;
That with a hand more swift and sure
The greater labour might be brought
To answer to his inward thought.
And as he laboured, his mind ran o'er
The various ships that were built of yore,
And above them all, and strangest of all
Towered the Great Harry, crank and tall,
Whose picture was hanging on the wall,
With bows and stern raised high in air,
And balconies hanging here and there,
And signal lanterns and flags afloat,
And eight round towers, like those that frown
From some old castle, looking down
Upon the drawbridge and the moat.

And he said with a smile, 'Our ship, I wis,
Shall be of another form than this!'

It was of another form, indeed;
Built for freight, and yet for speed,
A beautiful and gallant craft;
Broad in the beam, that the stress of the blast
Pressing down upon sail and mast,
Might not the sharp bows overwhelm;
Broad in the beam, but sloping aft
With graceful curve and slow degrees,
That she might be docile to the helm
And that the currents of parted seas,
Closing behind, with mighty force,
Might aid and not impede her course.

In the shipyard stood the Master,
    With the model of the vessel,
That should laugh at all disaster,
    And with wave and whirlwind wrestle!

Covering many a rood of ground,
Lay the timber piled around;
Timber of chestnut and elm and oak,
And scattered here and there, with these,
The knarred and crooked cedar knees;
Brought from regions far away,
From Pascagoula's sunny bay,
And the banks of the roaring Roanoke!
Oh! what a wondrous thing it is
To note how many wheels of toil
One thought, one word, can set in motion!
There's not a ship that sails the ocean,
But every climate, every soil,
Must bring its tribute, great or small,
And help to build the wooden wall!

The sun was rising o'er the sea,
And long the level shadows lay,
As if they, too, the beams would be
Of some great, airy argosy,

Framed and launched in a single day.
That silent architect, the sun,
Had hewn and laid them every one,
Ere the work of man was yet begun.
Beside the Master, when he spoke,
A youth, against an anchor leaning
Listened, to catch his slightest meaning.
Only the long waves, as they broke
In ripples on the pebbly beach,
Interrupted the old man's speech.
Beautiful they were, in sooth,
The old man and the fiery youth!
The old man, in whose busy brain
Many a ship that sailed the main
Was modelled o'er and o'er again; —
The fiery youth, who was to be
The heir of his dexterity,
The heir of his house, and his daughter's hand,
When he had built and launched from land
What the elder head had planned.

'Thus,' said he, 'will we build this ship!
Lay square the blocks upon the slip,
And follow well this plan of mine.
Choose the timbers with greatest care;
Of all that is unsound beware;
For only what is sound and strong
To this vessel shall belong.
Cedar of Maine and Georgia pine
Here together shall combine.
A goodly frame, and a goodly fame,
And the UNION be her name!
For the day that gives her to the sea
Shall give my daughter unto thee!'
The Master's word
Enraptured the young man heard;
And as he turned his face aside,
With a look of joy and a thrill of pride
Standing before
Her father's door,
He saw the form of his promised bride.

The sun shone on her golden hair,
And her cheek was glowing fresh and fair,
With the breath of morn and the soft sea air.
Like a beauteous barge was she,
Still at rest on the sandy beach,
Just beyond the billow's reach;
But he
Was the restless, seething, stormy sea!

Ah, how skilful grows the hand
That obeyeth Love's command!
It is the heart and not the brain,
That to the highest doth attain,
And he who followeth Love's behest
Far exceedeth all the rest!
Thus with the rising of the sun
Was the noble task begun,
And soon throughout the shipyard's bounds
Were heard the intermingled sounds
Of axes and of mallets, plied
With vigorous arms on every side;
Plied so deftly and so well,
That, ere the shadows of evening fell,
The keel of oak for a noble ship,
Scarfed and bolted, straight and strong,
Was lying ready, and stretched along
The blocks, well placed upon the slip.
Happy, thrice happy, every one
Who sees his labour well begun,
And not perplexed and multiplied,
By idly waiting for time and tide!

And when the hot, long day was o'er,
The young man at the Master's door
Sat with the maiden calm and still.
And within the porch, a little more
Removed beyond the evening chill,
The father sat, and told them tales
Of wrecks in the great September gales,
Of pirates upon the Spanish Main,
And ships that never came back again,

The chance and change of a sailor's life,
Want and plenty, rest and strife,
His roving fancy, like the wind,
That nothing can stay and nothing can bind,
And the magic charm of foreign lands,
With shadows of palms, and shining sands,
Where the tumbling surf,
O'er the coral reefs of Madagascar,
Washes the feet of the swarthy Lascar,
As he lies alone and asleep on the turf.
And the trembling maiden held her breath
At the tales of that awful, pitiless sea,
With all its terror and mystery,
The dim, dark sea, so like unto Death,
That divides and yet unites mankind!
And whenever the old man paused, a gleam
From the bowl of his pipe would awhile illume
The silent group in the twilight gloom,
And thoughtful faces, as in a dream;
And for a moment one might mark
What had been hidden by the dark,
That the head of the maiden lay at rest,
Tenderly, on the young man's breast!

Day by day the vessel grew,
With timbers fashioned strong and true,
Stemson and keelson and sternson-knee,
Till, framed with perfect symmetry,
A skeleton ship rose up to view!
All around the bows and along the side
The heavy hammers and mallets plied,
Till, after many a week, at length,
Wonderful for form and strength,
Sublime in its enormous bulk,
Loomed aloft the shadowy hulk!
And around it columns of smoke, upwreathing,
Rose from the boiling, bubbling, seething
Caldron, that glowed,
And overflowed
With the black tar, heated for the sheathing.
And amid the clamours

Of clattering hammers,
He who listened heard now and then
The song of the Master and his men : –

'Build me straight, O worthy Master,
   Staunch and strong, a goodly vessel,
That shall laugh at all disaster,
   And with wave and whirlwind wrestle !'

With oaken brace and copper band,
Lay the rudder on the sand,
That, like a thought, should have control
Over the movement of the whole ;
And near it the anchor, whose giant hand
Would reach down and grapple with the land,
And immovable and fast
Hold the great ship against the bellowing blast !
And at the bows an image stood,
By a cunning artist carved in wood,
With robes of white, that far behind
Seemed to be fluttering in the wind.
It was not shaped in a classic mould,
Not like a Nymph or Goddess of old,
Or Naiad rising from the water,
But modelled from the Master's daughter !
On many a dreary and misty night,
'Twill be seen by the rays of the signal light,
Speeding along through the rain and the dark,
Like a ghost in its snow-white sark,
The pilot of some phantom bark,
Guiding the vessel, in its flight,
By a path none other knows aright !
Behold, at last
Each tall and tapering mast
Is swung into its place ;
Shrouds and stays
Holding it firm and fast !

Long ago,
In the deer-haunted forests of Maine,
When upon mountain and plain

Lay the snow,
They fell, – those lordly pines !
Those grand, majestic pines !
Mid shouts and cheers
The jaded steers,
Panting beneath the goad,
Dragged down the weary, winding road
Those captive kings so straight and tall.
To be shorn of their streaming hair,
And, naked and bare,
To feel the stress and the strain
Of the wind and the reeling main,
Whose roar
Would remind them for evermore
Of their native forests they should not see again.

And everywhere
The slender, graceful spars
Poise aloft in the air,
And at the mast-head,
White, blue, and red,
A flag unrolls the stripes and stars.
Ah ! when the wanderer, lonely, friendless,
In foreign harbours shall behold
That flag unrolled,
'Twill be as a friendly hand
Stretched out from his native land,
Filling his heart with memories sweet and endless !

All is finished ! and at length
Has come the bridal day
Of beauty and of strength.
To-day the vessel shall be launched !
With fleecy clouds the sky is blanched,
And o'er the bay,
Slowly, in all his splendours dight,
The great sun rises to behold the sight.

The ocean old,
Centuries old,
Strong as youth, and as uncontrolled,

Paces restless to and fro,
Up and down the sands of gold.
His beating heart is not at rest;
And far and wide,
With ceaseless flow,
His beard of snow
Heaves with the heaving of his breast.
He waits impatient for his bride.
There she stands,
With her foot upon the sands,
Decked with flags and streamers gay,
In honour of her marriage day,
Her snow-white signals fluttering, blending,
Round her like a veil descending,
Ready to be
The bride of the gray, old sea.

On the deck another bride
Is standing by her lover's side.
Shadows from the flags and shrouds,
Like the shadows cast by clouds,
Broken by many a sunny fleck,
Fall around them on the deck.

The prayer is said,
The service read,
The joyous bridegroom bows his head.
And in tears the good old Master
Shakes the brown hand of his son,
Kisses his daughter's glowing cheek
In silence, for he cannot speak,
And ever faster
Down his own the tears begin to run.
The worthy pastor –
The shepherd of that wandering flock,
That has the ocean for its wold,
That has the vessel for its fold,
Leaping ever from rock to rock –
Spake, with accents mild and clear,
Words of warning, words of cheer,
But tedious to the bridegroom's ear.

He knew the chart
Of the sailor's heart,
All its pleasures and its griefs,
All its shallows and rocky reefs,
All those secret currents, that flow
With such resistless undertow,
And lift and drift, with terrible force,
The will from its moorings and its course,
Therefore he spake, and thus said he : —
'Like unto ships far off at sea,
Outward or homeward bound, are we.
Before, behind and all around,
Floats and swings the horizon's bound,
Seems at its distant rim to rise
And climb the crystal wall of the skies,
And then again to turn and sink,
As if we could slide from its outer brink.
Ah ! it is not the sea,
It is not the sea that sinks and shelves,
But ourselves
That rock and rise
With endless and uneasy motion,
Now touching the very skies,
Now sinking into the depths of ocean.
Ah ! if our souls but poise and swing
Like the compass in its brazen ring,
Ever level and ever true
To the toil and the task we have to do,
We shall sail securely, and safely reach
The Fortunate Isles, on whose shining beach
The sights we see, and the sounds we hear,
Will be those of joy and not of fear !'

Then the Master,
With a gesture of command,
Waved his hand ;
And at the word,
Loud and sudden there was heard,
All around them and below,
The sound of hammers, blow on blow,
Knocking away the shores and spurs.

And see ! she stirs !
She starts, — she moves, — she seems to feel
The thrill of life along her keel,
And, spurning with her foot the ground,
With one exulting, joyous, bound,
She leaps into the ocean's arms !
And lo ! from the assembled crowd
There rose a shout, prolonged and loud,
That to the ocean seemed to say, —
'Take her, O bridegroom, old and gray,
Take her to thy protecting arms,
With all her youth and all her charms !'
How beautiful she is ! How fair
She lies within those arms, that press
Her form with many a soft caress
Of tenderness and watchful care !
Sail forth into the sea, O ship !
Through wind and wave, right onward steer !
The moistened eye, the trembling lip,
Are not the signs of doubt or fear.
Sail forth into the sea of life,
O gentle, loving, trusting wife,
And safe from all adversity
Upon the bosom of that sea
Thy comings and thy goings be !
For gentleness and love and trust
Prevail o'er angry wave and gust ;
And in the wreck of noble lives
Something immortal still survives !

Thou, too, sail on, O Ship of State !
Sail on, O UNION, strong and great !
Humanity with all its fears,
With all the hopes of future years,
Is hanging breathless on thy fate !
We know what Master laid thy keel,
What Workmen wrought thy ribs of steel,
Who made each mast, and sail, and rope,
What anvils rang, what hammers beat,
In what a forge and what a heat
Were shaped the anchors of thy hope !

Fear not each sudden sound and shock,
'Tis of the wave and not the rock ;
'Tis but the flapping of the sail,
And not a rent made by the gale !
In spite of rock and tempest's roar,
In spite of false lights on the shore,
Sail on, nor fear to breast the sea !
Our hearts, our hopes, are all with thee,
Our hearts, our hopes, our prayers, our tears,
Our faith triumphant o'er our fears,
Are all with thee, – are all with thee !

Twilight

The twilight is sad and cloudy,
  The wind blows wild and free,
And like the wings of sea-birds
  Flash the white caps of the sea.

But in the fisherman's cottage
  There shines a ruddier light
And a little face at the window
  Peers out into the night.

Close, close it is pressed to the window,
  As if those childish eyes
Were looking into the darkness,
  To see some form arise.

And a woman's waving shadow
  Is passing to and fro,
Now rising to the ceiling,
  Now bowing and bending low.

What tale do the roaring ocean,
  And the night-wind, bleak and wild,
As they beat at the crazy casement,
  Tell to that little child?

And why do the roaring ocean,
  And the night-wind, wild and bleak,
As they beat at the heart of the mother,
  Drive the colour from her cheek?

Sir Humphrey Gilbert

Southward with fleet of ice
  Sailed the corsair Death;
Wild and fast blew the blast,
  And the east-wind was his breath.

His lordly ships of ice
  Glistened in the sun;
On each side, like pennons wide,
  Flashing crystal streamlets run.

His sails of white sea-mist
  Dripped with silver rain;
But where he passed there were cast
  Leaden shadows o'er the main.

Eastward from Campobello
  Sir Humphrey Gilbert sailed;
Three days or more seaward he bore,
  Then, alas! the land-wind failed.

Alas! the land-wind failed,
  And ice-cold grew the night;
And never more, on sea or shore,
  Should Sir Humphrey see the light.

He sat upon the deck,
  The Book was in his hand;
'Do not fear! Heaven is as near,'
  He said, 'by water as by land!'

In the first watch of the night,
  Without a signal's sound,
Out of the sea, mysteriously,
  The fleet of Death rose all around.

The moon and the evening star
  Were hanging in the shrouds;

Every mast, as it passed,
   Seemed to rake the passing clouds.

They grappled with their prize,
   At midnight black and cold!
As of a rock was the shock;
   Heavily the ground-swell rolled.

Southward through day and dark,
   They drift in close embrace,
With mist and rain, to the Spanish Main;
   Yet there seems no change of place.

Southward, for ever southward,
   They drift through dark and day;
And like a dream, in the Gulf Stream
   Sinking, vanish all away.

The Fire of Drift-Wood

We sat within the farmhouse old,
   Whose windows, looking o'er the bay,
Gave to the sea-breeze, damp and cold,
   An easy entrance, night and day.

Not far away we saw the port, –
   The strange, old-fashioned, silent town, –
The lighthouse, – the dismantled fort, –
   The wooden houses, quaint and brown.

We sat and talked until the night,
   Descending, filled the little room;
Our faces faded from the sight,
   Our voices only broke the gloom.

We spake of many a vanished scene,
   Of what we once had thought and said,
Of what had been, and might have been,
   And who was changed, and who was dead.

And all that fills the hearts of friends,
   When first they feel, with secret pain,
Their lives thenceforth have separate ends,
   And never can be one again;

The first slight swerving of the heart,
   That words are powerless to express,
And leave it still unsaid in part,
   Or say it in too great excess.

The very tones in which we spake
   Had something strange, I could but mark;
The leaves of memory seemed to make
   A mournful rustling in the dark.

Oft died the words upon our lips,
   As suddenly, from out the fire

Built of the wreck of stranded ships,
   The flames would leap and then expire.

And, as their splendour flashed and failed,
   We thought of wrecks upon the main, –
Of ships dismasted, that were hailed
   And sent no answer back again.

The windows, rattling in their frames, –
   The ocean, roaring up the beach, –
The gusty blast, – the bickering flames,
   All mingled vaguely in our speech;

Until they made themselves a part
   Of fancies floating through the brain,
The long-lost ventures of the heart,
   That send no answers back again.

O flames that glowed! O hearts that yearned!
   They were indeed too much akin,
The drift-wood fire without that burned,
   The thoughts that burned and glowed within.

The Builders

All are architects of Fate,
　Working in these walls of Time;
Some with massive deeds and great,
　Some with ornaments of rhyme.

Nothing useless is, or low;
　Each thing in its place is best;
And what seems but idle show
　Strengthens and supports the rest.

For the structure that we raise,
　Time is with materials filled;
Our to-days and yesterdays
　Are the blocks with which we build.

Truly shape and fashion these;
　Leave no yawning gaps between;
Think not, because no man sees,
　Such things will remain unseen.

In the elder days of Art,
　Builders wrought with greatest care
Each minute an unseen part;
　For the Gods see everywhere.

Let us do our work as well,
　Both the unseen and the seen!
Make the house, where Gods may dwell,
　Beautiful, entire, and clean.

Else our lives are incomplete,
　Standing in these walls of Time,
Broken stairways, where the feet
　Stumble as they seek to climb.

Build to-day, then, strong and sure,
　With a firm and ample base;

And ascending and secure
  Shall to-morrow find its place.

Thus alone can we attain
  To those turrets, where the eye
Sees the world as one vast plain,
  And one boundless reach of sky.

Sand of the Desert in an Hour-Glass

A handful of red sand, from the hot clime
   Of Arab deserts brought,
Within this glass becomes the spy of Time,
   The minister of Thought.

How many weary centuries has it been
   About those deserts blown !
How many strange vicissitudes has seen,
   How many histories known !

Perhaps the camels of the Ishmaelite
   Trampled and passed it o'er,
When into Egypt from the patriarch's sight
   His favourite son they bore.

Perhaps the feet of Moses, burnt and bare,
   Crushed it beneath their tread ;
Or Pharaoh's flashing wheels into the air
   Scattered it as they sped ;

Or Mary, with the Christ of Nazareth
   Held close in her caress,
Whose pilgrimage of hope and love and faith
   Illumed the wilderness ;

Or anchorites beneath Engaddi's palms
   Pacing the Dead Sea beach,
And singing slow their old Armenian psalms
   In half-articulate speech ;

Or caravans, that from Bassora's gate
   With westward steps depart ;
Or Mecca's pilgrims, confident of Fate,
   And resolute in heart !

These have passed over it, or may have passed !
   Now in this crystal tower

Imprisoned by some curious hand at last,
  It counts the passing hour.

And as I gaze, these narrow walls expand : –
  Before my dreamy eye
Stretches the desert with its shifting sand,
  Its unimpeded sky.

And borne aloft by the sustaining blast,
  This little golden thread
Dilates into a column high and vast,
  A form of fear and dread.

And onward, and across the setting sun,
  Across the boundless plain,
The column and its broader shadow run,
  Till thought pursues in vain.

The vision vanishes ! These walls again
  Shut out the lurid sun,
Shut out the hot, immeasurable plain ;
  The half-hour's sand is run !

The Open Window

The old house by the lindens
    Stood silent in the shade,
And on the gravelled pathway
    The light and shadow played.

I saw the nursery windows
    Wide open to the air;
But the faces of the children,
    They were no longer there.

The large Newfoundland house-dog
    Was standing by the door;
He looked for his little playmates,
    Who would return no more.

They walked not under the lindens,
    They played not in the hall;
But shadow, and silence, and sadness
    Were hanging over all.

The birds sang in the branches,
    With sweet, familiar tone;
But the voices of the children
    Will be heard in dreams alone!

And the boy that walked beside me
    He could not understand
Why closer in mine, ah! closer,
    I pressed his warm, soft hand!

The Singers

God sent his singers upon earth
With songs of sadness and of mirth,
That they might touch the hearts of men,
And bring them back to heaven again.

The first a youth, with soul of fire,
Held in his hand a golden lyre;
Through groves he wandered, and by streams,
Playing the music of our dreams.

The second, with a bearded face,
Stood singing in the market-place,
And stirred with accents deep and loud
The hearts of all the listening crowd.

A gray, old man, the third and last,
Sang in cathedrals dim and vast,
While the majestic organ rolled
Contrition from its mouths of gold.

And those who heard the Singers three
Disputed which the best might be;
For still their music seemed to start
Discordant echoes in each heart.

But the great Master said, 'I see
No best in kind, but in degree;
I gave a various gift to each,
To charm, to strengthen, and to teach.

'These are the three great chords of might,
And he whose ear is tuned aright
Will hear no discord in the three,
But the most perfect harmony.'

The Ladder of St Augustine

Saint Augustine! well hast thou said,
    That of our vices we can frame
A ladder, if we will but tread
    Beneath our feet each deed of shame!

All common things, each day's events,
    That with the hour begin and end,
Our pleasures and our discontents,
    Are rounds by which we may ascend.

The low desire, the base design,
    That makes another's virtues less;
The revel of the ruddy wine,
    And all occasions of excess;

The longing for ignoble things;
    The strife for triumph more than truth;
The hardening of the heart, that brings
    Irreverence for the dreams of youth;

All thoughts of ill; all evil deeds,
    That have their root in thoughts of ill;
Whatever hinders or impedes
    The action of the nobler will; –

All these must first be trampled down
    Beneath our feet, if we would gain
In the bright fields of fair renown
    The right of eminent domain.

We have not wings, we cannot soar;
    But we have feet to scale and climb
By slow degrees, by more and more,
    The cloudy summits of our time.

The mighty pyramids of stone
    That wedge-like cleave the desert airs,

When nearer seen, and better known,
  Are but gigantic flights of stairs.

The distant mountains, that uprear
  Their solid bastions to the skies,
Are crossed by pathways, that appear
  As we to higher levels rise.

The heights by great men reached and kept
  Were not attained by sudden flight,
But they, while their companions slept,
  Were toiling upward in the night.

Standing on what too long we bore
  With shoulders bent and downcast eyes,
We may discern – unseen before –
  A path to higher destinies.

Nor deem the irrevocable Past,
  As wholly wasted, wholly vain,
If, rising on its wrecks, at last
  To something nobler we attain.

The Warden of the Cinque Ports

A mist was driving down the British Channel,
  The day was just begun,
And through the window-panes, on floor and panel,
  Streamed the red autumn sun.

It glanced on flowing flag and rippling pennon,
  And the white sails of ships ;
And, from the frowning rampart, the black cannon
  Hailed it with feverish lips.

Sandwich and Romney, Hastings, Hythe, and Dover,
  Were all alert that day,
To see the French war-streamers speeding over,
  When the fog cleared away.

Sullen and silent, and like couchant lions,
  Their cannon, through the night,
Holding their breath, had watched, in grim defiance,
  The sea-coast opposite.

And now they roared at drum-beat from their stations
  On every citadel,
Each answering each, with morning salutations,
  That all was well.

And down the coast, all taking up the burden,
  Replied the distant forts,
As if to summon from his sleep the Warden
  And Lord of the Cinque Ports.

Him shall no sunshine from the fields of azure,
  No drum-beat from the wall,
No morning gun from the black fort's embrasure,
  Awaken with its call !

No more, surveying with an eye impartial
  The long line of the coast,

Shall the gaunt figure of the old Field-Marshal
  Be seen upon his post !

For in the night, unseen, a single warrior,
  In sombre harness mailed,
Dreaded of man, and surnamed the Destroyer,
  The rampart wall has scaled.

He passed into the chamber of the sleeper,
  The dark and silent room,
And as he entered, darker grew and deeper,
  The silence and the gloom.

He did not pause to parley or dissemble,
  But smote the Warden hoar ;
Ah ! what a blow ! that made all England tremble
  And groan from shore to shore.

Meanwhile without, the surly cannon waited,
  The sun rose bright o'erhead ;
Nothing in Nature's aspect intimated
  That a great man was dead.

Haunted Houses

All houses wherein men have lived and died
   Are haunted houses. Through the open doors
The harmless phantoms on their errands glide,
   With feet that make no sound upon the floors.

We meet them at the door-way, on the stair,
   Along the passages they come and go,
Impalpable impressions on the air,
   A sense of something moving to and fro.

There are more guests at table, than the hosts
   Invited; the illuminated hall
Is thronged with quiet, inoffensive ghosts,
   As silent as the pictures on the wall.

The stranger at my fireside cannot see
   The forms I see, nor hear the sounds I hear;
He but perceives what is; while unto me
   All that has been is visible and clear.

We have no title-deeds to house or lands;
   Owners and occupants of earlier dates
From graves forgotten stretch their dusty hands,
   And hold in mortmain still their old estates.

The spirit-world around this world of sense
   Floats like an atmosphere, and everywhere
Wafts through these earthly mists and vapours dense
   A vital breath of more ethereal air.

Our little lives are kept in equipoise
   By opposite attractions and desires;
The struggle of the instinct that enjoys,
   And the more noble instinct that aspires.

These perturbations, this perpetual jar
   Of earthly wants and aspirations high,

Come from the influence of an unseen star,
   An undiscovered planet in our sky.

And as the moon from some dark gate of cloud
   Throws o'er the sea a floating bridge of light,
Across whose trembling planks our fancies crowd,
   Into the realm of mystery and night, –

So from the world of spirits there descends
   A bridge of light, connecting it with this,
O'er whose unsteady floor, that sways and bends,
   Wander our thoughts above the dark abyss.

In the Churchyard at Cambridge

In the village churchyard she lies,
Dust is in her beautiful eyes,
   No more she breathes, nor feels, nor stirs;
At her feet and at her head
Lies a slave to attend the dead,
   But their dust is white as hers.

Was she a lady of high degree,
So much in love with the vanity
   And foolish pomp of this world of ours?
Or was it Christian charity,
And lowliness and humility,
   The richest and rarest of all dowers?

Who shall tell us? No one speaks;
No colour shoots into those cheeks,
   Either of anger or of pride,
At the rude question we have asked;
Nor will the mystery be unmasked
   By those who are sleeping at her side.

Hereafter? – And do you think to look
On the terrible pages of that Book
   To find her failings, faults, and errors?
Ah; you will then have other cares,
In your own shortcomings and despairs,
   In your own secret sins and terrors!

The Two Angels

Two angels, one of Life and one of Death,
   Passed o'er our village as the morning broke;
The dawn was on their faces, and beneath,
   The sombre houses hearsed with plumes of smoke.

Their attitude and aspect were the same,
   Alike their features and their robes of white;
But one was crowned with amaranth, as with flame,
   And one with asphodels, like flakes of light.

I saw them pause on their celestial way;
   Then said I, with deep fear and doubt oppressed,
'Beat not so loud, my heart, lest thou betray
   The place where thy beloved are at rest!'

And he who wore the crown of asphodels,
   Descending, at my door began to knock,
And my soul sank within me, as in wells
   The waters sink before an earthquake's shock.

I recognised the nameless agony,
   The terror and the tremor and the pain,
That oft before had filled or haunted me,
   And now returned with threefold strength again.

The door I opened to my heavenly guest,
   And listened, for I thought I heard God's voice;
And, knowing whatsoe'er he sent was best,
   Dared neither to lament nor to rejoice.

Then with a smile, that filled the house with light,
   'My errand is not Death, but Life,' he said;
And ere I answered, passing out of sight,
   On his celestial embassy he sped.

'Twas at thy door, O friend! and not at mine,
   The angel with the amaranthine wreath,

Pausing, descended, and with voice divine,
  Whispered a word that had a sound like Death.

Then fell upon the house a sudden gloom,
  A shadow on those features fair and thin;
And softly, from that hushed and darkened room,
  Two angels issued, where but one went in.

All is of God! If he but wave his hand,
  The mists collect, the rain falls thick and loud,
Till, with a smile of light on sea and land,
  Lo! he looks back from the departing cloud.

Angels of Life and Death alike are his;
  Without his leave they pass no threshold o'er;
Who, then, would wish or dare, believing this,
  Against his messengers to shut the door?

The Jewish Cemetery at Newport

How strange it seems ! These Hebrews in their graves,
　　Close by the street of this fair seaport town.
Silent beside the never-silent waves,
　　At rest in all this moving up and down !

The trees are white with dust, that o'er their sleep
　　Wave their broad curtains in the south-wind's breath,
While underneath such leafy tents they keep
　　The long, mysterious Exodus of Death.

And these sepulchral stones, so old and brown,
　　That pave with level flags their burial-place,
Seem like the tablets of the Law, thrown down
　　And broken by Moses at the mountain's base.

The very names recorded here are strange,
　　Of foreign accent, and of different climes :
Alvares and Rivera interchange
　　With Abraham and Jacob of old times.

'Blessed be God ! for he created Death !'
　　The mourners said, 'and Death is rest and peace' ;
Then added, in the certainty of faith,
　　'And giveth Life that never more shall cease.'

Closed are the portals of their Synagogue,
　　No Psalms of David now the silence break,
No Rabbi reads the ancient Decalogue
　　In the grand dialect the Prophets spake.

Gone are the living, but the dead remain,
　　And not neglected ; for a hand unseen,
Scattering its bounty, like a summer rain,
　　Still keeps their graves and their remembrance green.

How came they here ? What burst of Christian hate,
　　What persecution, merciless and blind,

Drove o'er the sea – that desert desolate –
   These Ishmaels and Hagars of mankind?

They lived in narrow streets and lanes obscure,
   Ghetto and Judenstrass, in mirk and mire;
Taught in the school of patience to endure
   The life of anguish and the death of fire.

All their lives long, with the unleavened bread
   And bitter herbs of exile and its fears,
The wasting famine of the heart they fed,
   And slaked its thirst with marah of their tears.

Anathema marantha! was the cry
   That rang from town to town, from street to street;
At every gate the accursed Mordecai
   Was mocked and jeered, and spurned by Christian feet.

Pride and humiliation hand in hand
   Walked with them through the world where'er they went;
Trampled and beaten were they as the sand,
   And yet unshaken as the continent.

For in the background figures vague and vast
   Of patriarchs and of prophets rose sublime,
And all the great traditions of the Past
   They saw reflected in the coming time.

And thus for ever with reverted look
   The mystic volume of the world they read,
Spelling it backward, like a Hebrew book.
   Till life became a Legend of the Dead.

But ah! what once has been shall be no more!
   The groaning earth in travail and in pain
Brings forth its races, but does not restore,
   And the dead nations never rise again.

My Lost Youth

Often I think of the beautiful town
   That is seated by the sea ;
Often in thought go up and down
The pleasant streets of that dear old town.
   And my youth comes back to me,
     And a verse of a Lapland song
     Is haunting my memory still :
  'A boy's will is the wind's will,
And the thoughts of youth are long, long thoughts.'

I can see the shadowy lines of its trees,
   And catch, in sudden gleams,
The sheen of the far-surrounding seas,
And islands that were the Hesperides
   Of all my boyish dreams.
     And the burden of that old song,
     It murmurs and whispers still :
  'A boy's will is the wind's will,
And the thoughts of youth are long, long thoughts.'

I remember the black wharves and the slips,
   And the sea-tides tossing free ;
And Spanish sailors with bearded lips,
And the beauty and mystery of the ships,
   And the magic of the sea.
     And the voice of that wayward song,
     Is singing and saying still :
  'A boy's will is the wind's will,
And the thoughts of youth are long, long thoughts.'

I remember the bulwarks by the shore,
   And the fort upon the hill ;
The sunrise gun, with its hollow roar,
The drum-beat repeated o'er and o'er,
   And the bugle wild and shrill.
     And the music of that old song
     Throbs in my memory still :

'A boy's will is the wind's will,
And the thoughts of youth are long, long thoughts.'

I remember the sea-fight far away,
    How it thundered o'er the tide !
And the dead captains, as they lay
In their graves, o'erlooking the tranquil bay,
    Where they in battle died.
        And the sound of that mournful song
        Goes through me with a thrill :
'A boy's will is the wind's will,
And the thoughts of youth are long, long thoughts.'

I can see the breezy dome of groves,
    The shadows of Deering's Woods ;
And the friendships old and the early loves
Come back with a Sabbath sound, as of doves
    In quiet neighbourhoods.
        And the verse of that sweet old song,
        It flutters and murmurs still :
'A boy's will is the wind's will,
And the thoughts of youth are long, long thoughts.'

I remember the gleams and glooms that dart
    Across the schoolboy's brain ;
The song and the silence in the heart,
That in part are prophecies, and in part
    Are longings wild and vain.
        And the voice of that fitful song
        Sings on, and is never still :
'A boy's will is the wind's will,
And the thoughts of youth are long, long thoughts.'

There are things of which I may not speak ;
    There are dreams that cannot die ;
There are thoughts that make the strong heart weak,
And bring a pallor into the cheek,
    And a mist before the eye.
        And the words to that fatal song
        Come over me like a chill :

'A boy's will is the wind's will,
And the thoughts of youth are long, long thoughts.'

Strange to me now are the forms I meet
   When I visit the dear old town;
But the native air is pure and sweet,
And the trees that o'ershadow each well-known street,
   As they balance up and down,
     Are singing the beautiful song,
     Are sighing and whispering still:
  'A boy's will is the wind's will,
And the thoughts of youth are long, long thoughts.'

And Deering's Woods are fresh and fair,
   And with joy that is almost pain
My heart goes back to wander there,
And among the dreams of the days that were,
   I find my lost youth again.
     And the strange and beautiful song,
     The groves are repeating it still:
  'A boy's will is the wind's will,
And the thoughts of youth are long, long thoughts.'

The Ropewalk

In that building, long and low,
With its windows all a-row,
    Like the port-holes of a hulk,
Human spiders spin and spin,
Backward down their threads so thin
    Dropping, each a hempen bulk.

At the end, an open door;
Squares of sunshine on the floor
    Light the long and dusky lane;
And the whirring of a wheel,
Dull and drowsy, makes me feel
    All its spokes are in my brain.

As the spinners to the end
Downward go and reascend,
    Gleam the long threads in the sun;
While within this brain of mine
Cobwebs brighter and more fine
    By the busy wheel are spun.

Two fair maidens in a swing,
Like white doves upon the wing,
    First before my vision pass;
Laughing, as their gentle hands
Closely clasp the twisted strands,
    At their shadow on the grass.

Then a booth of mountebanks,
With its smell of tan and planks,
    And a girl poised high in air
On a cord, in spangled dress,
With a faded loveliness,
    And a weary look of care.

Then a homestead among farms,
And a woman with bare arms
    Drawing water from a well;

As the bucket mounts apace,
With it mounts her own fair face,
   As at some magician's spell.

Then an old man in a tower,
Ringing loud the noontide hour,
   While the rope coils round and round
Like a serpent at his feet,
And again, in swift retreat,
   Nearly lifts him from the ground.

Then within a prison-yard,
Faces fixed, and stern, and hard,
   Laughter and indecent mirth ;
Ah ! it is the gallows-tree !
Breath of Christian charity,
   Blow, and sweep it from the earth !

Then a schoolboy, with his kite
Gleaming in a sky of light,
   And an eager, upward look ;
Steeds pursued through land and field ;
Fowlers with their snares concealed ;
   And an angler by a brook.

Ships rejoicing in the breeze,
Wrecks that float o'er unknown seas,
   Anchors dragged through faithless sand ;
Sea-fog drifting overhead,
And, with lessening line and lead,
   Sailors feeling for the land.

All these scenes do I behold,
These, and many left untold,
   In that building long and low ;
While the wheel goes round and round,
With a drowsy, dreamy sound,
   And the spinners backward go.

Something Left Undone

Labour with what zeal we will,
   Something still remains undone,
Something uncompleted still
   Waits the rising of the sun.

By the bedside, on the stair,
   At the threshold, near the gates,
With its menace or its prayer,
   Like a mendicant it waits ;

Waits, and will not go away ;
   Waits, and will not be gainsaid ;
By the cares of yesterday
   Each to-day is heavier made ;

Till at length the burden seems
   Greater than our strength can bear,
Heavy as the weight of dreams,
   Pressing on us everywhere.

And we stand from day to day,
   Like the dwarfs of times gone by,
Who, as Northern legends say,
   On their shoulders held the sky.

The Haunted Chamber

Each heart has its haunted chamber,
  Where the silent moonlight falls !
On the floor are mysterious footsteps,
  There are whispers along the walls !

And mine at times is haunted
  By phantoms of the Past,
As motionless as shadows
  By the silent moonlight cast.

A form sits by the window,
  That is not seen by day,
For as soon as the dawn approaches
  It vanishes away.

It sits there in the moonlight,
  Itself as pale and still,
And points with its airy finger
  Across the window-sill.

Without, before the window,
  There stands a gloomy pine,
Whose boughs wave upward and downward
  As wave these thoughts of mine.

And underneath its branches
  Is the grave of a little child,
Who died upon life's threshold,
  And never wept nor smiled.

What are ye, O pallid phantoms !
  That haunt my troubled brain ?
That vanish when day approaches,
  And at night return again ?

What are ye, O pallid phantoms !
  But the statues without breath,
That stand on the bridge overarching
  The silent river of death ?

The Meeting

After so long an absence
    At last we meet again :
Does the meeting give us pleasure,
    Or does it give us pain ?

The tree of life has been shaken,
    And but few of us linger now,
Like the Prophet's two or three berries
    In the top of the uppermost bough.

We cordially greet each other
    In the old, familiar tone ;
And we think, though we do not say it,
    How old and gray he is grown !

We speak of a Merry Christmas
    And many a Happy New Year ;
But each in his heart is thinking
    Of those that are not here.

We speak of friends and their fortunes,
    And of what they did and said,
Till the dead alone seem living,
    And the living alone seem dead.

And at last we hardly distinguish
    Between the ghosts and the guests ;
And a mist and shadow of sadness
    Steals over our merriest jests.

Vox Populi

When Mazárvan the magician
   Journeyed westward through Cathay,
Nothing heard he but the praises
   Of Badoura on his way.

But the lessening rumour ended
   When he came to Khaledan,
There the folk were talking only
   Of Prince Camaralzaman.

So it happens with the poets :
   Every province hath its own ;
Camaralzaman is famous
   Where Badoura is unknown.

Changed

From the outskirts of the town,
    Where of old the mile-stone stood,
Now a stranger, looking down
I behold the shadowy crown
    Of the dark and haunted wood.

Is it changed, or am I changed?
    Ah! the oaks are fresh and green,
But the friends with whom I ranged
Through their thickets are estranged
    By the years that intervene.

Bright as ever flows the sea,
    Bright as ever shines the sun,
But, alas! they seem to me
Not the sun that used to be,
    Not the tides that used to run.

The Brook and the Wave

The brooklet came from the mountain,
  As sang the bard of old,
Running with feet of silver
  Over the sands of gold !

Far away in the briny ocean
  There rolled a turbulent wave,
Now singing along the sea-beach,
  Now howling along the cave.

And the brooklet has found the billow,
  Though they flowed so far apart,
And has filled with its freshness and sweetness
  That turbulent, bitter heart !

Aftermath

When the Summer fields are mown,
When the birds are fledged and flown,
    And the dry leaves strew the path;
With the falling of the snow,
With the cawing of the crow,
Once again the fields we mow
    And gather in the aftermath.

Not the sweet, new grass with flowers
Is this harvesting of ours;
    Not the upland clover bloom;
But the rowen mixed with weeds,
Tangled tufts from marsh and meads,
Where the poppy drops its seeds
    In the silence and the gloom.

Palingenesis

I lay upon the headland-height, and listened
To the incessant sobbing of the sea
  In caverns under me,
And watched the waves, that tossed and fled and glistened
Until the rolling meadows of amethyst
  Melted away in mist.

Then suddenly, as one from sleep, I started;
For round about me all the sunny capes
  Seemed peopled with the shapes
Of those whom I had known in days departed,
Apparelled in the loveliness which gleams
  On faces seen in dreams.

A moment only, and the light and glory
Faded away, and the disconsolate shore
  Stood lonely as before;
And the wild-roses of the promontory
Around me shuddered in the wind, and shed
  Their petals of pale red.

There was an old belief that in the embers
Of all things their primordial form exists,
  And cunning alchemists
Could re-create the rose with all its members
From its own ashes, but without the bloom,
  Without the lost perfume.

Ah me! What wonder-working, occult science
Can from the ashes in our hearts once more
  The rose of youth restore?
What craft of alchemy can bid defiance
To time and change, and for a single hour
  Renew this phantom-flower?

'Oh, give me back,' I cried, 'the vanished splendours,
The breath of morn, and the exultant strife,
  When the swift stream of life

Bounds o'er its rocky channel, and surrenders
The pond, with all its lilies, for the leap
    Into the unknown deep !'

And the sea answered, with a lamentation,
Like some old prophet wailing, and it said,
    'Alas ! thy youth is dead !
It breathes no more, its heart has no pulsation ;
In the dark places with the dead of old
    It lies for ever cold !'

Then said I, 'From its consecrated cerements
I will not drag this sacred dust again,
    Only to give me pain ;
But, still remembering all the lost endearments,
Go on my way, like one who looks before,
    And turns to weep no more.'

Into what land of harvests, what plantations
Bright with autumnal foliage and the glow
    Of sunsets burning low ;
Beneath what midnight skies, whose constellations
Light up the spacious avenues between
    This world and the unseen !

Amid what friendly greetings and caresses,
What households, though not alien, yet not mine,
    What bowers of rest divine ;
To what temptations in lone wildernesses,
What famine of the heart, what pain and loss,
    The bearing of what cross !

I do not know ; nor will I vainly question
Those pages of the mystic book which hold
    The story still untold,
But without rash conjecture or suggestion
Turn its last leaves in reverence and good heed,
    Until 'The End' I read.

Concord

[NATHANIEL HAWTHORNE]

May 23, 1864

How beautiful it was, that one bright day
   In the long week of rain!
Though all its splendour could not chase away
   The omnipresent pain.

The lovely town was white with apple-blooms,
   And the great elms o'erhead
Dark shadows wove on their ærial looms
   Shot through with golden thread.

Across the meadows, by the gray old manse,
   The historic river flowed; —
I was as one who wanders in a trance,
   Unconscious of his road.

The faces of familiar friends seemed strange;
   Their voices I could hear,
And yet the words they uttered seemed to change
   Their meaning to my ear.

For the one face I looked for was not there,
   The one low voice was mute;
Only an unseen presence filled the air,
   And baffled my pursuit.

Now I look back, and meadow, manse, and stream
   Dimly my thought defines;
I only see — a dream within a dream —
   The hill-top hearsed with pines.

I only hear above his place of rest
   Their tender undertone,
The infinite longings of a troubled breast,
   The voice so like his own.

There in seclusion and remote from men
    The wizard hand lies cold,
Which at its topmost speed let fall the pen,
    And left the tale half told.

Ah ! who shall lift that wand of magic power,
    And the lost clue regain ?
The unfinished window in Aladdin's tower
    Unfinished must remain !

Giotto's Tower

How many lives, made beautiful and sweet
   By self-devotion and by self-restraint, —
   Whose pleasure is to run without complaint
   On unknown errands of the Paraclete, —
Wanting the reverence of unshodden feet,
   Fail of the nimbus which the artists paint
   Around the shining forehead of the saint,
   And are in their completeness incomplete !
In the old Tuscan town stands Giotto's tower,
   The lily of Florence blossoming in stone, —
   A vision, a delight, and a desire, —
The builder's perfect and centennial flower,
   That in the night of ages bloomed alone.
   But wanting still the glory of the spire.

To-morrow

'Tis late at night, and in the realm of sleep
  My little lambs are folded like the flocks;
  From room to room I hear the wakeful clocks
  Challenge the passing hour, like guards that keep
Their solitary watch on tower and steep;
  Far off I hear the crowing of the cocks,
  And through the opening door that time unlocks
  Feel the fresh breathing of To-morrow creep.
To-morrow! the mysterious, unknown guest,
  Who cries to me: 'Remember Barmecide,
  And tremble to be happy with the rest.'
And I make answer: 'I am satisfied;
  I dare not ask; I know not what is best;
  God hath already said what shall betide.'

On Translating the Divina Commedia

FIRST SONNET

Oft have I seen at some cathedral door
  A labourer, pausing in the dust and heat,
  Lay down his burden, and with reverent feet
  Enter, and cross himself, and on the floor
Kneel to repeat his paternoster o'er:
  Far off the noises of the world retreat;
  The loud vociferations of the street
  Become an undistinguishable roar.
So, as I enter here from day to day,
  And leave my burden at this minster-gate,
  Kneeling in prayer, and not ashamed to pray,
The tumult of the time disconsolate
  To inarticulate murmurs dies away,
While the eternal ages watch and wait.

SECOND SONNET

How strange the sculptures that adorn these towers;
  This crowd of statues, in whose folded sleeves
  Birds build their nests; while canopied with leaves
  Parvis and portal bloom like trellised bowers,
And the vast minster seems a cross of flowers!
  But fiends and dragons on the gargoyled eaves
  Watch the dead Christ between the living thieves,
  And, underneath, the traitor Judas lowers!
Ah! from what agonies of heart and brain,
  What exultations trampling on despair,
  What tenderness, what tears, what hate of wrong,
What passionate outcry of a soul in pain,
  Uprose this poem of the earth and air,
  This mediæval miracle of song!

THIRD SONNET

I enter, and I see thee in the gloom
  Of the long aisles, O poet saturnine!

And strive to make my steps keep pace with thine.
    The air is filled with some unknown perfume;
The congregation of the dead make room
    For thee to pass; the votive tapers shine;
    Like rooks that haunt Ravenna's groves of pine
The hovering echoes fly from tomb to tomb.
From the confessionals I hear arise
    Rehearsals of forgotten tragedies
    And lamentations from the crypts below;
And then a voice celestial that begins
    With the pathetic words, 'Although your sins
    As scarlet be,' and ends with 'as the snow.'

FOURTH SONNET

With snow-white veil and garments as of flame,
    She stands before thee, who so long ago
    Filled thy young heart with passion and the woe
    From which thy song and all its splendours came;
And while with stern rebuke she speaks thy name,
    The ice about thy heart melts as the snow
    On mountain heights, and in swift overflow
    Comes gushing from thy lips in sobs of shame.
Thou makest full confession; and a gleam,
    As of the dawn on some dark forest cast,
    Seems on thy lifted forehead to increase;
Lethe and Eunoe – the remembered dream
    And the forgotten sorrow – bring at last
    That perfect pardon which is perfect peace.

FIFTH SONNET

I lift mine eyes, and all the windows blaze
    With forms of Saints and holy men who died,
    Here martyred and hereafter glorified;
    And the great Rose upon its leaves displays
Christ's Triumph, and the angelic roundelays,
    With splendour upon splendour multiplied;
    And Beatrice again at Dante's side
    No more rebukes, but smiles her words of praise.
And then the organ sounds, and unseen choirs

Sing the old Latin hymns of peace and love
   And benedictions of the Holy Ghost;
And the melodious bells among the spires
   O'er all the house-tops and through heaven above
   Proclaim the elevation of the Host!

SIXTH SONNET

O star of morning and of liberty!
   O bringer of the light, whose splendour shines
   Above the darkness of the Apennines,
   Forerunner of the day that is to be!
The voices of the city and the sea,
   The voices of the mountains and the pines,
   Repeat thy song, till the familiar lines
   Are footpaths for the thought of Italy!
Thy fame is blown abroad from all the heights,
   Through all the nations, and a sound is heard,
   As of a mighty wind, and men devout,
Strangers of Rome, and the new proselytes,
   In their own language hear thy wondrous word,
   And many are amazed and many doubt.

Nature

As a fond mother, when the day is o'er,
    Leads by the hand her little child to bed,
    Half willing, half reluctant to be led,
    And leave his broken playthings on the floor,
Still gazing at them through the open door,
    Nor wholly reassured and comforted
    By promises of others in their stead,
    Which, though more splendid, may not please him more ;
So Nature deals with us, and takes away
    Our playthings one by one, and by the hand
    Leads us to rest so gently, that we go
Scarce knowing if we wished to go or stay,
    Being too full of sleep to understand
    How far the unknown transcends the what we know.

The Poets

O ye dead Poets, who are living still
   Immortal in your verse, though life be fled,
   And ye, O living Poets, who are dead
   Though ye are living, if neglect can kill,
Tell me if in the darkest hours of ill,
   With drops of anguish falling fast and red
   From the sharp crown of thorns upon your head,
   Ye were not glad your errand to fulfil?
Yes; for the gift and ministry of Song
   Have something in them so divinely sweet,
   It can assuage the bitterness of wrong;
Not in the clamour of the crowded street,
   Not in the shouts and plaudits of the throng,
   But in ourselves, are triumph and defeat.

The Broken Oar

Once upon Iceland's solitary strand
  A poet wandered with his book and pen,
  Seeking some final word, some sweet Amen,
  Wherewith to close the volume in his hand.
The billows rolled and plunged upon the sand,
  The circling sea-gulls swept beyond his ken,
  And from the parting cloud-rack now and then
  Flashed the red sunset over sea and land.
Then by the billows at his feet was tossed
  A broken oar; and carved thereon he read,
  'Oft was I weary, when I toiled at thee';
And like a man, who findeth what was lost,
  He wrote the words, then lifted up his head,
  And flung his useless pen into the sea.

Kéramos

1878

Turn, turn, my wheel! Turn round and round
Without a pause, without a sound:
  So spins the flying world away!
This clay, well mixed with marl and sand,
Follows the motion of my hand;
For some must follow, and some command,
  Though all are made of clay!

Thus sang the Potter at his task
Beneath the blossoming hawthorn-tree,
While o'er his features, like a mask,
The quilted sunshine and leaf-shade
Moved, as the boughs above him swayed,
And clothed him, till he seemed to be
A figure woven in tapestry,
So sumptuously was he arrayed
In that magnificent attire
Of sable tissue flaked with fire.
Like a magician he appeared,
A conjurer without book or beard;
And while he plied his magic art —
For it was magical to me —
I stood in silence and apart,
And wondered more and more to see
That shapeless, lifeless mass of clay
Rise up to meet the master's hand,
And now contract and now expand,
And even his slightest touch obey;
While ever in a thoughtful mood
He sang his ditty, and at times
Whistled a tune between the rhymes,
As a melodious interlude.

Turn, turn, my wheel! All things must change
To something new, to something strange;
  Nothing that is can pause or stay;
The moon will wax, the moon will wane,

The mist and cloud will turn to rain,
The rain to mist and cloud again,
  To-morrow be to-day.

Thus still the Potter sang, and still,
By some unconscious act of will,
The melody and even the words
Were intermingled with my thought,
As bits of coloured thread are caught
And woven into nests of birds.
And thus to regions far remote,
Beyond the ocean's vast expanse,
This wizard in the motley coat
Transported me on wings of song,
And by the northern shores of France
Bore me with restless speed along.

What land is this that seems to be
A mingling of the land and sea?
This land of sluices, dikes, and dunes?
This water-net, that tessellates
The landscape? This unending maze
Of gardens, through whose latticed gates
The imprisoned pinks and tulips gaze;
Where in the long summer afternoons
The sunshine, softened by the haze,
Comes streaming down as through a screen;
Where over the fields and pastures green
The painted ships float high in air,
And over all and everywhere
The sails of windmills sink and soar
Like wings of sea-gulls on the shore?

What land is this? Yon pretty town
Is Delft, with all its wares displayed;
The pride, the market-place, the crown
And centre of the Potter's trade.
See! every house and room is bright
With glimmers of reflected light
From plates that on the dresser shine;
Flagons to foam with Flemish beer,

Or sparkle with the Rhenish wine,
And pilgrim flasks with fleur-de-lis,
And ships upon a rolling sea,
And tankards pewter topped, and queer
With comic mask and musketeer !
Each hospitable chimney smiles
A welcome from its painted tiles ;
The parlour walls, the chamber floors,
The stairways and the corridors,
The borders of the garden walks,
Are beautiful with fadeless flowers,
That never droop in winds or showers,
And never wither on their stalks.

Turn, turn, my wheel ! All life is brief ;
What now is bud will soon be leaf,
    What now is leaf will soon decay ;
The wind blows east, the wind blows west ;
The blue eggs in the robin's nest
Will soon have wings and beak and breast,
    And flutter and fly away.

Now southward through the air I glide,
The song my only pursuivant,
And see across the landscape wide
The blue Charente, upon whose tide
The belfries and the spires of Saintes
Ripple and rock from side to side,
As, when an earthquake rends its walls,
A crumbling city reels and falls.

Who is it in the suburbs here,
This Potter, working with such cheer,
In this mean house, this mean attire,
His manly features bronzed with fire,
Whose figulines and rustic wares
Scarce find him bread from day to day ?
This madman, as the people say,
Who breaks his tables and his chairs
To feed his furnace fires, nor cares
Who goes unfed if they are fed,

Nor who may live if they are dead?
This alchemist with hollow cheeks
And sunken, searching eyes, who seeks,
By mingled earths and ores combined
With potency of fire, to find
Some new enamel, hard and bright,
His dream, his passion, his delight?

O Palissy! within thy breast
Burned the hot fever of unrest;
Thine was the prophet's vision, thine
The exultation, the divine
Insanity of noble minds,
That never falters nor abates,
But labours and endures and waits,
Till all that it foresees it finds,
Or what it cannot find creates!

Turn, turn, my wheel! This earthen jar
A touch can make, a touch can mar;
*   And shall it to the Potter say,*
What makest thou? Thou hast no hand?
As men who think to understand
A world by their Creator planned,
*   Who wiser is than they.*

Still guided by the dreamy song,
As in a trance I float along
Above the Pyrenean chain,
Above the fields and farms of Spain,
Above the bright Majorcan isle,
That lends its softened name to art, –
A spot, a dot upon the chart,
Whose little towns red-roofed with tile,
Are ruby-lustred with the light
Of blazing furnaces by night,
And crowned by day with wreaths of smoke.
Then eastward, wafted in my flight
On my enchanter's magic cloak,
I sail across the Tyrrhene Sea
Into the land of Italy,

And o'er the windy Apennines,
Mantled and musical with pines.

The palaces, the princely halls,
The doors of houses and the walls
Of churches and of belfry towers,
Cloister and castle, street and mart,
Are garlanded and gay with flowers
That blossom in the fields of art.
Here Gubbio's workshops gleam and glow
With brilliant, iridescent dyes,
The dazzling whiteness of the snow,
The cobalt blue of summer skies ;
And vase and scutcheon, cup and plate,
In perfect finish emulate
Faenza, Florence, Pesaro.

Forth from Urbino's gate there came
A youth with the angelic name
Of Raphael, in form and face
Himself angelic, and divine
In arts of colour and design.
From him Francesco Xanto caught
Something of his transcendent grace,
And into fictile fabrics wrought
Suggestions of the master's thought.
Nor less Maestro Giorgio shines
With madre-perl and golden lines
Of arabesques, and interweaves
His birds and fruits and flowers and leaves
About some landscape, shaded brown,
With olive tints on rock and town.
Behold this cup within whose bowl,
Upon a ground of deepest blue
With yellow-lustred stars o'erlaid,
Colours of every tint and hue
Mingle in one harmonious whole !
With large blue eyes and steadfast gaze,
Her yellow hair in net and braid,
Necklace and earrings all ablaze
With golden lustre o'er the glaze,

A woman's portrait; on the scroll,
Cana, the Beautiful! A name
Forgotten save for such brief fame
As this memorial can bestow, –
A gift some lover long ago
Gave with his heart to this fair dame.

A nobler title to renown
Is thine, O pleasant Tuscan town,
Seated beside the Arno's stream;
For Lucca della Robbia there
Created forms so wondrous fair,
They made thy sovereignty supreme.
These choristers with lips of stone,
Whose music is not heard, but seen,
Still chant, as from their organ-screen,
Their Maker's praise; nor these alone,
But the more fragile forms of clay,
Hardly less beautiful than they,
These saints and angels that adorn
The walls of hospitals, and tell
The story of good deeds so well
That poverty seems less forlorn,
And life more like a holiday.

Here in this old neglected church,
That long eludes the traveller's search,
Lies the dead bishop on his tomb;
Earth upon earth he slumbering lies,
Life-like and death-like in the gloom;
Garlands of fruit and flowers in bloom
And foliage deck his resting place;
A shadow in the sightless eyes,
A pallor on the patient face,
Made perfect by the furnace heat;
All earthly passions and desires
Burnt out by purgatorial fires;
Seeming to say, 'Our years are fleet,
And to the weary death is sweet.'

But the most wonderful of all
The ornaments on tomb and wall
That grace the fair Ausonian shores
Are those the faithful earth restores,
Near some Apulian town concealed,
In vineyard or in harvest field, –
Vases and urns and bas-reliefs,
Memorials of forgotten griefs,
Or records of heroic deeds
Of demigods and mighty chiefs:
Figures that almost move and speak,
And, buried amid mould and weeds,
Still in their attitudes attest
The presence of the graceful Greek, –
Achilles in his armour dressed,
Alcides with the Cretan bull,
And Aphrodite with her boy,
Or lovely Helena of Troy,
Still living and still beautiful.

Turn, turn, my wheel! 'Tis Nature's plan
The child should grow into the man,
  The man grow wrinkled, old, and gray;
In youth the heart exults and sings,
The pulses leap, the feet have wings;
In age the cricket chirps, and brings
  The harvest home of day.

And now the winds that southward blow,
And cool the hot Sicilian isle,
Bear me away. I see below
The long line of the Libyan Nile,
Flooding and feeding the parched land
With annual ebb and overflow,
A fallen palm whose branches lie
Beneath the Abyssinian sky,
Whose roots are in Egyptian sands.
On either bank huge water-wheels,
Belted with jars and dripping weeds,
Send forth their melancholy moans,
As if, in their gray mantles hid,

Dead anchorites of the Thebaid
Knelt on the shore and told their beads,
Beating their breasts with loud appeals
And penitential tears and groans.

This city, walled and thickly set
With glittering mosque and minaret,
Is Cairo, in whose gay bazaars
The dreaming traveller first inhales
The perfume of Arabian gales,
And sees the fabulous earthen jars,
Huge as were those wherein the maid
Morgiana found the Forty Thieves
Concealed in midnight ambuscade;
And seeing, more than half believes
The fascinating tales that run
Through all the Thousand Nights and One,
Told by the fair Scheherezade.

More strange and wonderful than these
Are the Egyptian deities,
Ammon, and Emeth, and the grand
Osiris, holding in his hand
The lotus; Isis, crowned and veiled;
The sacred Ibis, and the Sphinx;
Bracelets with blue enamelled links;
The Scarabee in emerald mailed,
Or spreading wide his funeral wings;
Lamps that perchance their night-watch kept
O'er Cleopatra while she slept, –
All plundered from the tombs of kings.

Turn, turn, my wheel! The human race
Of every tongue, of every place,
  Caucasian, Coptic, or Malay,
All that inhabit this great earth,
Whatever be their rank or worth,
Are kindred and allied by birth,
  And made of the same clay.

O'er desert sands, o'er gulf and bay,
O'er Ganges and o'er Himalay,
Bird-like I fly, and flying sing,
To flowery kingdoms of Cathay,
And bird-like poise on balanced wing
Above the town of King-te-tching,
A burning town, or seeming so, –
Three thousand furnaces that glow
Incessantly, and fill the air
With smoke uprising, gyre on gyre,
And painted by the lurid glare,
Of jets and flashes of red fire.

As leaves that in the autumn fall,
Spotted and veined with various hues,
Are swept along the avenues,
And lie in heaps by hedge and wall,
So from this grove of chimneys whirled
To all the markets of the world,
These porcelain leaves are wafted on, –
Light yellow leaves with spots and stains
Of violet and of crimson dye,
Or tender azure of a sky
Just washed by gentle April rains,
And beautiful with celadon.

Nor less the coarser household wares, –
The willow pattern, that we knew
In childhood, with its bridge of blue
Leading to unknown thoroughfares;
The solitary man who stares
At the white river flowing through
Its arches, the fantastic trees
And wild perspective of the view;
And intermingled among these
The tiles that in our nurseries
Filled us with wonder and delight,
Or haunted us in dreams at night.

And yonder by Nankin, behold!
The Tower of Porcelain, strange and old,

Uplifting to the astonished skies
Its ninefold painted balconies,
With balustrades of twining leaves,
And roofs of tile, beneath whose eaves
Hang porcelain bells that all the time
Ring with a soft, melodious chime;
While the whole fabric is ablaze
With varied tints, all fused in one
Great mass of colour, like a maze
Of flowers illumined by the sun.

Turn, turn, my wheel! What is begun
At daybreak must at dark be done,
  To-morrow will be another day;
To-morrow the hot furnace flame
Will search the heart and try the frame,
And stamp with honour or with shame
  These vessels made of clay.

Cradled and rocked in Eastern seas,
The islands of the Japanese
Beneath me lie; o'er lake and plain
The stork, the heron, and the crane
Through the clear realms of azure drift;
And on the hillside I can see
The villages of Imari,
Whose thronged and flaming workshops lift
Their twisted columns of smoke on high,
Cloud cloisters that in ruins lie,
With sunshine streaming through each rift,
And broken arches of blue sky.

All the bright flowers that fill the land,
Ripple of waves on rock or sand,
The snow on Fusiyama's cone,
The midnight heaven so thickly sown
With constellations of bright stars,
The leaves that rustle, the reeds that make
A whisper by each stream and lake,
The saffron dawn, the sunset red,
Are painted on these lovely jars;

Again the skylark sings, again
The stork, the heron, and the crane
Float through the azure overhead,
The counterfeit and counterpart
Of Nature reproduced in Art.

Art is the child of Nature; yes,
Her darling child, in whom we trace
The features of the mother's face,
Her aspect and her attitude,
All her majestic loveliness
Chastened and softened and subdued
Into a more attractive grace,
And with a human sense imbued.
He is the greatest artist, then,
Whether of pencil or of pen,
Who follows Nature. Never man,
As artist or as artisan,
Pursuing his own fantasies,
Can touch the human heart, or please,
Or satisfy our nobler needs,
As he who sets his willing feet
In Nature's footprints, light and fleet,
And follows fearless where she leads.

Thus mused I on that morn in May,
Wrapped in my visions like the Seer,
Whose eyes behold not what is near,
But only what is far away,
When, suddenly sounding peal on peal,
The church-bell from the neighbouring town
Proclaimed the welcome hour of noon.
The Potter heard, and stopped his wheel,
His apron on the grass threw down,
Whistled his quiet little tune,
Not overloud nor overlong,
And ended thus his simple song:

Stop, stop, my wheel! Too soon, too soon
The noon will be the afternoon,
   Too soon to-day be yesterday;

Behind us in our path we cast
The broken potsherds of the past,
And all are ground to dust at last,
   And trodden into clay!

Dedication

TO G. W. G.

With favouring winds, o'er sunlit seas,
We sailed for the Hesperides,
The land where golden apples grow;
But that, ah! that was long ago.

How far, since then, the ocean streams
Have swept us from that land of dreams,
That land of fiction and of truth,
The lost Atlantis of our youth!

Whither, ah, whither? Are not these
The tempest-haunted Hebrides,
Where sea-gulls scream, and breakers roar
And wreck and seaweed line the shore?

Ultima Thule! Utmost Isle!
Here in thy harbours for a while
We lower our sails; a while we rest
From the unending, endless quest.

Becalmed

Becalmed upon the sea of Thought,
Still unattained the land is sought,
My mind, with loosely-hanging sails,
Lies waiting the auspicious gales.

On either side, behind, before,
The ocean stretches like a floor, –
A level floor of amethyst,
Crowned by a golden dome of mist.

Blow, breath of inspiration, blow !
Shake and uplift this golden glow !
And fill the canvas of the mind
With wafts of thy celestial wind.

Blow, breath of song ! until I feel
The straining sail, the lifting keel,
The life of the awakening sea,
Its motion and its mystery !

Chimes

Sweet chimes! that in the loneliness of night
 Salute the passing hour, and in the dark
 And silent chambers of the household mark
 The movements of the myriad orbs of light!
Through my closed eyelids, by the inner sight,
 I see the constellations in the arc
 Of their great circles moving on, and hark!
 I almost hear them singing in their flight.
Better than sleep it is to lie awake
 O'er-canopied by the vast starry dome
 Of the immeasurable sky; to feel
The slumbering world sink under us, and make
 Hardly an eddy, – a mere rush of foam
 On the great sea beneath a sinking keel.

Four by the Clock

Four by the clock ! and yet not day ;
But the great world rolls and wheels away,
With its cities on land, and its ships at sea,
Into the dawn that is to be !

Only the lamp in the anchored bark
Sends its glimmer across the dark,
And the heavy breathing of the sea
Is the only sound that comes to me.

Elegiac Verse

I

Peradventure of old, some bard in Ionian Islands,
    Walking alone by the sea, hearing the wash of the waves,
Learned the secret from them of the beautiful verse elegiac,
    Breathing into his song motion and sound of the sea.

For as the wave of the sea, upheaving in long undulations,
    Plunges loud on the sand, pauses, and turns, and retreats,
So the Hexameter, rising and singing, with cadence sonorous,
    Falls; and in refluent rhythm back the Pentameter flows.

II

Not in his youth alone, but in age, may the heart of the poet
    Bloom into song, as the gorse blossoms in autumn and spring.

III

Not in tenderness wanting, yet rough are the rhymes of our
    poet;
    Though it be Jacob's voice, Esau's, alas! are the hands.

IV

Let us be grateful to writers for what is left in the inkstand;
    When to leave off is an art only attained by the few.

V

How can the Three be One? you ask me; I answer by asking,
    Hail and snow and rain, are they not three, and yet one?

VI

By the mirage uplifted the land floats vague in the ether,
    Ships and the shadows of ships hang in the motionless air;
So by the art of the poet our common life is uplifted,
    So, transfigured, the world floats in a luminous haze.

VII

Like a French poem is Life; being only perfect in structure
    When with the masculine rhymes mingled the feminine are.

VIII

Down from the mountain descends the brooklet, rejoicing in
    freedom;
    Little it dreams of the mill hid in the valley below;
Glad with the joy of existence, the child goes singing and
    laughing,
    Little dreaming what toils lie in the future concealed.

IX

As the ink from our pen, so flow our thoughts and our feelings
    When we begin to write, however sluggish before.

X

Like the Kingdom of Heaven, the Fountain of Youth is within
    us;
    If we seek it elsewhere, old shall we grow in the search.

XI

If you would hit the mark, you must aim a little above it;
    Every arrow that flies feels the attraction of earth.

XII

Wisely the Hebrews admit no Present tense in their language;
    While we are speaking the word, it is already the Past.

XIII

In the twilight of age all things seem strange and phantasmal,
    As between daylight and dark ghost-like the landscape
    appears.

XIV

Great is the art of beginning, but greater the art is of ending;
    Many a poem is marred by a superfluous verse.

A Fragment

Awake ! arise ! the hour is late !
   Angels are knocking at thy door !
They are in haste and cannot wait,
   And once departed come no more.

Awake ! arise ! the athlete's arm
   Loses its strength by too much rest ;
The fallow land, the untilled farm,
   Produces only weeds at best.

Possibilities

Where are the Poets, unto whom belong
   The Olympian heights ; whose singing shafts were sent
   Straight to the mark, and not from bows half bent,
   But with the utmost tension of the thong ?
Where are the stately argosies of song,
   Whose rushing keels made music as they went
   Sailing in search of some new continent,
   With all sail set, and steady winds and strong ?
Perhaps there lives some dreamy boy, untaught
   In schools, some graduate of the field or street,
   Who shall become a master of the art,
An admiral sailing the high seas of thought,
   Fearless and first and steering with his fleet
   For lands not yet laid down in any chart.

The Slave's Dream

Beside the ungathered rice he lay,
  His sickle in his hand;
His breast was bare, his matted hair
  Was buried in the sand.
Again, in the mist and shadow of sleep,
  He saw his Native Land.

Wide through the landscape of his dreams
  The lordly Niger flowed;
Beneath the palm-trees on the plain
  Once more a king he strode;
And heard the tinkling caravans
  Descend the mountain-road.

He saw once more his dark-eyed queen
  Among her children stand;
They clasped his neck, they kissed his cheeks,
  They held him by the hand! —
A tear burst from the sleeper's lids
  And fell into the sand.

And then at furious speed he rode
  Along the Niger's bank;
His bridle-reins were golden chains,
  And, with a martial clank,
At each leap he could feel his scabbard of steel
  Smiting his stallion's flank.

Before him, like a blood-red flag,
  The bright flamingoes flew;
From morn till night he followed their flight,
  O'er plains where the tamarind grew,
Till he saw the roofs of Caffre huts,
  And the ocean rose to view.

At night he heard the lion roar,
  And the hyena scream,
And the river-horse, as he crushed the reeds

Beside some hidden stream;
And it passed, like a glorious roll of drums,
  Through the triumph of his dream.

The forests, with their myriad tongues,
  Shouted of liberty;
And the Blast of the Desert cried aloud,
  With a voice so wild and free,
That he started in his sleep and smiled
  At their tempestuous glee.

He did not feel the driver's whip,
  Nor the burning heat of day;
For Death had illumined the Land of Sleep,
  And his lifeless body lay
A worn-out fetter, that the soul
  Had broken and thrown away!

Mezzo Cammin

Written at Boppard, on the Rhine,
August 25, 1842, just before leaving for home.

Half of my life is gone, and I have let
 The years slip from me and have not fulfilled
 The aspiration of my youth, to build
 Some tower of song with lofty parapet.
Not indolence, nor pleasure, nor the fret
 Of restless passions that would not be stilled,
 But sorrow, and a care that almost killed,
 Kept me from what I may accomplish yet;
Though, half-way up the hill, I see the Past
 Lying beneath me with its sounds and sights, –
 A city in the twilight dim and vast,
With smoking roofs, soft bells, and gleaming lights, –
 And hear above me on the autumnal blast
The cataract of Death far thundering from the heights.

The Cross of Snow

In the long, sleepless watches of the night,
    A gentle face – the face of one long dead –
    Looks at me from the wall, where round its head
    The night-lamp casts a halo of pale light.
Here in this room she died ; and soul more white
    Never through martyrdom of fire was led
    To its repose : nor can in books be read
    The legend of a life more benedight.
There is a mountain in the distant West
    That, sun-defying, in its deep ravines
    Displays a cross of snow upon its side.
Such is the cross I wear upon my breast
    These eighteen years, through all the changing scenes
    And seasons, changeless since the day she died.

Chaucer

An old man in a lodge within a park ;
  The chamber walls depicted all around
  With portraitures of huntsman, hawk, and hound,
  And the hurt deer. He listeneth to the lark,
Whose song comes with the sunshine through the dark
  Of painted glass in leaden lattice bound ;
  He listeneth and he laugheth at the sound,
  Then writeth in a book like any clerk.
He is the poet of the dawn, who wrote
  The Canterbury Tales, and his old age
  Made beautiful with song ; and as I read
I hear the crowing cock, I hear the note
  Of lark and linnet, and from every page
  Rise odours of ploughed field or flowery mead.

Milton

I pace the sounding sea-beach and behold
   How the voluminous billows roll and run,
   Upheaving and subsiding, while the sun
   Shines through their sheeted emerald far unrolled,
And the ninth wave, slow gathering fold by fold
   All its loose-flowing garments into one,
   Plunges upon the shore, and floods the dun
   Pale reach of sands, and changes them to gold.
So in majestic cadence rise and fall
   The mighty undulations of thy song,
   O sightless bard, England's Maeonides !
And ever and anon, high over all
   Uplifted, a ninth wave superb and strong,
Floods all the soul with its melodious seas.

The Tides

I saw the long line of the vacant shore,
  The sea-weed and the shells upon the sand,
  And the brown rocks left bare on every hand,
  As if the ebbing tide would flow no more.
Then heard I, more distinctly than before,
  The ocean breathe and its great breast expand,
  And hurrying came on the defenceless land
  The insurgent waters with tumultuous roar.
All thought and feeling and desire, I said,
  Love, laughter, and the exultant joy of song
  Have ebbed from me for ever! Suddenly o'er me
They swept again from their deep ocean bed,
  And in a tumult of delight, and strong
  As youth, and beautiful as youth, upbore me.

A Nameless Grave

'A soldier of the Union mustered out,'
  Is the inscription on an unknown grave
  At Newport News, beside the salt-sea wave,
  Nameless and dateless; sentinel or scout
Shot down in skirmish, or disastrous rout
  Of battle, when the loud artillery drave
  Its iron wedges through the ranks of brave
  And doomed battalions, storming the redoubt.
Thou unknown hero sleeping by the sea
  In thy forgotten grave! with secret shame
  I feel my pulses beat, my forehead burn,
When I remember thou hast given for me
  All that thou hadst, thy life, thy very name,
  And I can give thee nothing in return.

The Tide Rises, the Tide Falls

The tide rises, the tide falls,
The twilight darkens, the curlew calls;
Along the sea-sands damp and brown
The traveller hastens toward the town,
  And the tide rises, the tide falls.

Darkness settles on roofs and walls,
But the sea in the darkness calls and calls;
The little waves, with their soft white hands,
Efface the footprints in the sands,
  And the tide rises, the tide falls.

The morning breaks; the steeds in their stalls
Stamp and neigh, as the hostler calls;
The day returns, but nevermore
Returns the traveller to the shore,
  And the tide rises, the tide falls.

L'Envoi

Ye voices, that arose
After the Evening's close,
And whispered to my restless heart repose !

Go, breathe it in the ear
Of all who doubt and fear,
And say to them, 'Be of good cheer !'

Ye sounds, so low and calm,
That in the groves of balm
Seemed to me like an angel's psalm !

Go, mingle yet once more
With the perpetual roar
Of the pine forest, dark and hoar !

Tongues of the dead, not lost,
But speaking from death's frost,
Like fiery tongues at Pentecost !

Glimmer, as funeral lamps,
Amid the chills and damps
Of the vast plain where Death encamps !

INDEX OF FIRST LINES